BETWEEN MAN AND MAN

Martin Buber was born at Vienna in 1878. His youth was spent in Galicia at the home of his grandfather, the Hebrew scholar Salomon Buber, but he returned to Vienna to study philosophy in 1898. He was then for a time editor of two Zionist periodicals, *Welt* and *Der Jude*, until in 1923 he became a Professor of the Philosophy of Religion at the University of Frankfurt. That same year he published his great theological study *I and Thou*. Buber, whose contribution to the history and philosophy of religion is unsurpassed in this century, died in 1965.

BETWEEN MAN AND MAN

MARTIN BUBER

Translated and introduced by
Ronald Gregor Smith

COLLINS
Fount Paperbacks

First published by Kegan Paul, Trench, Trubner & Co. Ltd. 1947
First issued in the Fontana Library, Theology and Philosophy, 1961
First issued in Fount Paperbacks 1979
Fifth Impression September 1979

© Martin Buber, 1947

Made and printed in Great Britain by
William Collins Sons & Co Ltd, Glasgow

CONTENTS

I: DIALOGUE
(*Zwiesprache, 1929*)

SECTION ONE: DESCRIPTION

SECTION TWO: LIMITATION

SECTION THREE: CONFIRMATION

II: THE QUESTION TO THE SINGLE ONE
(*Die Frage an den Einzelnen, 1936*)

III: EDUCATION
(*Rede über das Erzieherische, 1926*)

IV: THE EDUCATION OF CHARACTER
(*Ueber Charaktererziehung, 1939*)

V: WHAT IS MAN?
(*Was ist der Mensch? 1938*)

CONTENTS

SECTION TWO: MODERN ATTEMPTS

Translator's Introduction

MARTIN BUBER was born in Vienna in 1878. In 1960 he was elected first President of the newly established National Academy of Sciences of the State of Israel. Over that long life-span he has been active and influential in many spheres, in psychology, educational theory, philosophy, theology and sociology. In association with that remarkable man, Franz Rosenzweig (1886-1929), he also began the immense task of translating the Bible into modern German.

But Buber cannot be easily classified. In a sense he belongs to none of the spheres he has influenced, but by his questions to them he calls them back to their real meaning. He has been called one of the few wise men of our time, and his wisdom may be described as the power to step over artificial boundaries, for the sake of true humanity.

That he was born a Jew, and has become increasingly conscious of his Jewishness, does not dispose of him. Rather, it discloses the real source of his power. He was brought up in Lemberg, in Galicia, by his grandfather, Salomon Buber, a noted scholar in the tradition of the Haskalah, or Jewish Enlightenment. He studied philosophy and the history of art at the universities of Vienna, Berlin, Leipzig and Zurich. But the pull of the Jewish tradition was strong. In the early years of this century he devoted himself to an intensive study of the teachings of Hasidism. It was not until 1923 that he was appointed to a Chair of Jewish Philosophy of Religion, later including Comparative Religion, at the University of Frankfurt. This lasted till 1933, and in 1938 he went to Palestine, to become Professor of Social Philosophy in the Hebrew University at Jerusalem. From this Chair he retired in 1951, since when he has lived in Jerusalem.

The present work is perhaps the best volume to serve as an introduction to Buber's many-sided thought. It was not a single production in the ordinary sense, since the five pieces of which it is composed were written—four in German and one in Hebrew—at various times over a whole decade. But for that very reason they give a view of the variety and richness of Buber's thought which is not so immediately clear in a single work. They are all, it is true, supplements to and illustrations of the guiding ideas of the earlier and now well-known work *I and Thou*. But each had its origin in a demand of the hour. Those who find *I and Thou* mysterious will find more particular illumination in the concrete themes treated here, in the more anecdotal style of *Dialogue,* the more discursive and philosophical form of *What Is Man?,* the straightforward criticism of Kierkegaard in *The Question to The Single One,* and the analysis of educational aims and ideals in the two remaining pieces in the volume. In Buber's own Foreword to this English edition the reader will find his lapidary descriptions of each item. Here we venture to sum up the book by saying that each part is like a signpost in a rich and variegated countryside, pointing back to Buber's increasing concern, which is I with Thou, man with man.

But this concern leads to a wide range of interest in the actual ongoing life of our society which effectively removes any danger of mere reiteration. *Between Man and Man* makes a real advance on *I and Thou* because Buber here turns to particulars, to human actions and ideals in such different realms as those of education, industrial relations, political action, philosophical enquiry, and conventional religious attitudes. He does this with such persistence, such delicacy and such absence of fanaticism that his revolutionary and exceptional stand may easily go unregarded. It is nevertheless likely that Buber's way of thought, more precisely, the stand which he takes, will be one of the chief supports for " that individual " or " single one " (in Kierkegaard's phrase), in the era of collectivism, of mass society and loss of the human subject, into which we are now moving. For it is as persons along with other persons that the essence of true humanity consists. This is not to be simply experienced, in the sense of being analysable as an inert object within our reach, nor simply understood, in the sense of being able to be established as part of a system of ideal ends; but it is to be grasped, in the sense of a mutual encounter in which each self in its wholeness meets another, and in the meeting decides to be for the other in a reciprocal movement which is at the same time of the essence of community. True humanity is community. In elaborating these ideas Buber's thought may be said to move simultaneously inwards, in a deepening of self-knowledge, and outwards, in a new and vivid awareness of life in the world with others. But the one aspect of the movement is impossible without the other.

The question whether Buber is concerned only with man, with a kind of anthropology of a naturalist order, has taken several forms in the course of discussion of his work. Pantheism, animism, mysticism have all been suggested as possible descriptions of the tendencies in his thought. A proper answer to these criticisms would require a detailed examination of his whole thought, and especially of its antecedents. It is sufficient to note here that Buber is not fairly faced, in the totality of his intention, when he is criticised from the standpoint of an alien theology or philosophy. For example, the criticism by neo-orthodox theologians, such as Karl Barth, that Buber's thought is restricted to anthropology, and thus loses the transcendental sanction for true humanity, misses the point. For it is precisely in his concern with man as man that Buber recognises, and acknowledges, the meeting with the " Eternal Thou," who comes again and again of grace to meet him. Like the Rabbi of whom he tells, who wished to write a book about Adam, the whole man, then decided not to write it, he is aware of the audacity of his effort. Behind his venture, moreover, there lie not only the common forms of the Western European tradition, but also (as I have already indicated) the tradition of Hasidism. This movement within Eastern European Jewry was, at its best, an intensively creative mystical movement, but it was a mysticism of the everyday, which obliterated the artificial distinction between the sacred and the secular. The concern with man in his wholeness along with others, the hallowing of the everyday, the refusal to separate religion off as something special, the response to the demand of each occasion as it comes, are elements which are strikingly expressed, in a practical, humorous, down-to-earth style, in the stories and legends which have been assiduously gathered and set down by Buber himself. The reader may look for himself into the wealth of this teaching.[1] It is this part of the background of Buber's thought which more than any other gives to it its remarkable concreteness and unity. Some knowledge of this Hasidist background is essential if misunderstanding, whether by too rigid disagreement or too hasty agreement, is to be avoided.

It is mainly as a consequence of this Hasidist influence that Buber is able to traverse various fields, of education, sociology, psychology, philosophy and theology, not as separate realms, but as one realm, though without confusion : one in the response of each man to the claim which rises up to meet him in them.

The question whether Buber has lost the transcendental side of experience, or reduced theology to anthropology, or God to an inner potentiality in man, a gnostic " spark," could indeed be answered in its own terms, if this were considered worth doing. Thus we might without difficulty refute the criticism about loss of transcendence by looking again at the central matter, man with man : here in fact is living transcendence, the other rising up against you, claiming your response. Or we might examine the meaning of the inner potentiality in man as in truth the sign of grace acting in and through man. Or we might consider whether a theology which is not afraid to talk of God in terms of man, the whole man, is not in truth the only kind of theology which makes it possible for man to talk with God.

But all these possible ways of arguing do not face Buber's work in the richness and the simplicity of its intention. This intention may be summed up as the presentation of a philosophy of the Word. For Buber all life is a dialogue in which the Word which is not of man comes to man.

[1] Cf. *Die Erzählungen der Chassidim*, Zurich, 1949; *Tales of the Hasidim*, London, 1956.

But this Word comes to man in and through the concerns of man, his decisions, his responsibilites, his responses. This Word is not bound to man, but neither is it absolutely transcendent. It is other than man, and it makes him free to be what he is destined to be. It is a Presence which is to be found in man himself, whom Buber calls (in the last words of *What Is Man?*) "the eternal meeting of the One with the Other."

RONALD GREGOR SMITH

Glasgow University, June 1960

FOREWORD

THE five works which I have brought together for English readers in this volume have arisen in connexion with my little book *I and Thou* (1923),[1] as filling out and applying what was said there, with particular regard to the needs of our time.

The first of these works, *Dialogue* (1929), proceeded from the desire to clarify the "dialogical" principle presented in *I and Thou*, to illustrate it and to make precise its relations to essential spheres of life.

The Question to the Single One, which contains some political inferences, is the elaboration of an address which I gave to the students of the three German-Swiss Universities at the close of 1933. The book appeared in Germany in 1936—astonishingly, since it attacks the life-basis of totalitarianism. The fact that it could be published with impunity is certainly to be explained from its not having been understood by the appropriate authorities.

There follow two addresses on major problems of education, the first given at the Third International Educational Conference at Heidelberg in 1925, the second at the National Conference of Jewish Teachers of Palestine at Tel-Aviv in 1939. Both addresses treat of the significance of the dialogical principle in the sphere of education, the first for its groundwork, the second for its most important task.

The volume concludes with my inaugural course of lectures as Professor of Social Philosophy at the Hebrew University of Jerusalem (1938). This course shows, in the unfolding of the question about the essence of man, that it is by beginning neither with the individual nor with the collectivity, but only with the reality of the mutual relation between man and man, that this essence can be grasped.   MARTIN BUBER

Jerusalem

[1] English edition (T. & T. Clark) Edinburgh, 1937, 2nd (revised) edition, 1958.

The translator has pleasure in acknowledging the generous help of Mr. Kurt Emmerich, who gave unstintingly of his time and knowledge in the earlier stages of the translation, and of the author himself, who read not only the entire MS. but also the proofs, and made countless valuable suggestions

DIALOGUE

Original Remembrance

THROUGH ALL sorts of changes the same dream, sometimes after an interval of several years, recurs to me. I name it the dream of the double cry. Its context is always much the same, a " primitive " world meagrely equipped. I find myself in a vast cave, like the Latomias of Syracuse, or in a mud building that reminds me when I awake of the villages of the *fellahin,* or on the fringe of a gigantic forest whose like I cannot remember having seen.

The dream begins in very different ways, but always with something extraordinary happening to me, for instance, with a small animal resembling a lion-cub (whose name I know in the dream but not when I awake) tearing the flesh from my arm and being forced only with an effort to loose its hold. The strange thing is that this first part of the dream story, which in the duration as well as the outer meaning of the incidents is easily the most important, always unrolls at a furious pace as though it did not matter. Then suddenly the pace abates : I stand there and cry out. In the view of the events which my waking consciousness has I should have to suppose that the cry I utter varies in accordance with what preceded it, and is sometimes joyous, sometimes fearful, sometimes even filled both with pain and with triumph. But in my morning recollection it is neither so expressive nor so various. Each time it is the same cry, inarticulate but in strict rhythm, rising and falling, swelling to a fulness which my throat could not endure were I awake, long and slow, quiet, quite slow and very long, a cry that is a song. When it ends my heart stops beating. But then, somewhere, far away, another cry moves towards me, another which is the same, the same cry uttered or sung by another voice. Yet it is not the same cry, certainly no "echo" of my cry but rather its true rejoinder, tone for tone not repeating mine, not even in a weakened form, but corresponding to mine, answering its tones—so much so, that mine, which at first had to my own ear no sound of questioning at all, now appear as questions, as a long series of questions, which now all receive a response. The response is no more capable of interpretation than the question. And yet the cries that meet the one cry that is the same do not seem to be the same as one another. Each time the voice is new. But now, as the reply ends, in the first moment after its dying fall, a certitude, true dream certitude comes to me that *now it has happened*. Nothing more. Just this, and in this way—*now it has happened*. If I should try to explain it, it means that that happening which gave rise to my cry has only now, with the rejoinder, really and undoubtedly happened.

After this manner the dream has recurred each time—till once, the last time, now two years ago. At first it was as usual (it was the dream with the animal), my cry died away, again my heart stood still. But then there was quiet. There came no answering call. I listened, I heard no sound. For I *awaited* the response for the first time; hitherto it had always surprised me, as though I had never heard it before. Awaited, it failed to come. But now something happened with me. As though I had till now had no other access from the world to sensation save that of the ear and now discovered myself as a being simply equipped with senses, both those clothed in the bodily organs and the naked senses, so I exposed myself to the distance, open to all sensation and perception. And then, not from a distance but from the air round about me, noiselessly, came the answer. Really it did not come; it was there. It had been there—so I may explain it—even before my cry : there it was, and now, when I laid myself open to it, it let itself be received by me. I received it as completely into my perception as ever I received the rejoinder in one of the earlier dreams. If I were to report with what I heard it

I should have to say "with every pore of my body." As ever the rejoinder came in one of the earlier dreams this corresponded to and answered my cry. It exceeded the earlier rejoinder in an unknown perfection which is hard to define, for it resides in the fact that it was already there.

When I had reached an end of receiving it, I felt again that certainty, pealing out more than ever, that *now it has happened.*

Silence which is Communication

Just as the most eager speaking at one another does not make a conversation (this is most clearly shown in that curious sport, aptly termed discussion, that is "breaking apart," which is indulged in by men who are to some extent gifted with the ability to think), so for a conversation no sound is necessary, not even a gesture. Speech can renounce all the media of sense, and it is still speech.

Of course I am not thinking of lovers' tender silence, resting in one another, the expression and discernment of which can be satisfied by a glance, indeed by the mere sharing of a gaze which is rich in inward relations. Nor am I thinking of the mystical shared silence, such as is reported of the Franciscan Aegidius and Louis of France (or, almost identically, of two rabbis of the Hasidim) who, meeting once, did not utter a word, but "taking their stand in the reflection of the divine Face" experienced one another. For here too there is still the expression of a gesture, of the physical attitude of the one to the other.

What I am thinking of I will make clear by example. Imagine two men sitting beside one another in any kind of solitude of the world. They do not speak with one another, they do not look at one another, not once have they turned to one another. They are not in one another's confidence, the one knows nothing of the other's career, early that morning they got to know one another in the course of their travels. In this moment neither is thinking of the other; we do not need to know what their thoughts

are. The one is sitting on the common seat obviously after
his usual manner, calm, hospitably disposed to everything
that may come. His being seems to say it is too little to be
ready, one must also be really *there*. The other, whose
attitude does not betray him, is a man who holds himself
in reserve, withholds himself. But if we know about
him we know that a childhood's spell is laid on him, that
his withholding of himself is something other than an attitude, behind all attitude is entrenched the impenetrable
inability to communicate himself. And now—let us
imagine that this is one of the hours which succeed in
bursting asunder the seven iron bands about our heart—
imperceptibly the spell is lifted. But even now the man
does not speak a word, does not stir a finger. Yet he does
something. The lifting of the spell has happened to him
—no matter from where—without his doing. But this is
what he does now : he releases in himself a reserve over
which only he himself has power. Unreservedly communication streams from him, and the silence bears it to his
neighbour. Indeed it was intended for him, and he receives it unreservedly as he receives all genuine destiny
that meets him. He will be able to tell no one, not even
himself, what he has experienced. What does he now
"know" of the other? No more knowing is needed. For
where unreserve has ruled, even wordlessly, between men,
the word of dialogue has happened sacramentally.

Opinions and the Factual

Human dialogue, therefore, although it has its distinc-
tive life in the sign, that is in sound and gesture (the
letters of language have their place in this only in special
instances, as when, between friends in a meeting, notes
describing the atmosphere skim back and forth across the
table), can exist without the sign, but admittedly not in an
objectively comprehensible form. On the other hand an
element of communication, however inward, seems to
belong to its essence. But in its highest moments dialogue
reaches out even beyond these boundaries. It is completed

outside contents, even the most personal, which are or can be communicated. Moreover it is completed not in some " mystical " event, but in one that is in the precise sense factual, thoroughly dovetailed into the common human world and the concrete time-sequence.

One might indeed be inclined to concede this as valid for the special realm of the erotic. But I do not intend to bring even this in here as an explanation. For Eros is in reality much more strangely composed than in Plato's genealogical myth, and the erotic is in no way, as might be supposed, purely a compressing and unfolding of dia-logue. Rather do I know no other realm where, as in this one (to be spoken of later), dialogue and monologue are so mingled and opposed. Many celebrated ecstasies of love are nothing but the lover's delight in the possibilities of his own person which are actualized in unexpected fulness.

I would rather think of something unpretentious yet significant—of the glances which strangers exchange in a busy street as they pass one another with unchanging pace. Some of these glances, though not charged with destiny, nevertheless reveal to one another two dialogical natures.

But I can really show what I have in mind only by events which open into a genuine change from communi-cation to communion, that is, in an embodiment of the word of dialogue.

What I am here concerned with cannot be conveyed in ideas to a reader. But we may represent it by examples—provided that, where the matter is important, we do not eschew taking examples from the inmost recesses of the personal life. For where else should the like be found?

My friendship with one now dead arose in an incident that may be described, if you will, as a broken-off conver-sation. The date is Easter 1914. Some men from different European peoples had met in an undefined presentiment of the catastrophe, in order to make preparations for an attempt to establish a supra-national authority. The con-versations were marked by that unreserve, whose substance and fruitfulness I have scarcely ever experienced so strongly. It had such an effect on all who took part that the fictitious fell away and every word was an actuality. Then as we discussed the composition of the larger circle from which public initiative should proceed (it was decided that it should meet in August of the same year) one of us, a man of passionate concentration and judicial power of love, raised the consideration that too many Jews had been nominated, so that several countries would be represented in unseemly proportion by their Jews. Though similar reflections were not foreign to my own mind, since I hold that Jewry can gain an effective and more than merely stimulating share in the building of a steadfast world of peace only in its own community and not in scattered members, they seemed to me, expressed in this way, to be tainted in their justice. Obstinate Jew that I am, I protested against the protest. I no longer know how from that I came to speak of Jesus and to say that we Jews knew him from within, in the impulses and stirrings of his Jewish being, in a way that remains inaccessible to the peoples submissive to him. " In a way that remains inaccessible to you "—so I directly addressed the former clergyman. He stood up, I too stood, we looked into the heart of one another's eyes. " It is gone," he said, and before everyone we gave one another the kiss of brotherhood.

The discussion of the situation between Jews and Christians had been transformed into a bond between the Christian and the Jew. In this transformation dialogue was fulfilled. Opinions were gone, in a bodily way the factual took place.

Disputations in Religion

Here I expect two objections, one weighty and one powerful.

One argument against me takes this form. When it is a question of essential views, of views concerning *Weltanschauung*, the conversation *must* not be broken off in such a way. Each must expose himself wholly, in a real way, in his humanly unavoidable partiality, and thereby ex-

perience himself in a real way as limited by the other, so
that the two suffer together the destiny of our conditioned
nature and meet one another in it.

To this I answer that the experience of being limited is
included in what I refer to; but so too is the experience
of overcoming it together. This cannot be completed on
the level of *Weltanschauung,* but on that of reality.
Neither needs to give up his point of view; only, in that
unexpectedly they do something and unexpectedly something happens to them which is called a covenant, they
enter a realm where the law of the point of view no longer
holds. They too suffer the destiny of our conditioned
nature, but they honour it most highly when, as is permitted to us, they let themselves run free of it for an
immortal moment. They had already met one another
when each in his soul so turned to the other that from
then on, making him present, he spoke really to and
towards him.

The other objection, which comes from a quite different,
in fact from the opposite, side is to the effect that this
may be true so far as the province of the point of view
reaches, but it ceases to be true for a confession of faith.
Two believers in conflict about their doctrines are concerned with the execution of the divine will, not with a
fleeting personal agreement. For the man who is so
related to his faith that he is able to die or to slay for it
there can be no realm where the law of the faith ceases to
hold. It is laid on him to help truth to victory, he does
not let himself be misled by sentiments. The man holding
a different, that is a false, belief must be converted, or at
least instructed; direct contact with him can be achieved
only outside the advocacy of the faith, it cannot proceed
from it. The thesis of religious disputation cannot be
allowed to " go."

This objection derives its power from its indifference
to the non-binding character of the relativized spirit—a
character which is accepted as a matter of course. I can
answer it adequately only by a confession.

I have not the possibility of judging Luther, who
refused fellowship with Zwingli in Marburg, or Calvin

who furthered the death of Servetus. For Luther and
Calvin believe that the Word of God has so descended
among men that it can be clearly known and must therefore be exclusively advocated. I do not believe that; the
Word of God crosses my vision like a falling star to whose
fire the meteorite will bear witness without making it light
up for me, and I myself can only bear witness to the light
but not produce the stone and say "This is it." But this
difference of faith is by no means to be understood merely
as a subjective one. It is not based on the fact that we
who live to-day are weak in faith, and it will remain even
if our faith is ever so much strengthened. The situation of
the world itself, in the most serious sense, more precisely
the relation between God and man, has changed. And this
change is certainly not comprehended in its essence by our
thinking only of the darkening, so familiar to us, of the
supreme light, only of the night of our being, empty of
revelation. It is the night of an expectation—not of a
vague hope, but of an expectation. We expect a theophany
of which we know nothing but the place, and the place is
called community. In the public catacombs of this expectation there is no single God's Word which can be
clearly known and advocated, but the words delivered are
clarified for us in our human situation of being turned to
one another. There is no obedience to the coming one
without loyalty to his creature. To have experienced this
is our way.

A time of genuine religious conversations is beginning—
not those so-called but fictitious conversations where none
regarded and addressed his partner in reality, but genuine
dialogues, speech from certainty to certainty, but also
from one open-hearted person to another open-hearted
person. Only then will genuine common life appear, not
that of an identical content of faith which is alleged to be
found in all religions, but that of the situation, of anguish
and of expectation.

Setting of the Question

The life of dialogue is not limited to men's traffic with one another; it is, it has shown itself to be, a relation of men to one another that is only represented in their traffic.

Accordingly, even if speech and communication may be dispensed with, the life of dialogue seems, from what we may perceive, to have inextricably joined to it as its minimum constitution one thing, the mutuality of the inner action. Two men bound together in dialogue must obviously be turned to one another, they must therefore—no matter with what measure of activity or indeed of consciousness of activity—have turned to one another.

It is good to put this forward so crudely and formally. For behind the formulating question about the limits of a category under discussion is hidden a question which bursts all formulas asunder.

Observing, Looking On, Becoming Aware

We may distinguish three ways in which we are able to perceive a man who is living before our eyes. (I am not thinking of an object of scientific knowledge, of which I do not speak here.) The object of our perception does not need to know of us, of our being there. It does not matter at this point whether he stands in a relation or has a standpoint towards the perceiver.

The *observer* is wholly intent on fixing the observed man in his mind, on " noting " him. He probes him and writes him up. That is, he is diligent to write up as many " traits " as possible. He lies in wait for them, that none may escape him. The object consists of traits, and it is known what lies behind each of them. Knowledge of the human system of expression constantly incorporates in the instant the newly appearing individual variations, and remains applicable. A face is nothing but physiognomy, movements nothing but gestures of expression.

The *onlooker* is not at all intent. He takes up the position which lets him see the object freely, and undisturbed awaits what will be presented to him. Only at the beginning may he be ruled by purpose, everything beyond that is involuntary. He does not go around taking notes indiscriminately, he lets himself go, he is not in the least afraid of forgetting something ("Forgetting is good," he says). He gives his memory no tasks, he trusts its organic work which preserves what is worth preserving. He does not lead in the grass as green fodder, as the observer does; he turns it and lets the sun shine on it. He pays no attention to traits ("Traits lead astray," he says). What stands out for him from the object is what is not "character" and not "expression" ("The interesting is not important," he says). All great artists have been onlookers.

But there is a perception of a decisively different kind.

The onlooker and the observer are similarly orientated, in that they have a position, namely, the very desire to perceive the man who is living before our eyes. Moreover, this man is for them an object separated from themselves and their personal life, who can in fact for this sole reason be "properly" perceived. Consequently what they experience in this way, whether it is, as with the observer, a sum of traits, or, as with the onlooker, an existence, neither demands action from them nor inflicts destiny on them. But rather the whole is given over to the aloof fields of æsthesis.

It is a different matter when in a receptive hour of my personal life a man meets me about whom there is something, which I cannot grasp in any objective way at all, that "says something" to me. That does not mean, says to me what manner of man this is, what is going on in him, and the like. But it means, says something *to me*, addresses something to me, speaks something that enters my own life. It can be something about this man, for instance that he needs me. But it can also be something about myself. The man himself in his relation to me has nothing to do with what is said. He has no relation to me, he has indeed not noticed me at all. It is not he who says it to me, as that solitary man silently confessed his secret to his neighbour on the seat; but *it* says it.

To understand "say" as a metaphor is not to understand. The phrase "that doesn't say a thing to me" is an outworn metaphor; but the saying I am referring to is real speech. In the house of speech are many mansions, and this is one of the inner.

The effect of having this said to me is completely different from that of looking on and observing. I cannot depict or denote or describe the man in whom, through whom, something has been said to me. Were I to attempt it, that would be the end of saying. This man is not my object; I have got to do with him. Perhaps I have to accomplish something about him; but perhaps I have only to learn something, and it is only a matter of my "accepting." It may be that I have to answer at once, to this very man before me; it may be that the saying has a long and manifold transmission before it, and that I am to answer some other person at some other time and place, in who knows what kind of speech, and that it is now only a matter of taking the answering on myself. But in each instance a word demanding an answer has happened to me.

We may term this way of perception *becoming aware*.

It by no means needs to be a man of whom I become aware. It can be an animal, a plant, a stone. No kind of appearance or event is fundamentally excluded from the series of the things through which from time to time something is said to me. Nothing can refuse to be the vessel for the Word. The limits of the possibility of dialogue are the limits of awareness.

The Signs

Each of us is encased in an armour whose task is to ward off signs. Signs happen to us without respite, living means being addressed, we would need only to present ourselves and to perceive. But the risk is too dangerous for us, the soundless thunderings seem to threaten us with annihilation, and from generation to generation we perfect the defence apparatus. All our knowledge assures us, " Be calm, everything happens as it must happen, but nothing is directed at you, you are not meant; it is just ' the world,' you can experience it as you like, but whatever you make of it in yourself proceeds from you alone, nothing is required of you, you are not addressed, all is quiet."

Each of us is encased in an armour which we soon, out of familiarity, no longer notice. There are only moments which penetrate it and stir the soul to sensibility. And when such a moment has imposed itself on us and we then take notice and ask ourselves, " Has anything particular taken place? Was it not of the kind I meet every day?" then we may reply to ourselves, " Nothing particular, indeed, it is like this every day, only we are not there every day."

The signs of address are not something extraordinary, something that steps out of the order of things, they are just what goes on time and again, just what goes on in any case, nothing is added by the address. The waves of the æther roar on always, but for most of the time we have turned off our receivers.

What occurs to me addresses me. In what occurs to me the world-happening addresses me. Only by sterilizing it, removing the seed of address from it, can I take what occurs to me as a part of the world-happening which does not refer to me. The interlocking sterilized system into which all this only needs to be dovetailed is man's titanic work. Mankind has pressed speech too into the service of this work.

From out of this tower of the ages the objection will be levelled against me, if some of its doorkeepers should pay any attention to such trains of thought, that it is nothing but a variety of primitive superstition to hold that cosmic and telluric happenings have for the life of the human person a direct meaning that can be grasped. For instead of understanding an event physically, biologically, sociologically (for which I, inclined as I always have been to

admire genuine acts of research, think a great deal, when
those who carry them out only know what they are doing
and do not lose sight of the limits of the realm in which
they are moving), these keepers say, an attempt is being
made to get behind the event's alleged significance, and
for this there is no place in a reasonable world continuum
of space and time.

Thus, then, unexpectedly I seem to have fallen into the
company of the augurs, of whom, as is well-known, there
are remarkable modern varieties.

But whether they haruspicate or cast a horoscope their
signs have this peculiarity that they are in a dictionary,
even if not necessarily a written one. It does not matter
how esoteric the information that is handed down : he
who searches out the signs is *well up in* what life's juncture
this or that sign means. Nor does it matter that special
difficulties of separation and combination are created by
the meeting of several signs of different kinds. For you
can " look it up in the dictionary." The common signature
of all this business is that it is for all time : things remain
the same, they are discovered once for all, rules, laws, and
analogical conclusions may be employed throughout.
What is commonly termed superstition, that is, perverse
faith, appears to me rather as perverse knowledge (1).
From " superstition " about the number 13 an unbroken
ladder leads into the dizziest heights of gnosis. This is not
even the aping of a real faith.

Real faith—if I may so term presenting ourselves and
perceiving—begins when the dictionary is put down, when
you are done with it. What occurs to me says something
to me, but what it says to me cannot be revealed by any
esoteric information; for it has never been said before nor
is it composed of sounds that have ever been said. It can
neither be interpreted nor translated, I can have it neither
explained nor displayed; it is not a *what* at all, it is said
into my very life; it is no experience that can be remem-
bered independently of the situation, it remains the address
of that moment and cannot be isolated, it remains the
question of a questioner and will have its answer.

(It remains the question. For that is the other great contrast between all the business of interpreting signs and the speech of signs which I mean here : this speech never gives information or appeasement.)

Faith stands in the stream of "happening but once" which is spanned by knowledge. All the emergency structures of analogy and typology are indispensable for the work of the human spirit, but to step on them when the question of the questioner steps up to you, to me, would be running away. Lived life is tested and fulfilled in the stream alone.

With all deference to the world continuum of space and time I know as a living truth only concrete world reality which is constantly, in every moment, reached out to me. I can separate it into its component parts, I can compare them and distribute them into groups of similar phenomena, I can derive them from earlier and reduce them to simpler phenomena; and when I have done all this I have not touched my concrete world reality. Inseparable, incomparable, irreducible, now, happening once only, it gazes upon me with a horrifying look. So in Stravinsky's ballet the director of the wandering marionette show wants to point out to the people at the annual fair that a pierrot who terrified them is nothing but a wisp of straw in clothes : he tears it asunder—and collapses, gibbering, for on the roof of the booth the *living* Petrouchka sits and laughs at him.

The true name of concrete reality is the creation which is entrusted to me and to every man. In it the signs of address are given to us.

A Conversion

In my earlier years the "religious" was for me the exception. There were hours that were taken out of the course of things. From somewhere or other the firm crust of everyday was pierced. Then the reliable permanence of appearances broke down; the attack which took place burst its law asunder. "Religious experience" was the experience of an otherness which did not fit into the con-

text of life. It could begin with something customary, with
consideration of some familiar object, but which then
became unexpectedly mysterious and uncanny, finally
lighting a way into the lightning-pierced darkness of the
mystery itself. But also, without any intermediate stage,
time could be torn apart—first the firm world's structure
then the still firmer self-assurance flew apart and you were
delivered to fulness. The " religious " lifted you out. Over
there now lay the accustomed existence with its affairs, but
here illumination and ecstasy and rapture held, without
time or sequence. Thus your own being encompassed a life
here and a life beyond, and there was no bond but the
actual moment of the transition.

The illegitimacy of such a division of the temporal life,
which is streaming to death and eternity and which only in
fulfilling its temporality can be fulfilled in face of these,
was brought home to me by an everyday event, an event
of judgment, judging with that sentence from closed lips
and an unmoved glance such as the ongoing course of
things loves to pronounce.

What happened was no more than that one forenoon,
after a morning of " religious " enthusiasm, I had a visit
from an unknown young man, without being there in
spirit. I certainly did not fail to let the meeting be friendly,
I did not treat him any more remissly than all his contemporaries who were in the habit of seeking me out about this
time of day as an oracle that is ready to listen to reason. I
conversed attentively and openly with him—only I omitted
to guess the questions which he did not put. Later, not
long after, I learned from one of his friends—he himself
was no longer alive—the essential content of these questions; I learned that he had come to me not casually, but
borne by destiny, not for a chat but for a decision. He
had come to me, he had come in this hour. What do we
expect when we are in despair and yet go to a man?
Surely a presence by means of which we are told that
nevertheless there is meaning.

Since then I have given up the " religious " which is
nothing but the exception, extraction, exaltation, ecstasy;
or it has given me up. I possess nothing but the everyday

out of which I am never taken. The mystery is no longer disclosed, it has escaped or it has made its dwelling here where everything happens as it happens. I know no fulness but each mortal hour's fulness of claim and responsibility. Though far from being equal to it, yet I know that in the claim I am claimed and may respond in responsibility, and know who speaks and demands a response.

I do not know much more. If that is religion then it is just *everything*, simply all that is lived in its possibility of dialogue. Here is space also for religion's highest forms. As when you pray you do not thereby remove yourself from this life of yours but in your praying refer your thought to it, even though it may be in order to yield it; so too in the unprecedented and surprising, when you are called upon from above, required, chosen, empowered, sent, you with this your mortal bit of life are referred to, this moment is not extracted from it, it rests on what has been and beckons to the remainder which has still to be lived, you are not swallowed up in a fulness without obligation, you are willed for the life of communion.

Who Speaks?

In the signs of life which happens to us we are addressed. Who speaks?

It would not avail us to give for reply the word "God," if we do not give it out of that decisive hour of personal existence when we had to forget everything we imagined we knew of God, when we dared to keep nothing handed down or learned or self-contrived, no shred of knowledge, and were plunged into the night.

When we rise out of it into the new life and there begin to receive the signs, what can we know of that which—of him who gives them to us? Only what we experience from time to time from the signs themselves. If we name the speaker of this speech God, then it is always the God of a moment, a moment God.

I will now use a *gauche* comparison, since I know no right one.

When we really understand a poem, all we know of
the poet is what we learn of him in the poem—no biographical wisdom is of value for the pure understanding
of what is to be understood : the *I* which approaches us is
the subject of this single poem. But when we read other
poems by the poet in the same true way their subjects
combine in all their multiplicity, completing and confirm-
ing one another, to form the one polyphony of the person's existence.

In such a way, out of the givers of the signs, the speakers
of the words in lived life, out of the moment Gods there
arises for us with a single identity the Lord of the voice,
the One.

Above and Below

Above and below are bound to one another. The word
of him who wishes to speak with men without speaking
with God is not fulfilled; but the word of him who
wishes to speak with God without speaking with men goes
astray.

There is a tale that a man inspired by God once went
out from the creaturely realms into the vast waste. There
he wandered till he came to the gates of the mystery. He
knocked. From within came the cry : " What do you
want here?" He said, " I have proclaimed your praise in
the ears of mortals, but they were deaf to me. So I come
to you that you yourself may hear me and reply." " Turn
back," came the cry from within. " Here is no ear for you.
I have sunk my hearing in the deafness of mortals."

True address from God directs man into the place of
lived speech, where the voices of the creatures grope past
one another, and in their very missing of one another
succeed in reaching the eternal partner.

Responsibility

The idea of responsibility is to be brought back from

the province of specialized ethics, of an "ought" that swings free in the air, into that of lived life. Genuine responsibility exists only where there is real responding.

Responding to what?

To what happens to one, to what is to be seen and heard and felt. Each concrete hour allotted to the person, with its content drawn from the world and from destiny, is speech for the man who is attentive. Attentive, for no more than that is needed in order to make a beginning with the reading of the signs that are given to you. For that very reason, as I have already indicated, the whole apparatus of our civilization is necessary to preserve men from this attentiveness and its consequences. For the attentive man would no longer, as his custom is, "master" the situation the very moment after it stepped up to him : it would be laid upon him to go up to and into it. Moreover, nothing that he believed he possessed as always available would help him, no knowledge and no technique, no system and no programme, for now he would have to do with what cannot be classified, with concretion itself. This speech has no alphabet, each of its sounds is a new creation and only to be grasped as such.

It will, then, be expected of the attentive man that he faces creation as it happens. It happens as speech, and not as speech rushing out over his head but as speech directed precisely at him. And if one were to ask another if he too heard and he said he did, they would have agreed only about an experiencing and not about something experienced.

But the sounds of which the speech consists—I repeat it in order to remove the misunderstanding, which is perhaps still possible, that I referred to something extraordinary and larger than life—are the events of the personal everyday life. In them, as they now are, "great" or "small," we are addressed, and those which count as great, yield no greater signs than the others.

Our attitude, however, is not yet decided through our becoming aware of the signs. We can still wrap silence about us—a reply characteristic of a significant type of the age—or we can step aside into the accustomed way;

although both times we carry away a wound that is not to be forgotten in any productivity or any narcotism. Yet it can happen that we venture to respond, stammering perhaps—the soul is but rarely able to attain to surer articulation—but it is an honest stammering, as when sense and throat are united about what is to be said, but the throat is too horrified at it to utter purely the already composed sense. The words of our response are spoken in the speech, untranslatable like the address, of doing and letting —whereby the doing may behave like a letting and the letting like a doing. What we say in this way with the being is our entering upon the situation, into the situation, which has at this moment stepped up to us, whose appearance we did not and could not know, for its like has not yet been.

Nor are we now finished with it, we have to give up that expectation : a situation of which we have become aware is never finished with, but we subdue it into the substance of lived life. Only then, true to the moment, do we experience a life that is something other than a sum of moments. We respond to the moment, but at the same time we respond on its behalf, we answer for it. A newly-created concrete reality has been laid in our arms; we answer for it. A dog has looked at you, you answer for its glance, a child has clutched your hand, you answer for its touch, a host of men moves about you, you answer for their need (2).

Morality and Religion

Responsibility which does not respond to a word is a metaphor of morality. Factually, responsibility only exists when the court is there to which I am responsible, and "self-responsibility" has reality only when the "self" to which I am responsible becomes transparent into the absolute. But he who practises real responsibility in the life of dialogue does not need to name the speaker of the word to which he is responding—he knows him in the word's substance which presses on and in, assuming the cadence of an inwardness, and stirs him in his heart of hearts. A man can ward off with all his strength the belief that " God " is there, and he tastes him in the strict sacrament of dialogue.

Yet let it not be supposed that I make morality questionable in order to glorify religion. Religion, certainly, has this advantage over morality, that it is a phenomenon and not a postulate, and further that it is able to include composure as well as determination. The reality of morality, the demand of the demander, has a place in religion, but the reality of religion, the unconditioned being of the demander, has no place in morality. Nevertheless, when religion does itself justice and asserts itself, it is much more dubious than morality, just because it is more actual and inclusive. Religion as risk, which is ready to give itself up, is the nourishing stream of the arteries; as system, possessing, assured and assuring, religion which believes in religion is the veins' blood, which ceases to circulate. And if there is nothing that can so hide the face of our fellow-man as morality can, religion can hide from us as nothing else can the face of God. Principle there, dogma here, I appreciate the " objective " compactness of dogma, but behind both there lies in wait the—profane or holy—war against the situation's power of dialogue, there lies in wait the " once-for-all " which resists the unforeseeable moment. Dogma, even when its claim of origin remains uncontested, has become the most exalted form of invulnerability against revelation. Revelation will tolerate no perfect tense, but man with the arts of his craze for security props it up to perfectedness.

The Realms

THE REALMS of the life of dialogue and the life of monologue do not coincide with the realms of dialogue and monologue even when forms without sound and even without gesture are included. There are not merely great spheres of the life of dialogue which in appearance are not dialogue, there is also dialogue which is not the dialogue of life, that is, it has the appearance but not the essence of dialogue. At times, indeed, it seems as though there were only this kind of dialogue.

I know three kinds. There is genuine dialogue—no matter whether spoken or silent—where each of the participants really has in mind the other or others in their present and particular being and turns to them with the intention of establishing a living mutual relation between himself and them. There is technical dialogue, which is prompted solely by the need of objective understanding. And there is monologue disguised as dialogue, in which two or more men, meeting in space, speak each with himself in strangely tortuous and circuitous ways and yet imagine they have escaped the torment of being thrown back on their own resources. The first kind, as I have said, has become rare; where it arises, in no matter how "unspiritual" a form, witness is borne on behalf of the continuance of the organic substance of the human spirit. The second belongs to the inalienable sterling quality of "modern existence." But real dialogue is here continually hidden in all kinds of odd corners and, occasionally in an unseemly way, breaks surface surprisingly and inopportunely—certainly still oftener it is arrogantly tolerated than downright scandalizing—as in the tone of a railway guard's voice, in the glance of an old newspaper vendor, in the smile of the chimney-sweeper. And the third. . . .

A *debate* in which the thoughts are not expressed in

the way in which they existed in the mind but in the speaking are so pointed that they may strike home in the sharpest way, and moreover without the men that are spoken to being regarded in any way present as persons; a *conversation* characterized by the need neither to communicate something, nor to learn something, nor to influence someone, nor to come into connexion with someone, but solely by the desire to have one's own self-reliance confirmed by marking the impression that is made, or if it has become unsteady to have it strengthened; a *friendly chat* in which each regards himself as absolute and legitimate and the other as relativized and questionable; a *lovers' talk* in which both partners alike enjoy their own glorious soul and their precious experience—what an underworld of faceless spectres of dialogue!

The life of dialogue is not one in which you have much to do with men, but one in which you really have to do with those with whom you have to do. It is not the solitary man who lives the life of monologue, but he who is incapable of making real in the context of being the community in which, in the context of his destiny, he moves. It is, in fact, solitude which is able to show the innermost nature of the contrast. He who is living the life of dialogue receives in the ordinary course of the hours something that is said and feels himself approached for an answer. But also in the vast blankness of, say, a companionless mountain wandering that which confronts him, rich in change, does not leave him. He who is living the life of monologue is never aware of the other as something that is absolutely not himself and at the same time something with which he nevertheless communicates. Solitude for him can mean mounting richness of visions and thoughts but never the deep intercourse, captured in a new depth, with the incomprehensibly real. Nature for him is either an *état d'âme*, hence a " living through " in himself, or it is a passive object of knowledge, either idealistically brought within the soul or realistically alienated. It does not become for him a word apprehended with senses of beholding and feeling.

Being, lived in dialogue, receives even in extreme dereliction a harsh and strengthening sense of reciprocity; being, lived in monologue, will not, even in the tenderest intimacy, grope out over the outlines of the self.

This must not be confused with the contrast between "egoism" and "altruism" conceived by some moralists. I know people who are absorbed in "social activity" and have never spoken from being to being with a fellowman. I know others who have no personal relation except to their enemies, but stand in such a relation to them that it is the enemies' fault if the relation does not flourish into one of dialogue.

Nor is dialogic to be identified with love. I know no one in any time who has succeeded in loving every man he met. Even Jesus obviously loved of "sinners" only the loose, lovable sinners, sinners against the Law; not those who were settled and loyal to their inheritance and sinned against him and his message. Yet to the latter as to the former he stood in a direct relation. Dialogic is not to be identified with love. But love without dialogic, without real outgoing to the other, reaching to the other, and companying with the other, the love remaining with itself —this is called Lucifer.

Certainly in order to be able to go out to the other you must have the starting place, you must have been, you must be, with yourself. Dialogue between mere individuals is only a sketch, only in dialogue between persons is the sketch filled in. But by what could a man from being an individual so really become a person as by the strict and sweet experiences of dialogue which teach him the boundless contents of the boundary?

What is said here is the real contrary of the cry, heard at times in twilight ages, for universal unreserve. He who can be unreserved with each passer-by has no substance to lose; but he who cannot stand in a direct relation to each one who meets him has a fulness which is futile. Luther is wrong to change the Hebrew "companion" (out of which the Seventy had already made one who is near, a neighbour) into "nearest" (3). If everything concrete is equally near, equally nearest, life with the world ceases to have articulation and structure, it ceases to have human meaning. But nothing needs to mediate between me and one of my companions in the companionship of creation, whenever we come near one another, because we are bound up in relation to the same centre.

The Basic Movements

I term basic movement an essential action of man (it may be understood as an " inner " action, but it is not there unless it is there to the very tension of the eyes' muscles and the very action of the foot as it walks), round which an essential attitude is built up. I do not think of this happening in time, as though the single action preceded the lasting attitude; the latter rather has its truth in the accomplishing, over and over again, of the basic movement, without forethought but also without habit. Otherwise the attitude would have only æsthetic or perhaps also political significance, as a beautiful and as an effective lie. The familiar maxim, "An attitude must first be adopted, the rest follows of itself " ceases to be true in the circle of essential action and essential attitude—that is, where we are concerned with the wholeness of the person.

The basic movement of the life of dialogue is the turning towards the other. That, indeed, seems to happen every hour and quite trivially. If you look at someone and address him you turn to him, of course with the body, but also in the requisite measure with the soul, in that you direct your attention to him. But what of all this is an essential action, done with the essential being? In this way, that out of the incomprehensibility of what lies to hand this one person steps forth and becomes a presence. Now to our perception the world ceases to be an insignificant multiplicity of points to one of which we pay momentary attention. Rather it is a limitless tumult round a narrow breakwater, brightly outlined and able to bear heavy loads—limitless, but limited by the breakwater, so that, though not engirdled, it has become finite in itself, been given form, released from its own indifference. And yet none of the contacts of each hour is unworthy to take

up from our essential being as much as it may. For no
man is without strength for expression, and our turning
towards him brings about a reply, however imperceptible,
however quickly smothered, in a looking and sounding
forth of the soul that are perhaps dissipating in mere
inwardness and yet do exist. The notion of modern man
that this turning to the other is sentimental and does not
correspond to the compression of life to-day is a grotesque
error, just as his affirmation that turning to the other is
impractical in the bustle of this life to-day is only the
masked confession of his weakness of initiative when confronted with the state of the time. He lets it dictate to him
what is possible or permissible, instead of stipulating, as
an unruffled partner, what is to be stipulated to the state
of *every* time, namely, what space and what form it is
bound to concede to creaturely existence.

The basic movement of the life of monologue is not
turning away as opposed to turning towards; it is " reflexion " (4).

When I was eleven years of age, spending the summer
on my grandparents' estate, I used, as often as I could do
it unobserved, to steal into the stable and gently stroke
the neck of my darling, a broad dapple-grey horse. It was
not a casual delight but a great, certainly friendly, but
also deeply stirring happening. If I am to explain it now,
beginning from the still very fresh memory of my hand,
I must say that what I experienced in touch with the
animal was the Other, the immense otherness of the Other,
which, however, did not remain strange like the otherness
of the ox and the ram, but rather let me draw near and
touch it. When I stroked the mighty mane, sometimes
marvellously smooth-combed, at other times just as astonishingly wild, and felt the life beneath my hand, it was as
though the element of vitality itself bordered on my skin,
something that was not I, was certainly not akin to me,
palpably the other, not just another, really the Other
itself; and yet it let me approach, confided itself to me,
placed itself elementally in the relation of *Thou* and *Thou*
with me. The horse, even when I had not begun by pour-
ing oats for him into the manger, very gently raised his

massive head, ears flicking, then snorted quietly, as a conspirator gives a signal meant to be recognizable only by his fellow-conspirator; and I was approved. But once—I do not know what came over the child, at any rate it was childlike enough—it struck me about the stroking, what fun it gave me, and suddenly I became conscious of my hand. The game went on as before, but something had changed, it was no longer the same thing. And the next day, after giving him a rich feed, when I stroked my friend's head he did not raise his head. A few years later, when I thought back to the incident, I no longer supposed that the animal had noticed my defection. But at the time I considered myself judged.

Reflexion is something different from egoism and even from " egotism." It is not that a man is concerned with himself, considers himself, fingers himself, enjoys, idolizes and bemoans himself; all that can be added, but it is not integral to reflexion. (Similarly, to the turning towards the other, completing it, there can be added the realizing of the other in his particular existence, even the encompassing of him, so that the situations common to him and oneself are experienced also from his, the other's, end.) I term it reflexion when a man withdraws from accepting with his essential being another person in his particularity —a particularity which is by no means to be circumscribed by the circle of his own self, and though it substantially touches and moves his soul is in no way immanent in it— and lets the other exist only as his own experience, only as a " part of myself." For then dialogue becomes a fiction, the mysterious intercourse between two human worlds only a game, and in the rejection of the real life confronting him the essence of all reality begins to disintegrate.

The Wordless Depths

Sometimes I hear it said that every *I and Thou* is only superficial, deep down word and response cease to exist, there is only the one primal being unconfronted by another. We should plunge into the silent unity, but for the rest leave its relativity to the life to be lived, instead of imposing on it this absolutized *I* and absolutized *Thou* with their dialogue.

Now from my own unforgettable experience I know well that there is a state in which the bonds of the personal nature of life seem to have fallen away from us and we experience an undivided unity. But I do not know— what the soul willingly imagines and indeed is bound to imagine (mine too once did it)—that in this I had attained to a union with the primal being or the godhead. That is an exaggeration no longer permitted to the responsible understanding. Responsibly—that is, as a man holding his ground before reality—I can elicit from those experiences only that in them I reached an undifferentiable unity of myself without form or content. I may call this an original pre-biographical unity and suppose that it is hidden unchanged beneath all biographical change, all development and complication of the soul. Nevertheless, in the honest and sober account of the responsible understanding this unity is nothing but the unity of this soul of mine, whose "ground" I have reached, so much so, beneath all formations and contents, that my spirit has no choice but to understand it as the groundless (5). But the basic unity of my own soul is certainly beyond the reach of all the multiplicity it has hitherto received from life, though not in the least beyond individuation, or the multiplicity of all the souls in the world of which it is one—existing but once, single, unique, irreducible, this creaturely one : one of the human souls and not the "soul of the All"; a defined and particular being and not "Being"; the creaturely basic unity of a creature, bound to God as in the instant before release the creature is to the *creator spiritus*, not bound to God as the creature to the *creator spiritus* in the moment of release.

The unity of his own self is not distinguishable in the man's feeling from unity in general. For he who in the act or event of absorption is sunk beneath the realm of all multiplicity that holds sway in the soul cannot experience the cessation of multiplicity except as unity itself. That is, he experiences the cessation of his own multiplicity as the cessation of mutuality, as revealed or fulfilled absence of otherness. The being which has become one can no longer understand itself on this side of individuation nor indeed on this side of *I and Thou*. For to the border experience of the soul " one " must apparently mean the same as " the One."

But in the actuality of lived life the man in such a moment is not above but beneath the creaturely situation, which is mightier and truer than all ecstasies. He is not above but beneath dialogue. He is not nearer the God who is hidden above *I and Thou*, and he is farther from the God who is turned to men and who gives himself as the *I* to a *Thou* and the *Thou* to an *I*, than that other who in prayer and service and life does not step out of the position of confrontation and awaits no wordless unity, except that which perhaps bodily death discloses.

Nevertheless, even he who lives the life of dialogue knows a lived unity : the unity of *life*, as that which once truly won is no more torn by any changes, not ripped asunder into the everyday creaturely life and the " deified " exalted hours; the unity of unbroken, raptureless perseverance in concreteness, in which the word is heard and a stammering answer dared.

Of Thinking

To all unprejudiced reflection it is clear that all *art* is from its origin essentially of the nature of dialogue. All music calls to an ear not the musician's own, all sculpture to an eye not the sculptor's, architecture in addition calls to the step as it walks in the building. They all say, to him who receives them, something (not a " feeling " but a perceived mystery) that can be said only in this one language. But there seems to cling to *thought* something of the life of monologue to which communication takes a second, secondary place. Thought seems to arise in monologue. Is it so? Is there here—where, as the philosophers say, pure subject separates itself from the concrete person in order to establish and stabilize a world for itself—a citadel which rises towering over the life of dialogue, inaccessible to it, in which man-with-himself, the single one, suffers and triumphs in glorious solitude?

Plato has repeatedly called thinking a voiceless colloquy of the soul with itself. Everyone who has really thought knows that within this remarkable process there is a stage at which an " inner " court is questioned and replies. But that is not the arising of the thought but the first trying and testing of what has arisen. The arising of the thought does not take place in colloquy with oneself. The character of monologue does not belong to the insight into a basic relation with which cognitive thought begins; nor to the grasping, limiting and compressing of the insight; nor to its moulding into the independent conceptual form; nor to the reception of this form, with the bestowal of relations, the dovetailing and soldering, into an order of conceptual forms; nor, finally, to the expression and clarification in language (which till now had only a technical and reserved symbolic function). Rather are elements of dialogue to be discovered here. It is not himself that the thinker addresses in the stages of the thought's growth, in their answerings, but as it were the basic relation in face of which he has to answer for his insight, or the order in face of which he has to answer for the newly arrived conceptual form. And it is a misunderstanding of the dynamic of the event of thought to suppose that these apostrophizings of a being existing in nature or in ideas are " really " colloquies with the self.

But also the first trying and testing of the thought, when it is provisionally completed, before the " inner " court, in the platonic sense the stage of monologue, has besides the familiar form of its appearance another form in which dialogue plays a great part, well-known to Plato if to anyone. There he who is approached for judgment is not the empirical self but the *genius*, the spirit I am intended to become, the image-self, before which the new thought is borne for approval, that is, for taking up into its own consummating thinking.

And now from another dimension which even this lease of power does not satisfy there appears the longing for a trying and testing in the sphere of pure dialogue. Here the function of receiving is no longer given over to the *Thou-I* but to a genuine *Thou* which either remains one that is thought and yet is felt as supremely living and "other," or else is embodied in an intimate person. "Man," says Wilhelm von Humboldt in his significant treatise on *The Dual Number* (1827), "longs even for the sake of his mere thinking for a *Thou* corresponding to the *I*. The conception appears to him to reach its definiteness and certainty only when it reflects from another power of thought. It is produced by being torn away from the moving mass of representation and shaped in face of the subject into the object. But the objectivity appears in a still more complete form if this separation does not go on in the subject alone, if he really sees the thought outside himself; and this is possible only in another being, representing and thinking like himself. And between one power of thought and another there is no other mediator but speech." This reference, simplified to an aphorism, recurs with Ludwig Feuerbach in 1843 : "True dialectic is not a monologue of the solitary thinker with himself, it is a dialogue between *I* and *Thou*."

But this saying points beyond that "reflecting" to the fact that even in the original stage of the proper act of thought the inner action might take place in relation to a genuine and not merely an "inward" (Novalis) *Thou*. And where modern philosophy is most earnest in the desire to ask its questions on the basis of human existence, situation and present, in some modifications an important further step is taken. Here it is certainly no longer just that the *Thou* is ready to receive and disposed to philosophize along with the *I*. Rather, and pre-eminently, we have the *Thou* in opposition because we truly have the other who thinks other things in another way. So, too, it is not a matter of a game of draughts in the tower of a castle in the air, but of the binding business of life on the hard earth, in which one is inexorably aware of the otherness of the other but does not at all contest it without realizing it; one takes up its nature into one's own thinking, thinks in relation to it, addresses it in thought.

This man of modern philosophy, however, who in this way no longer thinks in the untouchable province of pure ideation, but thinks in reality—does he think in reality? Not solely in a reality framed by thought? Is the other, whom he accepts and receives in this way, not solely the other framed by thought, and therefore unreal? Does the thinker of whom we are speaking hold his own with the bodily fact of otherness?

If we are serious about thinking between *I* and *Thou* then it is not enough to cast our thoughts towards the other subject of thought framed by thought. We should also, with the thinking, precisely with the thinking, live towards the other man, who is not framed by thought but bodily present before us; we should live towards his concrete life. We should live not towards another thinker of whom we wish to know nothing beyond his thinking but, even if the other is a thinker, towards his bodily life over and above his thinking—rather, towards his person, to which, to be sure, the activity of thinking also belongs.

When will the action of thinking endure, include, and refer to the presence of the living man facing us? When will the dialectic of thought become dialogic, an unsentimental, unrelaxed dialogue in the strict terms of thought with the man present at the moment?

Eros

The Greeks distinguished between a powerful, world-begetting Eros and one which was light and whose sphere was the soul; and also between a heavenly and a profane Eros. Neither seems to me to indicate an absolute distinction. For the primal god Desire from whom the world is derived, is the very one who in the form of a " tender elfin spirit " (Jacob Grimm) enters into the sphere of souls and in an arbitrary daimonic way carries out here, as mediator of the pollination of being, his cosmogonic work : he is the great pollen-bearing butterfly of psychogenesis. And the Pandemos (assuming it is a genuine Eros and not a Priapos impudently pretending to be the higher one) needs only to stir his wings to let the primal fire be revealed in the body's games.

Of course, the matter in question is whether Eros has not forfeited the power of flight and is now condemned to live among tough mortals and govern their mortality's paltry gestures of love. For the souls of lovers do to one another what they do; but lame-winged beneath the rule of the lame-winged one (for his power and powerlessness are always shown in theirs) they cower where they are, each in his den, instead of soaring out each to the beloved partner and there, in the beyond which has come near, " knowing " (6).

Those who are loyal to the strong-winged Eros of dialogue know the beloved being. They experience his particular life in simple presence—not as a thing seen and touched, but from the innervations to his movements, from the " inner " to his " outer." But by this I mean nothing but the bipolar experience, and—more than a swinging over and away in the instant—a contemporaneity at rest. That inclination of the head over there—you feel how the soul enjoins it on the neck, you feel it not on your neck but on that one over there, on the beloved one, and yet you yourself are not as it were snatched away, you are here, in the feeling self-being, and you receive the inclination of the head, its injunction, as the answer to the word of your own silence. In contemporaneity at rest you make and you experience dialogue. The two who are loyal to the Eros of dialogue, who love one another, receive the common event from the other's side as well, that is, they receive it from the two sides, and thus for the first time understand in a bodily way what an event is.

The kingdom of the lame-winged Eros is a world of mirrors and mirrorings. But where the winged one holds sway there is no mirroring. For there I, the lover, turn to this other human being, the beloved, in his otherness, his independence, his self-reality, and turn to him with all the power of intention of my own heart. I certainly turn to him as to one who is there turning to me, but in that very reality, not comprehensible by me but rather comprehending me, in which I am there turning to him. I do not assimilate into my own soul that which lives and faces me, I vow it faithfully to myself and myself to it, I vow, I have faith (7).

The Eros of dialogue has the simplicity of fulness; the Eros of monologue is manifold. Many years I have wandered through the land of men, and have not yet reached an end of studying the varieties of the " erotic man " (as the vassal of the broken-winged one at times describes himself). There a lover stamps around and is in love only with his passion. There one is wearing his differentiated feelings like medal-ribbons. There one is enjoying the adventures of his own fascinating effect. There one is gazing enraptured at the spectacle of his own supposed surrender. There one is collecting excitement. There one is displaying his " power." There one is preening himself with borrowed vitality. There one is delighting to exist simultaneously as himself and as an idol very unlike himself. There one is warming himself at the blaze of what has fallen to his lot. There one is experimenting. And so on and on—all the manifold monologists with their mirrors, in the apartment of the most intimate dialogue !

I have spoken of the small fry, but I have had more in mind the leviathans. There are some who stipulate to the object they propose to devour that both the doing as a holy right and the suffering as a sacred duty are what is to be called heroic love. I know of " leaders " who with their grip not only cast into confusion the plasma of the growing human being but also disintegrate it radically, so that it can no longer be moulded. They relish this power of their influence, and at the same time deceive themselves and their herd into imagining they are moulders of youthful souls, and call on *Eros,* who is inaccessible to the *profanum vulgus,* as the tutelary god of this work.

They are all beating the air. Only he who himself turns to the other human being and opens himself to him receives the world in him. Only the being whose otherness, accepted by my being, lives and faces me in the whole compression of existence, brings the radiance of eternity to me. Only when two say to one another with all that they are, " It is *Thou*," is the indwelling of the Present Being between them (8).

Community

In the view customary to-day, which is defined by politics, the only important thing in groups, in the present as in history, is what they aim at and what they accomplish. Significance is ascribed to what goes on within them only in so far as it influences the group's action with regard to its aim. Thus it is conceded to a band conspiring to conquer the state power that the comradeship which fills it is of value, just because it strengthens the band's reliable assault power. Precise obedience will do as well, if enthusiastic drill makes up for the associates remaining strangers to one another; there are indeed good grounds for preferring the rigid system. If the group is striving even to reach a higher form of society then it can seem dangerous if in the life of the group itself something of this higher form begins to be realized in embryo. For from such a premature seriousness a suppression of the " effective " impetus is feared. The opinion apparently is that the man who whiles away his time as a guest on an oasis may be accounted lost for the project of irrigating the Sahara.

By this simplified mode of valuation the real and individual worth of a group remains as uncomprehended as when we judge a person by his effect alone and not by his qualities. The perversion of thought grows when chatter is added about sacrifice of being, about renunciation of self-realization, where possible with a reference to the favourite metaphor of the dung. Happiness, possession, power, authority, life can be renounced, but sacrifice of being is a sublime absurdity. And no moment, if it has to vouch for its relation to reality, can call upon any kind of later, future moments for whose sake, in order to make them fat, it has remained so lean.

The feeling of community does not reign where the desired change of institutions is wrested in common, but without community, from a resisting world. It reigns where the fight that is fought takes place from the position of a community struggling for its own reality as a community. But the future too is decided here at the same time; all political "achievements" are at best auxiliary troops to the effect which changes the very core, and which is wrought on the unsurveyable ways of secret history by the moment of realization. No way leads to any other goal but to that which is like it.

But who in all these massed, mingled, marching collectivities still perceives what that is for which he supposes he is striving—what community is? They have all surrendered to its counterpart. Collectivity is not a binding but a bundling together: individuals packed together, armed and equipped in common, with only as much life from man to man as will inflame the marching step. But community, growing community (which is all we have known so far) is the being no longer side by side but *with* one another of a multitude of persons. And this multitude, though it also moves towards one goal, yet experiences everywhere a turning to, a dynamic facing of, the others, a flowing from *I* to *Thou*. Community is where community happens. Collectivity is based on an organized atrophy of personal existence, community on its increase and confirmation in life lived towards one other. The modern zeal for collectivity is a flight from community's testing and consecration of the person, a flight from the vital dialogic, demanding the staking of the self, which is in the heart of the world.

The men of the "collective" look down superciliously on the "sentimentality" of the generation before them, of the age of the "youth movement." Then the concern, wide-ranging and deeply-pondered, was with the problem of all life's relations, "community" was aimed at and made a problem at the same time. They went round in circles and never left the mark. But now there is commanding and marching, for now there is the "cause." The false paths of subjectivity have been left behind and the road of objectivism, going straight for its goal, has been reached. But as there existed a pseudo-subjectivity with the former, since the elementary force of being a subject was lacking, so with the latter there exists a pseudo-objectivism, since one is here fitted not into a world but into a worldless faction. As in the former all songs in praise of freedom were sung into the void, because only freeing from bonds was known, but not freeing to responsibility, so in the latter even the noblest hymns on author-ity are a misunderstanding. For in fact they strengthen only the semblance of authority which has been won by speeches and cries; behind this authority is hidden an absence of consistency draped in the mighty folds of the attitude. But genuine authority, celebrated in those hymns, the authority of the genuine charismatic in his steady response to the lord of Charis, has remained unknown to the political sphere of the present. Superficially the two generations are different in kind to the extent of contra-diction, in truth they are stuck in the same chaotic con-dition. The man of the youth movement, pondering his problems, was concerned (whatever the particular matter at different times) with his very own share in it, he " experi-enced " his *I* without pledging a self—in order not to have to pledge a self in response and responsibility. The man of the collective undertaking, striding to action, succeeded beforehand in getting rid of himself and thus radically escaping the question of pledging a self. Progress is never-theless to be recorded. With the former monologue pre-sented itself as dialogue. With the latter it is considerably simpler, for the life of monologue is by their desire driven out from most men, or they are broken of the habit; and the others, who give the orders, have at least no need to feign any dialogic.

Dialogue and monologue are silenced. Bundled to-gether, men march without *Thou* and without *I*, those of the left who want to abolish memory, and those of the right who want to regulate it : hostile and separated hosts, they march into the common abyss.

Conversation with the Opponent

I HOPE FOR two kinds of readers for these thoughts : for the *amicus* who knows about the reality to which I am pointing with a finger I should like to be able to stretch out like Grünewald's Baptist; and for the *hostis* or *adversarius* who denies this reality and therefore contends with me, because I point to it (in his view misleadingly) as to a reality. Thus he takes what is said here just as seriously as I myself do, after long waiting writing what is to be written—just as seriously, only with the negative sign. The mere *inimicus*, as which I regard everyone who wishes to relegate me to the realm of ideology and there let my thoughts count, I would gladly dispense with.

I need say nothing at this point to the *amicus*. The hour of common mortality and the common way strikes in his and in my ears as though we stood even in the same place with one another and knew one another.

But it is not enough to tell the *adversarius* here what I am pointing at—the hiddenness of his personal life, his secret, and that, stepping over a carefully avoided threshold, he will discover what he denies. It is not enough. I dare not turn aside his gravest objection. I must accept it, as and where it is raised, and must answer.

So now the *adversarius* sits, facing me in his actual form as he appears in accordance with the spirit of the time, and speaks, more above and beyond me than towards and to me, in accents and attitude customary in the universal duel, free of personal relation.

" In all this the actuality of our present life, the conditioned nature of life as a whole, is not taken into account. All that you speak of takes place in the never-never-land, not in the social context of the world in which we spend our days, and by which if by anything our reality is defined. Your 'two men' sit on a solitary seat, obviously during a holiday journey. In a big city office you would not be able to let them sit, they would not reach the 'sacramental' there. Your 'interrupted conversation' takes place between intellectuals who have leisure a couple of months before the huge mass event to spin fantasies of its prevention through a spiritual influence. That may be quite interesting for people who are not taken up with any duty. But is the business employee to 'communicate himself without reserve' to his colleagues? Is the worker at the conveyor belt to 'feel himself addressed in what he experiences'? Is the leader of a gigantic technical undertaking to 'practise the responsibility of dialogue'? You demand that we enter into the situation which approaches us, and you neglect the enduring situation in which everyone of us, so far as we share in the life of the community, is elementally placed. In spite of all references to concreteness, all that is pre-war individualism in a revised edition."

And I. out of a deep consciousness of how almost impossible it is to think in common, if only in opposition, where there is no common experience, reply.

Before all, dear opponent, if we are to converse with one another and not at and past one another, I beg you to notice that I do not demand. I have no call to that and no authority for it. I try only to say that there is something, and to indicate how it is made : I simply record. And how could the life of dialogue be demanded? There is no ordering of dialogue. It is not that you *are* to answer but that you *are able*.

You are really able. The life of dialogue is no privilege of intellectual activity like dialectic. It does not begin in the upper story of humanity. It begins no higher than where humanity begins. There are no gifted and ungifted here, only those who give themselves and those who withhold themselves. And he who gives himself to-morrow is not noted to-day, even he himself does not know that he has it in himself, that we have it in ourselves, he will just find it, " and finding be amazed."

You put before me the man taken up with duty and

business. Yes, precisely him I mean, him in the factory, in the shop, in the office, in the mine, on the tractor, at the printing-press : man. I do not seek for men. I do not seek men out for myself, I accept those who are there, I have them, I have him, in mind, the yoked, the wheel-treading, the conditioned. Dialogue is not an affair of spiritual luxury and spiritual luxuriousness, it is a matter of creation, of the creature, and he is that, the man of whom I speak, he is a creature, trivial and irreplaceable.

In my thoughts about the life of dialogue I have had to choose the examples as " purely " and as much in the form of paradigm as memory presented them to me in order to make myself intelligible about what has become so unfamiliar, in fact so sunk in oblivion. For this reason I appear to draw my tales from the province which you term the " intellectual," in reality only from the province where things succeed, are rounded off, in fact are exemplary. But I am not concerned with the pure; I am concerned with the turbid, the repressed, the pedestrian, with toil and dull contraryness—and with the break-through. With the break-through and not with a perfection, and moreover with the break-through not out of despair with its murderous and renewing powers; no, not with the great catastrophic break-through which happens once for all (it is fitting to be silent for a while about that, even in one's own heart), but with the breaking through from the status of the dully-tempered disagreeableness, obstinacy, and contraryness in which the man, whom I pluck at random out of the tumult, is living and out of which he can and at times does break through.

Whither? Into nothing exalted, heroic or holy, into no Either and no Or, only into this tiny strictness and grace of every day, where I have to do with just the very same " reality " with whose duty and business I am taken up in such a way, glance to glance, look to look, word to word, that I experience it as reached to me and myself to it, it as spoken to me and myself to it. And now in all the clanking of routine that I called my reality, there appears to me, homely and glorious, the effective reality, creaturely and given to me in trust and responsibility. We do not find meaning lying in things nor do we put it into things, but between us and things it can happen.

It is not sufficient, dear opponent, first of all to ascribe to me the pathos of "all or nothing" and then to prove the impossibility of my alleged demand. I know neither what all nor what nothing is, the one appears to me to be as inhuman and contrived as the other. What I am meaning is the simple *quantum satis* of that which this man in this hour of his life is able to fulfil and to receive—if he gives himself. That is, if he does not let himself be deceived by the compact plausibility that there are places excluded from creation, that he works in such a place and is able to return to creation when his shift is over; or that creation is outstripped, that it once was but is irrevocably over, now there is business and now it is a case of stripping off all romanticism, gritting the teeth and getting through with what is recognized as necessary. I say—if he does not let himself be deceived.

No factory and no office is so abandoned by creation that a creative glance could not fly up from one working-place to another, from desk to desk, a sober and brotherly glance which guarantees the reality of creation which is happening—*quantum satis*. And nothing is so valuable a service of dialogue between God and man as such an unsentimental and unreserved exchange of glances between two men in an alien place.

But is it irrevocably an alien place? Must henceforth, through all the world's ages, the life of the being which is yoked to business be divided in two, into alien "work" and home "recovery"? More, since evenings and Sundays cannot be freed of the workday character but are unavoidably stamped with it, must such a life be divided out between the business of work and the business of recovery without a remainder of directness, of unregulated surplus—of freedom? (And the freedom I mean is established by no new order of society.)

Or does there already stir, beneath all dissatisfactions that can be satisfied, an unknown and primal and deep dissatisfaction for which there is as yet no recipe of satisfaction anywhere, but which will grow to such mightiness that it dictates to the technical leaders, the promoters, the inventors, and says, "Go on with your rationalizing, but humanize the rationalizing *ratio* in yourselves. Let it introduce the living man into its purposes and its calculations, him who longs to stand in a mutual relation with the world." Dear opponent, does the longing already stir in the depths—an impulse to great construction or a tiny spark of the last revolution—to fill business with the life of dialogue? That is, in the formulation of the *quantum satis,* the longing for an order of work in which business is so continually soaked in vital dialogic as the tasks to be fulfilled by it allow? And of the extent to which they can allow it there is scarcely an inkling to-day, in an hour when the question which I put is at the mercy of the fanatics, blind to reality, who conform to the time, and of the heralds, blind to possibility, of the impervious tragedy of the world.

Be clear what it means when a worker can experience even his relation to the machine as one of dialogue, when, for instance, a compositor tells that he has understood the machine's humming as "a merry and grateful smile at me for helping it to set aside the difficulties and obstructions which disturbed and bruised and pained it, so that now it could run free." Must even you not think then of the story of Androclus and the Lion?

But when a man draws a lifeless thing into his passionate longing for dialogue, lending it independence and as it were a soul, then there may dawn in him the presentiment of a world-wide dialogue, a dialogue with the world-happening that steps up to him even in his environment, which consists partly of things. Or do you seriously think that the giving and taking of signs halts on the threshold of that business where an honest and open spirit is found?

You ask with a laugh, can the leader of a great technical undertaking practise the responsibility of dialogue? He can. For he practises it when he makes present to himself in its concreteness, so far as he can, *quantum satis,* the business which he leads. He practises it when he experiences it, instead of as a structure of mechanical centres of force and their organic servants (among which latter there is for him no differentiation but the functional one), as an association of persons with faces and names and biographies, bound together by a work that is represented by, but does not consist of, the achievements of a complicated mechanism. He practises it when he is inwardly aware, with a latent and disciplined fantasy, of the multitude of these persons, whom naturally he cannot separately know and remember as such; so that now, when one of them for some reason or other steps really as an individual into the circle of his vision and the realm of his decision, he is aware of him without strain not as a number with a human mask but as a person. He practises it when he comprehends and handles these persons as persons—for the greatest part necessarily indirectly, by means of a system of mediation which varies according to the extent, nature and structure of the undertaking, but also directly, in the parts which concern him by way of organization. Naturally at first both camps, that of capital and that of the proletariat, will decry his masterly attitude of fantasy as fantastic nonsense and his practical attitude to persons as dilettantist. But just as naturally only until his increased figures of production accredit him in their eyes. (By this of course is not to be implied that those increases necessarily come to pass : between truth and success there is no pre-stabilized harmony.) Then, to be sure, something worse will follow. He will be pragmatically imitated, that is, people will try to use his " procedure " without his way of thinking and imagining. But this demoniac element inherent in spiritual history (think only of all the magicizing of religion) will, I think, shipwreck here on the power of discrimination in men's souls. And meanwhile it is to be hoped that a new generation will arise, learning from what is alive, and will take all this in real seriousness as he does.

Unmistakably men are more and more determined by " circumstances." Not only the absolute mass but also the relative might of social objectives is growing. As one determined partially by them the individual stands in each moment before concrete reality which wishes to reach out to him and receive an answer from him; laden with the situation he meets new situations. And yet in all the multiplicity and complexity he has remained Adam. Even now a real decision is made in him, whether he faces the speech of God articulated to him in things and events—or escapes. And a creative glance towards his fellow-creature can at times suffice for response.

Man is in a growing measure sociologically determined. But this growing is the maturing of a task not in the "ought" but in the "may" and in "need," in longing and in grace. It is a matter of renouncing the pantechnical mania or habit with its easy "mastery" of every situation; of taking everything up into the might of dialogue of the genuine life, from the trivial mysteries of everyday to the majesty of destructive destiny.

The task becomes more and more difficult, and more and more essential, the fulfilment more and more impeded and more and more rich in decision. All the regulated chaos of the age waits for the break-through, and wherever a man perceives and responds, he is working to that end.

II

THE QUESTION TO THE SINGLE ONE

Responsibility is the navel-string of creation.—P.B.

The Unique One and the Single One

ONLY BY COMING up against the category of the "Single One," (9) and by making it a concept of the utmost clarity, did Sören Kierkegaard become the one who presented Christianity as a paradoxical problem for the single "Christian." He was only able to do this owing to the radical nature of his solitariness. His " single one " cannot be understood without his solitariness, which differed in kind from the solitariness of one of the earlier Christian thinkers, such as Augustine or Pascal, whose name one would like to link with his. It is not irrelevant that beside Augustine stood a mother and beside Pascal a sister, who maintained the organic connexion with the world as only a woman as the envoy of elemental life can; whereas the central event of Kierkegaard's life and the core of the crystallization of his thought was the renunciation of Regina Olsen as representing woman and the world. Nor may this solitariness be compared with that of a monk or a hermit : for him the renunciation stands essentially only at the beginning, and even if it must be ever anew achieved and practised, it is not that which is the life theme, the basic problem, and the stuff out of which all teaching is woven. But for Kierkegaard this is just what renunciation is. It is embodied in the category of the single one, " the category through which, from the religious standpoint, time and history and the race must pass " (Kierkegaard, 1847).

By means of an opposition we can first of all be precisely aware what the single one, in a special and specially important sense, is not. A few years before Kierkegaard outlined his *Report to History* under the title *The Point of View for my Work as an Author,* in whose *Two Notes* the category of the Single One found its adequate formulation, Max Stirner published his book about "The Unique One" (10). This too is a border concept like the single one, but one from the other end. Stirner, a pathetic nominalist and unmasker of ideas, wanted to dissolve the alleged remains of German idealism (as which he regarded Ludwig Feuerbach) by raising not the thinking subject nor man but the concrete present individual as "the exclusive I" to be the bearer of the world, that is, of "his" world.

Here this Unique One "consuming himself" in "self-enjoyment" is the only one who has primary existence; only the man who comes to such a possession and consciousness of himself has primary existence—on account of the "unity and omnipotence of our I that is sufficient to itself, for it lets nothing be but itself." Thus the question of an essential relation between him and the other is eliminated as well. He has no essential relation except to himself (Stirner's alleged "living participation" "in the person of the other" is without essence, since the other has in his eyes no primary existence). That is, he has only that remarkable relation with the self which does not lack certain magical possibilities (since all other existence becomes the haunting of ghosts that are half in bonds, half free), but is so empty of any genuine power to enter into relation that it is better to describe as a relation only that in which not only *I* but also *Thou* can be said. This border product of a German Protagoras is usually underrated: the loss of reality which responsibility and truth have suffered in our time has here if not its spiritual origin certainly its exact conceptual prediction. "The man who belongs to himself alone . . . is by origin free, for he acknowledges nothing but himself," and "True is what is Mine" are formulas which forecast a congealing of the soul unsuspected by Stirner in all his rhetorical assurance. But also many a rigid collective *We,* which rejects a superior authority, is easily understood as a translation from the speech of the Unique One into that of the *Group-I* which acknowledges nothing but itself—carried out against Stirner's intention, who hotly opposes any plural version.

Kierkegaard's Single One has this in common with its counterpoint, Stirner's Unique One, that both are border categories; it has no more in common than this, but also it has no less.

The category of the Single One, too, means not the subject or "man," but concrete singularity; yet not the individual who is detecting his existence, but rather the person who is finding himself. But the finding himself, however primally remote from Stirner's "utilize thyself," is not akin either to that "know thyself" which apparently troubled Kierkegaard very much. For it means a becoming, and moreover in a weight of seriousness that only became possible, at least for the West, through Christianity. It is therefore a becoming which (though Kierkegaard says that his category was used by Socrates "for the dissolution of heathendom") is decisively different from that effected by the Socratic "delivery." "No-one is excluded from being a Single One except him who excludes himself by wishing to be 'crowd.'" Here not only is "Single One" opposed to "crowd," but also becoming is opposed to a particular mode of being which evades becoming. That may still be in tune with Socratic thought. But what does it mean, to become a Single One? Kierkegaard's account shows clearly that the nature of his category is no longer Socratic. It runs, "to fulfil the first condition of all religiosity" is "to be a single man." It is for this reason that the "Single One" is "the category through which, from the religious standpoint, time and history and the race must pass."

Since the concept of religiosity has since lost its definiteness, what Kierkegaard means must be more precisely defined. He cannot mean that to become a Single One is the presupposition of a condition of the soul, called religiosity. It is not a matter of a condition of the soul but a matter of existence in that strict sense in which—precisely by fulfilling the personal life—it steps in its essence over the boundary of the person. Then being, familiar being, becomes unfamiliar and no longer signifies my being but my participation in the Present Being. That this is what Kierkegaard means is expressed in the fundamental word that the Single One " corresponds " to God. In Kierkegaard's account, then, the concept " of all religiosity " has to be more precisely defined by " of all religious reality." But since this also is all too exposed to the epidemic sickening of the word in our time, by which every word is at once covered with the leprosy of routine and changed into a slogan, we must go further, as far as possible, and, giving up vexatious " religion," take a risk, but a necessary risk, and explain the phrase as meaning " of all human dealings with God." That Kierkegaard means this is shown by his reference to a " speaking with God." And indeed a man can have dealings with God only as a Single One, as a man who has become a Single One. This is so expressed in the Old Testament, though there a people too meets the Godhead as a people, that it time and again lets only a named person, Enoch, Noah, " have dealings with Elohim." Not before a man can say *I* in perfect reality—that is, finding himself—can he in perfect reality say *Thou*—that is, to God. And even if he does it in a community he can only do it " alone." " As the ' Single One ' he [every man] is alone, alone in the whole world, alone before God." That is—what Kierkegaard, strangely, does not think of—thoroughly unsocratic : in the words " the divine gives me a sign " Socrates's " religiosity " is represented, significant for all ages; but the words " I am alone before God " are unthinkable as coming from him. Kierkegaard's " alone " is no longer of Socrates; it is of Abraham—Genesis 12. 1 and 22. 2, alike demand in the same " Go before thee " the power to free oneself of all bonds, the bonds to the world of fathers and to the world of sons; and it is of Christ.

Clarity demands a further twofold distinction. First, with respect to mysticism. It too lets the man be alone before God but not as the Single One. The relation to God which it thinks of is the absorption of the *I*, and the Single One ceases to exist if he cannot—even in devoting himself—say *I*. As mysticism will not permit God to assume the servant's form of the speaking and acting person, of a creator, of a revealer, and to tread the way of the Passion through time as the partner of history, suffering along with it all destiny, so it forbids man, as the Single One persisting as such, from really praying and serving and loving such as is possible only by an *I* to a *Thou*. Mysticism only tolerates the Single One in order that he may radically melt away. But Kierkegaard knows, at any rate in relation to God, what love is, and thus he knows that there is no self-love that is not self-deceit (since he who loves—and it is he who matters—loves only the other and essentially not himself), but that without being and remaining oneself there is no love.

The second necessary distinction is with respect to Stirner's " Unique One." (For the sake of conceptual precision this expression is to be preferred to the more humanistic ones, such as Stendhal's *égotiste*.)

A preliminary distinction must be made with respect to so-called individualism, which has also produced a " religious " variety. The Single One, the person ready and able for the " standing alone before God," is the counterpart of what still, in no distant time, was called—in a term which is treason to the spirit of Goethe—personality, and man's becoming a Single One is the counterpart of " personal development." All individualism, whether it is styled æsthetic or ethical or religious, has a cheap and ready pleasure in man provided he is " developing." In other words, " ethical " and " religious " individualism are only inflexions of the " æsthetic " (which is as little genuine *æsthesis* as those are genuine *ethos* and genuine *religio*).

Morality and piety, where they have in this way become an autonomous aim, must also be reckoned among the show-pieces and shows of a spirit that no longer knows about Being but only about its mirrorings.

Where individualism ceases to be wanton Stirner begins. He is also, it is true, concerned with the " shaping of free personality," but in the sense of a severance of the " self " from the world : he is concerned with the tearing apart of his existential bindings and bonds, with breaking free from all ontic otherness of things and of lives, which now may only serve as "nourishment" of his selfhood. The contrapuntal position of Stirner's Unique One to Kierkegaard's Single One becomes clearest when the questions of responsibility and truth are raised.

For Stirner both are bound to be false questions. But it is important to see that intending to destroy both basic ideas he has destroyed only their routine forms and thus, contrary to his whole intention, has prepared for their purification and renewal. Historically-minded contemporaries have spoken disparagingly of him as a modern sophist; since then the function of the sophists, and consequently of their like, of dissolving and preparing, has been recognized. Stirner may have understood Hegel just as little as Protagoras did Heraclitus; but even as it is meaningless to reproach Protagoras with laying waste the gardens of the great cosmologist, so Stirner is untouched by being ridiculed as the unsuspecting and profane interloper in the fields of post-kantian philosophy. Stirner is not, any more than the sophists are, a curious interlude in the history of human thought. Like them he is an ἐπεισόδιον in the original sense. In his monologue the action secretly changes, what follows is a new thing—as Protagoras leads towards his contemporary Socrates, Stirner leads towards his contemporary Kierkegaard.

Responsibility presupposes one who addresses me primarily, that is, from a realm independent of myself, and to whom I am answerable. He addresses me about something that he has entrusted to me and that I am bound to take care of loyally. He addresses me from his trust and I respond in my loyalty or refuse to respond in my disloyalty, or I had fallen into disloyalty and wrestle free of it by the loyalty of the response. To be so answerable to a trusting person about an entrusted matter that loyalty and disloyalty step into the light of day (but both are not of the same right, for now loyalty, born again, is permitted to conquer disloyalty)—this is the reality of responsibility. Where no primary address and claim can touch me, for everything is " My property," responsibility has become a phantom. At the same time life's character of mutuality is dissipated. He who ceases to make a response ceases to hear the Word.

But this reality of responsibility is not what is questioned by Stirner; it is unknown to him. He simply does not know what of elemental reality happens between life and life, he does not know the mysteries of address and answer, claim and disclaim, word and response. He has not experienced this because it can only be experienced when one is not closed to the otherness, the ontic and primal otherness of the other (to the primal otherness of the other, which of course, even when the other is God, must not be confined to a "wholly otherness"). What Stirner with his destructive power successfully attacks is the substitute for a reality that is no longer believed : the fictitious responsibility in face of reason, of an idea, a nature, an institution, of all manner of illustrious ghosts, all that in its essence is not a person and hence cannot really, like father and mother, prince and master, husband and friend, like God, make you answerable. He wishes to show the nothingness of the word which has decayed into a phrase; he has never known the living world, he unveils what he knows. Ignorant of the reality whose appearance is appearance, he proves its nature to be appearance. Stirner dissolves the dissolution. "What you call responsibility is a lie!" he cries, and he is right : it is a lie. But there is a truth. And the way to it lies freer after the lie has been seen through.

Kierkegaard means true responsibility when, rushing in a parabola past Stirner, he speaks thus of the crowd and the Single One : "Being in a crowd either releases from repentance and responsibility or weakens the responsibility of the Single One, since the crowd leaves only a fragment of responsibility to him." These words, to which I intend to return, no longer have in view any illusion of a responsibility without a receiver, but genuine responsibility, recognized once more, in which the demander demands of me the entrusted good and I must open my hands or they petrify.

Stirner has unmasked as unreal the responsibility which is only ethical by exposing the non-existence of the alleged receivers as such. Kierkegaard has proclaimed anew the responsibility which is in faith.

And as with responsibility so with truth itself : here the parabolic meeting becomes still uncannier.

" Truth . . . exists only—in your head." " The truth is a—creature." " For Me there is no truth, for nothing passes beyond Me." " So long as you believe in the truth you do not believe in yourself. . . . You alone are the truth." What Stirner undertakes here is the dissolution of *possessed* truth, of " truth " as a general good that can be taken into possession and possessed, that is at once independent of and accessible to the person. He does not undertake this like the sophists and other sceptics by means of epistemology. He does not seem to have been acquainted with the epistemological method; he is as audaciously naive in his behaviour as though Hume and Kant had never lived. But neither wou'd the epistemology have achieved for him what he needed; for it, and the solipsist theory as well, leads only to the knowing subject and not to the concrete human person at which Stirner aims with undeviating fanaticism. The means by which he undertakes the dissolution of possessed truth is the demonstration that it is conditioned by the person. " True is what is Mine." There already lies hidden the fundamental principle of our day, " what I take as true is defined by what I am." To this two sentences may be taken as alternatives or as a combination—to Stirner's horror, certainly, but in logical continuation as an inseparable exposition—first the sentence " And what I am is conditioned by my complexes," and second the sentence " And what I am is conditioned by the class I belong to," with all its variants. Stirner is the involuntary father of modern psychological and sociological relativizings which for their part (to anticipate) are at once true and false.

But again Stirner is right, again he dissolves the dissolution. *Possessed* truth is not even a creature, it is a ghost, a succubus with which a man may succeed in effectively imagining he is living, but with which he cannot live. You cannot devour the truth, it is not served up anywhere in the world, you cannot even gape at it, for it is not an object. And yet there does exist a participation in the being of inaccessible truth—for the man who stands its test. There exists a real relation of the whole human person to the unpossessed, unpossessable truth, and it is completed only in standing its test. This real relation, whatever it is called, is the relation to the Present Being.

The re-discovery of truth, which has been disenthroned in the human world by the semblance of truth, but which is in truth eternally irremovable, which cannot be possessed but which can be served, and for which service can be given by perceiving *and* standing test, is accomplished by Kierkegaard in a paradoxical series of sentences. It begins with the words, " He who communicates it [the truth] is only a Single One. And then its communication is again only for the Single One; for this view of life, ' the Single One,' is the very truth." You must listen carefully. Not that the Single One exists and not that he should exist is described as the truth, but " this view of life " which consists in the Single One's existing, and which is hence also simply identified with him. To be the Single One is the communication of the truth, that is, the human truth. " The crowd," says Kierkegaard, " produces positions of advantage in human life," which " overlook in time and the world the eternal truth—the Single One." " You alone are the truth " is what Stirner says. " The Single One is the truth," is what is said here. That is the uncanny parabolic phenomenon of words to which I have referred. In " a time of dissolution " (Kierkegaard) there is the blank point at which the No and the Yes move up to and past one another with all their power, but purely objectively and without consciousness. Now Kierkegaard continues : " The truth cannot be communicated and received except as it were before God's eyes, by God's help; so that God is there, is the medium as he is the truth. . . . For God is the truth and its medium." Thus " ' The Single One ' is the truth " and " God is the truth." That is true because the Single One " corresponds " to God. Hence Kierkegaard can say that the category of the ' Single One ' is and remains " the fixed point which can resist pantheist confusion." The Single One corresponds to God. For

" man is akin to the Godhead." In Old Testament language, the Single One realizes the " image " of God precisely through having become a Single One. In the language in which alone a generation, wrestling with the problem of truth, succumbing to it, turning from it, but also exploring it ever anew, can understand the conquest, the Single One existentially stands the test of the appearing truth by " the personal existence expressing what is said " [I would say " what is unsaid "]. There is this human side of truth—in human existence. God is the truth because he is, the Single One is the truth because he reaches his existence.

Stirner has dissolved the truth which is only noetic, and against all his knowledge and desire cleared a space into which Kierkegaard's believed and tested truth has stepped, the truth which can no longer be obtained and possessed by the *noesis* alone, but which must be existentially realized in order to be inwardly known and communicated.

But there is still a third and last contact and repulsion. For Stirner every man is the Unique One if only he discards all ideological ballast (to which for him the religious belongs) and settles down as owner of his world-property. For Kierkegaard " every, absolutely every man " " can and ought " to be " the Single One "—only he must . . . what, indeed, must he? He must become a Single One. For " the matter is thus : this category cannot be taught by precept; it is something that you can *do,* it is an *art* . . . and moreover an art whose practice could cost the artist, in time, his life." But when we investigate closely to see if there is a nearer definition anywhere, even if not precisely one that can be taught by precept, one will be found—no more than one, no more than a single word, but it is found : it is " obey." It is at any rate what is under all circumstances prohibited to Stirner's Unique One by his author. It is easy to discover that behind all Stirner's prohibitions to his Unique One this stands as the real, comprehensive and decisive prohibition. With this one verb Kierkegaard finally thrusts off the spirit which, without either of them knowing, has approached so near, too near, in the time of dissolution.

And yet—the illumination of our time makes it visible—the two, primally different, primally strange to one another, concerning one another in nothing but with one another concerning us, work together, not a hundred years ago but to-day, the one announcing decay as decay, the other proving the eternal structure to be inviolable. To renounce obedience to any usurping lord is Stirner's demand; Kierkegaard has none of his own—he repeats the ancient, misused, desecrated, outworn, inviolable "obey the Lord." If a man becomes the Single One "then the obedience is all right" even in the time of dissolution, where otherwise the obedience is not all right.

Stirner leads out of all kinds of alleys into the open country where each is the Unique One and the world is his property. There they bustle in futile and non-committal life, and nothing comes of it but bustle, till one after the other begins to notice what this country is called. Kierkegaard leads to a "narrow pass"; his task is "where possible to induce the many, to invite them, to stir them to press through this narrow pass, 'the Single One,' through which, note well, none passes unless he becomes 'the Single One,' since in the concept itself the opposite is excluded." I think, however, that in actual history the way to this narrow pass is through that open country that first is called individual egoism and then collective egoism and, finally, by its true name, despair.

But is there really a way through the narrow pass? Can one really become the Single One?

"I myself do not assert of myself," says Kierkegaard, "that I am that one. For I have indeed fought for it, but have not yet grasped it, and am in the continued fight continually reminded that it is beyond human strength to be 'the Single One' in the highest sense."

"In the highest sense"—that is spoken with a Christian and a christological reference, it manifests the paradox of the Christian task. But it is also convincing to the non-christian. It has in it the assertion that no man can say of himself that he has become the Single One, since a higher sense of the category always remains unfulfilled beyond him; but it also has in it the assertion that every man can nevertheless become a Single One. Both are true.

"The eternal, the decisive, can be worked for only where one man is; and to become this one man, which all men can, means to let oneself be helped by God." This is a way.

And yet it is not the way; for reasons of which I have not spoken in this section and of which I now have to speak.

The Single One and his Thou

Kierkegaard's " to become a Single One " is, as we have seen, not meant Socratically. The goal of this becoming is not the " right " life, but the entry into a relation. " To become " means here to become *for* something, " for " in the strict sense which simply transcends the circle of the person himself. It means to be made ready for the one relation which can be entered into only by the Single One, the one; the relation for whose sake man exists.

This relation is an exclusive one, the exclusive one, and this means, according to Kierkegaard, that it is the excluding relation, excluding all others; more precisely, that it is the relation which in virtue of its unique, essential life expels all other relations into the realm of the unessential.

"Everyone should be chary about having to do with ' the others,' and should essentially speak only with God and with himself," he says in the exposition of the category. Everyone, so it is to be understood, because everyone can be the one.

The joining of the " with God " with the " with himself " is a serious incompatibility that nothing can mitigate. All the enthusiasm of the philosophers for monologue, from Plato to Nietzsche, does not touch the simple experience of faith that speaking with God is something *toto genere* different from " speaking with oneself "; whereas, remarkably, it is not something *toto genere* different from speaking with another human being. For in the latter case there is common the fact of being approached, grasped, addressed, which cannot be anticipated in any depth of the soul; but in the former case it is not common in spite of all the soul's adventures in doubling roles—games, intoxications, dreams, visions, surprises, overwhelmings, overpowerings—in spite of all tensions and divisions, and all the noble and strong images for traffic with oneself. " Then one became two "—that can never become *ontically* true, just as the reverse " one and one at one " of mysticism can never be ontically true. Only when I have to do with another essentially, that is, in such a way that he is no longer a phenomenon of my *I*, but instead is my *Thou*, do I experience the reality of speech with another—in the irrefragable genuineness of mutuality. *Abyssus abyssum 'amat*—what that means the soul first experiences when it reaches its frontier and finds itself faced by one that is simply not the soul itself and yet is a self.

But on this point Kierkegaard seems to correct himself. In the passage in his *Journals* where he asks the question, " And how does one become a Single One?" the answer begins with the formulation, obviously more valid in the problem under discussion, that one should be, " regarding the highest concerns, related solely to God."

If, in this sentence, the word " highest " is understood as limiting in its content, then the phrase is self-evident : the highest concerns can be put only to the highest. But it cannot be meant in this way; this is clear from the other sentence, " Everyone should. . . ." If both are held together, then Kierkegaard's meaning is evident that the Single One has to do *essentially* (is not " chary ") only with God.

But thereby the category of the Single One, which has scarcely been properly discovered, is already fatefully misunderstood.

Kierkegaard, the Christian concerned with " contemporaneity " with Jesus, here contradicts his master.

To the question—which was not merely aimed at " tempting " him, but was rather a current and significant controversial question of the time—which was the allinclusive and fundamental commandment, the " great " commandment, Jesus replied by connecting the two Old Testament commandments between which above all the choice lay: "love God with all your might" and "love your neighbour as one like yourself" (11). Both are to be "loved," God and the "neighbour" (i.e. not man in general, but the man who meets me time and again in the context of life), but in different ways. The neighbour is to be loved "as one like myself" (not "as I love myself"; in the last reality one does not love oneself, but one should rather learn to love oneself through love of one's neighbour), to whom, then, I should show love as I wish it may be shown to me. But God is to be loved with all my soul and all my might. By connecting the two Jesus brings to light the Old Testament truth that God and man are not rivals. Exclusive love to God ("with *all* your heart") is, *because he is God,* inclusive love, ready to accept and include all love. It is not himself that God creates, not himself he redeems, even when he "reveals himself" it is not himself he reveals: his revelation does not have himself as object. He limits himself in all his limitlessness, he makes room for the creatures, and so, in love to him, he makes room for love to the creatures.

"In order to come to love," says Kierkegaard about his renunciation of Regina Olsen, "I had to remove the object." That is sublimely to misunderstand God. Creation is not a hurdle on the road to God, it is the road itself. We are created along with one another and directed to a life with one another. Creatures are placed in my way so that I, their fellow-creature, by means of them and with them find the way to God. A God reached by their exclusion would not be the God of all lives in whom all life is fulfilled. A God in whom only the parallel lines of single approaches intersect is more akin to the "God of the philosophers" than to the "God of Abraham and Isaac and Jacob." God wants us to come to him by means of the Reginas he has created and not by renunciation of them. If we remove the object, then—we have removed the object altogether. Without an object, artificially producing the object from the abundance of the human spirit and calling it God, this love has its being in the void.

"The matter must be brought back to the monastery from which Luther broke out." So Kierkegaard defines the task of the time. "Monastery" can here mean only the institutional safeguarding of man from an essential relation, inclusive of his whole being, to any others but God. And certainly to one so safeguarded the orientation towards the point called God is made possible with a precision not to be attained otherwise. But what "God" in this case means is in fact only the end-point of a human line of orientation. But the real God lets no shorter line reach him than each man's longest, which is the line embracing the world that is accessible to this man. For he, the real God, is the creator, and all beings stand before him in relation to one another in his creation, becoming useful in living with one another for his creative purpose. To teach an acosmic relation to God is not to know the creator. Acosmic worship of a God of whom one knows, along with Kierkegaard, that it is of his grace "that he wills to be a person in relation to you," is Marcionism, and not even consistent Marcionism; for this worship does not separate the creator and the redeemer as it would have to do if it were consistent.

But one must not overlook the fact that Kierkegaard is not at all concerned to put Luther breaking out of the monastery in the wrong. On one occasion he treats Luther's marriage as something removed from all natural personal life, all directness between man and wife, as a symbolic action, a deed representing and expressing the turning-point of the spiritual history of the west. "The most important thing," he makes Luther say, "is that it becomes notorious that I am married." But behind Luther's marrying Katharina there emerges, unnamed but clear, Kierkegaard's not marrying Regina. "Put the other way round, one could say . . . in defiance of the whole nineteenth century I cannot marry." Here there is added as a new perspective the qualitative difference between historical epochs. Certainly, on Kierkegaard's view it is true for both ages that the Single One should not have to do essentially with any others but God, and according to him, then, Luther speaks not essentially but only symbolic-

ally with Katharina; though bound to the world he remains essentially worldless and "alone before God." But
the symbolic actions are opposed : by the one the word of
a new bond with the world—even if perhaps in the end a
bond that is not binding—is spoken to the one century;
by the other the word of a new and in any event binding
renunciation is spoken to the other century. What is the
reason? Because the nineteenth century has given itself
up to the "crowd," and "the crowd is untruth."

But now two things are possible. Either the bond with
the world preached with his life by Luther is in Kierkegaard's view not binding or "essential" or necessary for
the leading of Luther's age to God. But that would make
Luther one who lets what is not binding be effective as
something that is binding, who has a different thing to say
for men than he has for God, and who treats the sacrament
as though it were fulfilled outside God; it would make
Luther one in whose symbolic action no authority could
reside. Or else on the other hand the bond with the world
preached with his life by Luther is in Kierkegaard's view
binding and essential and necessary for leading to God.
Then the difference between the two epochs, which is for
the rest indubitably a qualitative one, would have a say
in what is basically independent of history, more so than
birth and death—the relation of the Single One to God.
For the essential quality of this relation cannot be of one
kind in the former century and of another in the latter; it
cannot in the one go right through the world and in the
other go over and beyond the world. Human representa-
tions of the relation change, the truth of the relation is
unchangeable because it stands in eternal mutuality; it is
not man who defines his approach to it but the creator
who in the unambiguity of man's creation has instituted
the approach.

It is certainly not possible to speak of God other than
dialectically, for he does not come under the principle of
contradiction. Yet there is a limit of dialectic where
assertion ceases but where there is knowledge. Who is
there who confesses the God whom Kierkegaard and I
confess, who could suppose in decisive insight that God

wants *Thou* to be truly said only to him, and to all others only an unessential and fundamentally invalid word—that God demands of us to choose between him and his creation? The objection is raised that the world as a fallen world is not to be identified with the creation. But what fall of the world could be so mighty that it could *for him* break it away from being his creation? That would be to make the action of the world into one more powerful than God's action and into one compelling him.

The essential is not that we should see things as standing out from God nor as being absorbed in him, but that we should "see things in God," the things themselves. To apply this to our relations with creatures: only when all relations, uncurtailed, are taken into the one relation, do we set the ring of our life's world round the sun of being.

Certainly that is the most difficult thing, and man in order to be able to do it must let himself be helped from time to time by an inner-worldly "monastery." Our relations to creatures incessantly threaten to get incapsulated. As the world itself is sustained in its independence as the world through striving to be closed to God, though as creation it is open to him, so every great bond of man—though in it he has perceived his connexion with the infinite—defends itself vigorously against continually debouching into the infinite. Here the monastic forms of life in the world, the loneliness in the midst of life into which we turn as into hostelries, help us to prevent the connexion between the conditioned bonds and the one unconditioned bond from slackening. This too, if we do not wish to see our participation in the Present Being dying off, is an imperative interchange, the systole to the diastole of the soul; and the loneliness must know the quality of strictness, of a monastery's strictness, in order to do its work. But it must never wish to tear us away from creatures, never refuse to dismiss us to them. By that it would act contrary to its own law and would close us, instead of enabling us, as is its office, to keep open the gates of finitude.

Kierkegaard does not conceal from us for a moment

that his resistance to a bond with the world, his religious
doctrine of loneliness, is based on personal nature and personal destiny. He confesses that he "ceased to have
common speech" with men. He notes that the finest
moment in his life is in the bath-house, before he dives into
the water: "I have nothing more to do with the world."
He exposes before our eyes some of the roots of his
"melancholy." He knows precisely what has brought him
to the point of being chary about having to do with others
and of essentially speaking only with God and with himself. And yet, as soon as he begins with the "direct" language, he expresses it as an imperative: let *everyone* do
so. Continually he points to his own shadow—and wants
to leap across it. He is a being excepted and exposed, and
certainly so are we all, for so is man as man. But Kierkegaard has moved to the fringe of being excepted and exposed, and maintains equilibrium only by means of the
unheard-of balance of his "author's" reticently communi-
cative existence with the complicated safeguards of all the
"pseudonyms"; whereas we are not on the fringe, and
that is no "not yet" nor any sort of compromising, no
shirking of melancholy; it is organic continuance and grace
of preservation and significant for the future of the spirit.
Kierkegaard behaves in our sight like a schizophrenist, who
tries to win over the beloved individual into "his" world
as if it were the true one. But it is not the true one. We,
ourselves wandering on the narrow ridge, must not shrink
from the sight of the jutting rock on which he stands over
the abyss; nor may we step on it. We have much to learn
from him, but not the final lesson.

Our rejection can be supported by Kierkegaard's own
teaching. He describes "the ethical" as "the only means
by which God communicates with 'man'" (1853). The
context of the teaching naturally keeps at a distance the
danger of understanding this in the sense of an absolutiz-
ing of the ethical. But it must be understood so that not
merely an autarkic ethic but also an autarkic religion is
inadmissible; so that as the ethical cannot be freed from
the religious neither can the religious from the ethical
without ceasing to do justice to the present truth. The

ethical no longer appears here, as in Kierkegaard's earlier thought, as a "stage" from which a "leap" leads to the religious, a leap by which a level is reached that is quite different and has a different meaning; but it dwells in the religious, in faith and service. This ethical can no longer mean a morality belonging to a realm of relativity and time and again overtaken and invalidated by the religious, but it means an *essential* action and suffering in relation to men, which are co-ordinated with the essential relation to God. But only he who has to do with men essentially can essentially act and suffer in relation to them. If the ethical is the only means by which God communicates with man then I am forbidden to speak essentially only with God and myself. And so indeed it is. I do not say that Kierkegaard on his rock, alone with the mercy of the Merciful, is false; I say only that you and I are forbidden.

Kierkegaard is deeply conscious of the dubiousness which arises from the negativizing extension of the category of the Single One. "The frightful thing," he writes in his Journal, and we read it, as he wrote it, with fear and trembling, "is that precisely the highest form of piety, to let everything earthly go, can be the highest egoism." Here obviously a distinction is made according to motives, and the idea of egoism used here is an idea of motivation. If we put in its place an objective idea, an idea of a state of affairs, the sentence is changed to a still more frightful one : "Precisely what appears to us as the highest form of piety—to let everything earthly go—is the highest egoism."

Is it true that the Single One "corresponds" to God? Does he realize the "image" of God solely by having become a Single One? One thing is lacking for that to be —and it is the decisive thing.

"Certainly," says Kierkegaard, "God is no egoist, but he is the infinite Ego." Yet thereby too little is said of the God whom we confess—if one dares to say anything at all. He hovers over his creation not as over a chaos, he embraces it. He is the infinite *I* that makes every *It* into his *Thou*.

The Single One corresponds to God when he in his human way embraces the bit of the world offered to him as God embraces his creation in his divine way. He realizes the image when, as much he can in a personal way, he says *Thou* with his being to the beings living round about him.

No-one can so refute Kierkegaard as Kierkegaard himself. Reasoning with and judging himself, he corrects his own spirit from its depths, often before it has uttered itself. In 1843 Kierkegaard enters this unforgettable confession in his Journal : " Had I had faith I would have stayed with Regina." By this he means, " If I had really believed that ' with God all things are possible,' hence also the resolution of this—my melancholy, my powerlessness, my fear, my alienation, fraught with destiny, from woman and from the world—then I would have stayed with Regina." But while meaning this he says something different, too, namely, that the Single One, if he really believes, and that means if he is really a Single One (which, as we saw, he has become for the one relation of faith), can and may have to do essentially with another. And behind this there lurks the extreme that he who can and may also *ought to* do this. " The only means by which God communicates with man is the ethical." But the ethical in its plain truth means to help God by loving his creation in his creatures, by loving it towards him. For this, to be sure, one must let oneself be helped by him.

" The Single One is the category through which, from the religious standpoint, time and history and the race must pass." What is this " religious standpoint "? One beside others? The standpoint towards God, gained by standing aside from all others? God one object beside other objects, the chosen one beside the rejected ones? God as Regina's successful rival? Is that still God? Is that not merely an object adapted to the religious genius? (Note that I am not speaking of true holiness for which, as it hallows *everything,* there is no " religious standpoint ".) Religious genius? Can there be religious geniuses? Is that not a *contradictio in adiecto*? Can the religious be a specification? " Religious geniuses " are theological geni-

uses. Their God is the God of the theologians. Admittedly,
that is not the God of the philosophers, but neither is it
the God of Abraham and Isaac and Jacob. The God of the
theologians, too, is a logicized God, and so is even the
God of a theology which will speak only dialectically and
makes light of the principle of contradiction. So long as
they practise theology they do not get away from religion
as a specification. When Pascal in a volcanic hour made
that stammering distinction between God and God he was
no genius but a man experiencing the primal glow of faith;
but at other times he was a theological genius and dwelt in
a specifying religion, out of which the happening of that
hour had lifted him.

Religion as a specification misses its mark. God is not
an object beside objects and hence cannot be reached by
renunciation of objects. God, indeed, is not the cosmos
but far less is he Being *minus* cosmos. He is not to be
found by subtraction and not to be loved by reduction.

The Single One and the Body Politic

Kierkegaard's thought circles round the fact that he
essentially renounced an essential relation to a definite
person. He did not resign this casually, or in the relativity
of the many experiences and decisions of life, or with the
soul alone, but essentially. The essential nature of his
renunciation, its downright positive essentiality, is what he
wants to express by saying, " In defiance of the whole
nineteenth century I cannot marry." The renunciation
becomes essential through its representing in concrete biography the renunciation of an essential relation to the
world as that which hinders being alone before God.
Moreover, as I have already said, this does not happen
just once, as when a man enters a monastery and has
thereby cut himself off from the world and lives outside
it as one who has done this; but it is peculiarly enduring :
the renunciation becomes the zero of a spiritual graph
whose every point is determined in relation to this zero.
It is in this way that the graph receives its true existential

character, by means of which it has provided the impulse
to a new philosophy and a new theology. And certainly
there goes along with this secularly significant concreteness of biography the curiously manifold motivation—
which is undoubtedly legitimate, and is to be found piece-
meal in the soundings of inwardness—of the renunciation
which Kierkegaard expresses directly and indirectly by
suggestion and concealment. But beyond that, on a closer
consideration it is to be noted that there arises, between the
renunciation and an increasingly strong point of view and
attitude which is finally expressed with penetrating clarity
in the *Two Notes* to the *Report to History,* a secret and
unexpressed connexion important for Kierkegaard and for
us.

" The crowd is untruth." " This consideration of life,
the Single One, is the truth." " No-one is excluded from
becoming a Single One except him who excludes himself
by wanting to be crowd." And again, " ' The Single One '
is the category of the spirit, of spiritual awakening and
revival, and is as sharply opposed to politics as possible."
The Single One and the crowd, the " spirit " and " politics "—this opposition is not to be separated from that into
which Kierkegaard enters with the world, expressing it
symbolically by means of his renunciation.

Kierkegaard does not marry " in defiance of the whole
nineteenth century." What he describes as the nineteenth
century is the " age of dissolution," the age of which he
says that a single man " cannot help it or save it," he can
" only express that it is going under "—going under, if it
cannot reach God through the " narrow pass." And
Kierkegaard does not marry, in a symbolic action of negation, in defiance of this age, because it is the age of the
" crowd " and the age of " politics." Luther married in
symbolic action, because he wanted to lead the believing
man of his age out of a rigid religious separation, which
finally separated him from grace itself, to a life with God
in the world. Kierkegaard does not marry (this of course
is not part of the manifold subjective motivation but is the
objective meaning of the symbol) because he wants to lead
the unbelieving man of his age, who is entangled in the

crowd, to become single, to the solitary life of faith, to being alone before God. Certainly, " to marry or not to marry " is the representative question when the monastery is in view. If the Single One really must be, as Kierkegaard thinks, a man who does not have to do essentially with others, then marriage hinders him if he takes it seriously—and if he does not take it seriously then, in spite of Kierkegaard's remark about Luther, it cannot be understood how he as an existing person can be " the truth." For man, with whom alone Kierkegaard is fundamentally concerned, there is the additional factor that in his view woman stands " quite differently from man in a dangerous rapport to finitude." But there is still a special additional matter which I shall now make clear.

If one makes a fairly comprehensive survey of the whole labyrinthine structure of Kierkegaard's thought about renunciation it will be recognized that he is speaking not solely of a hard, hard-won renunciation, bought with the heart's blood, of life with a person; but in addition of the downright positively valued renunciation of the life (conditioned by life with a person) with an impersonal being, which in the foreground of the happening is called " people," in its background " the crowd." This being, however, in its essence—of which Kierkegaard knows or wants to know nothing—refutes these descriptions as caricatures and acknowledges as its true name only that of a *res publica,* in English " the body politic." When Kierkegaard says the category of the " Single One " is " as sharply opposed as possible to politics," he obviously means an activity that has essentially lost touch with its origin the *polis.* But this activity, however degenerate, is one of the decisive manifestations of the body politic. Every degeneration indicates its genus, and in such a way that the degeneration is never related to the genus simply as present to past, but as in a distorted face the distortion is related to the form persisting beneath it. The body politic, which is sometimes also called the " world," that is, the human world, seeks, knowingly or unknowingly, to realize in its genuine formations men's turning to one another in the context of creation. The false formations distort but they cannot eliminate the eternal origin. Kierkegaard in his horror of malformation turns away. But the man who has not ceased to love the human world in all its abasement sees even to-day genuine form. Supposing that the crowd is untruth, it is only a state of affairs in the body politic; how truth is here related to untruth must be part and parcel of the true question to the Single One, and that warning against the crowd can be only its preface.

From this point that special matter can be made clear of which I said that it is an additional reason for Kierkegaard's considering marriage to be an impediment. Marriage, essentially understood, brings one into an essential relation to the "world"; more precisely, to the body politic, to its malformation and its genuine form, to its sickness and its health. Marriage, as the decisive union of one with another, confronts one with the body politic and its destiny—man can no longer shirk that confrontation in marriage, he can only prove himself in it or fail. The isolated person, who is unmarried or whose marriage is only a fiction, can maintain himself in isolation; the " community " of marriage is part of the great community, joining with its own problems the general problems, bound up with its hope of salvation to the hope of the great life that in its most miserable state is called the crowd. He who " has entered on marriage," who has entered into marriage, has been in earnest, in the intention of the sacrament, with the fact that the other *is*; with the fact that I cannot legitimately share in the Present Being without sharing in the being of the other; with the fact that I cannot answer the lifelong address of God to me without answering at the same time for the other; with the fact that I cannot be answerable without being at the same time answerable for the other as one who is entrusted to me. But thereby a man has decisively entered into relation with otherness; and the basic structure of otherness, in many ways uncanny but never quite unholy or incapable of being hallowed, in which I and the others who meet me in my life are inwoven, is the body politic. It is to this, into this, that marriage intends to lead us. Kierkegaard himself makes one of his pseudonyms, the "married man" of the *Stages,* express this, though in the style of a lower point of view which is meant to be overcome by a higher. But it is a lower point of view only when trivialized, there is no higher, because to be raised above the situation in which we are set never yields in truth a higher point of view. Marriage is the exemplary bond, it carries us as does none other into the greater bondage, and only as those who are bound can we reach the freedom of the children of God. Expressed with a view to the man, the woman certainly stands "in a dangerous rapport to finitude," and finitude is certainly the danger, for nothing threatens us so sharply as that we remain clinging to it. But our hope of salvation is forged on this very danger, for our human way to the infinite leads only through fulfilled finitude.

This person is other, essentially other than myself, and this otherness of his is what I mean, because I mean him; I confirm it; I wish his otherness to exist, because I wish his particular being to exist. That is the basic principle of marriage and from this basis it leads, if it is real marriage, to insight into the right and the legitimacy of otherness and to that vital acknowledgment of many-faced otherness —even in the contradiction and conflict with it—from which dealings with the body politic receive their religious ethos. That the men with whom I am bound up in the body politic and with whom I have directly or indirectly to do, are essentially other than myself, that this one or that one does not have merely a different mind, or way of thinking or feeling, or a different conviction or attitude, but has also a different perception of the world, a different recognition and order of meaning, a different touch from the religions of existence, a different faith, a different soil : to affirm all this, to affirm it in the way of a creature, in the midst of the hard situations of conflict, without relaxing their real seriousness, is the way by which we may officiate as helpers in this wide realm entrusted to us as well, and from which alone we are from time to time permitted to touch in our doubts, in humility and upright investigation, on the other's " truth " or " untruth," " justice " or " injustice." But to this we are led by marriage, if it is real, with a power for which there is scarcely a substitute, by its steady experiencing of the life-substance of the other as other, and still more by its crises and the overcoming of them which rises out of the organic depths, whenever the monster of otherness, which but now blew on us with its icy demon's breath and now is redeemed by our risen affirmation of the other, which knows and destroys all negation, is transformed into the mighty angel of union of which we dreamed in our mother's womb.

Of course, there is a difference between the private sphere of existence, to which marriage belongs, and the public sphere of existence. *Identification* takes place in a qualitatively different way in each. The private sphere is that with which a man, at any rate in the healthy epochs of its existence, can in all concreteness identify himself without regard to individual differentiation, such as the bodily and spiritual one between members of a family. This identification can take place by his saying in all concreteness *We, I,* of this family or band of his. (A genuine band stands in this respect on the side of the private sphere, in another respect it is on the side of the public sphere.) And when he says this he means not merely the whole, but also the single persons recognized and affirmed by him in their particular being. Identification with the public sphere of existence, on the other hand, is not really able to embrace the concrete persons in a concrete way. Thus I say of my nation " we," and this can be raised to the power of an elementary " That is I." But as soon as concretion, direction to the persons of whom the nation consists, enters in, there is a cleavage, and knowledge of the unbridgable multiple otherness permeates the identification in a broad stream. If the like happened to a province of private existence then it would either itself become of questionable value or it would pass over into public existence. For the relation to public existence every such test can be a proof and strengthening.

There are, however, two basic attitudes in which identification with public existence wards off the concretion, the direction to actual persons, and either transitorily or enduringly asserts itself. Very different from one another though they are, they often exercise almost the same effect. The one derives from the act of enthusiasm of "historic" hours : the crowd is actualized, enters into the action and is transfigured in it, and the person, overpowered by delirious ecstasy, is submerged in the movement of public existence. Here there is no contesting and impeding knowledge about the otherness of other persons : the transfiguration of the crowd eclipses all otherness, and the fiery impulse to identification can beget a real "family" feeling for the unknown man who walks in a demonstration or in the enthusiastic confusion of the streets runs into one's arms.

The other basic attitude is passive and constant. It is the accustomed joining in public opinion and in public "taking of a position." Here the crowd remains latent, it does not appear as a crowd, but only becomes effective. And, as is known, this happens in such a way that I am either completely excused from forming an opinion and a decision, or as it were convicted, in a murky recess of inwardness, of the invalidity of my opinions and decisions, and in their stead fitted out with ones that are approved as valid. By this means I am not in the least made aware of others since the same thing happens to them and their otherness has been varnished over.

Of these two basic attitudes the first is of such a kind that it snatches us out and away from confrontation with the great form of otherness in public existence, from the most difficult of the inner-worldly tasks, and raises us enthusiastically into the historical paradise of crowds. The second undermines the ground on which confrontation is to be carried out; it rubs out the pathetic signs of otherness and then convinces us by the evidence of our own eyes that uniformity is the real thing.

It is from this point that Kierkegaard's confusion of public existence, or the body politic, with the crowd, is to be understood. He knows the body politic, indeed, also in the form of the State, which is for him, however, only a fact in the world of relativity which is foreign to transcendence; it is respectable, but without significance for the individual's religious relation. And then he knows a crowd which is not respectable, but which has the deepest negative significance, indeed concerning transcendence, but as compact devilry.

This confusion which is in increasing measure heavy with consequences for the thought of our time must be opposed with the force of distinction.

A man in the crowd is a stick stuck in a bundle moving through the water, abandoned to the current or being pushed by a pole from the bank in this or that direction. Even if it seems to the stick at times that it is moving by its own motion it has in fact none of its own; and the bundle, too, in which it drifts has only an illusion of self-propulsion. I do not know if Kierkegaard is right when he says that the crowd is untruth—I should rather describe it as non-truth since (in distinction from some of its masters) it is not on the same plane as the truth, it is not in the least opposed to it. But it is certainly "un-freedom." In what un-freedom consists cannot be adequately learned under the pressure of fate, whether it is the compulsion of need or of men; for there still remains the rebellion of the inmost heart, the tacit appeal to the secrecy of eternity. It can be adequately learned only when you are tied up in the bundle of the crowd, sharing its opinions and desires, and only dully perceiving that you are in this condition.

The man who is living with the body politic is quite different. He is not bundled, but bound. He is bound up in relation to it, betrothed to it, married to it, therefore suffering his destiny along with it; rather, simply suffering it, always willing and ready to suffer it, but not abandoning himself blindly to any of its movements, rather confronting each movement watchfully and carefully that it does not miss truth and loyalty. He sees powers press on and sees God's hands in their supreme power held up on high, that the mortal immortals there below may be able to decide for themselves. He knows that in all his weakness he is put into the service of decision. If it is the crowd, remote from, opposed to, decision which swarms round him, he does not put up with it. At the place where he stands, whether lifted up or unnoticed, he does what he can, with the powers he possesses, whether compressed predominance or the word which fades, to make the crowd no longer a crowd. Otherness enshrouds him, the otherness to which he is betrothed. But he takes it up into his life only in the form of *the* other, time and again the other, the other who meets him, who is sought, lifted out of the crowd, the " companion." Even if he has to speak to the crowd he seeks the person, for a people can find and find again its truth only through persons, through persons standing their test. *That* is the Single One who " changes the crowd into Single Ones "—how could it be one who remains far from the crowd? It cannot be one who is reserved, only one who is given; given, not given over. It is a paradoxical work to which he sets his soul, to make the crowd no longer a crowd. It is to bring out from the crowd and set on the way of creation which leads to the Kingdom. And if he does not achieve much he has time, he has God's own time. For the man who loves God and his companion in one—though he remains in all the frailty of humanity—receives God for his companion.

" The Single One " is not the man who has to do with God essentially, and only unessentially with others, who is unconditionally concerned with God and conditionally with the body politic. The Single One is the man for whom the reality of relation with God as an exclusive relation includes and encompasses the possibility of relation with all otherness, and for whom the whole body politic, the reservoir of otherness, offers just enough otherness for him to pass his life with it.

The Single One in Responsibility

The category of the Single One has changed. It cannot be that the relation of the human person to God is established by the subtraction of the world. The Single One must therefore take his world, what of the world is extended and entrusted to him in his life, without any reduction into his life's devotion: he must let his world partake

unabated of its essentiality. It cannot be that the Single
One finds God's hands when he stretches his hands out
and away beyond creation. He must put his arms round
the vexatious world, whose true name is creation; only
then do his fingers reach the realm of lightning and of
grace. It cannot be that the spirit of reduction reigns in
the relation of faith as well. The Single One who lives
in his relation of faith must wish to have it fulfilled in the
uncurtailed measure of the life he lives. He must face the
hour which approaches him, the biographical and historical hour, just as it is, in its whole world content and
apparently senseless contradiction, without weakening the
impact of otherness in it. He must hear the message, stark
and untransfigured, which is delivered to him out of this
hour, presented by this situation as it arrives. Nor must he
translate for himself its wild and crude profaneness into
the chastely religious : he must recognize that the question
put to him, with which the speech of the situation is fraught
—whether it sounds with angels' or with devils' tongues
—remains God's question to him, of course without the
devils thereby being turned into angels. It is a question
wondrously tuned in the wild crude sound. And he, the
Single One, must answer, by what he does and does not
do, he must accept and answer for the hour, the hour of
the world, of all the world, as that which is given to him,
entrusted to him. Reduction is forbidden; you are not at
liberty to select what suits you, the whole cruel hour is at
stake, the whole claims you, and you must answer—Him.

You must hear the claim, however unharmoniously it
strikes your ear—and let no-one interfere; give the answer
from the depths, where a breath of what has been
breathed in still hovers—and let no-one prompt you.

This arch-command, for whose sake the Bible makes its
God *speak* from the very time of creation, defines anew,
when it is heard, the relation of the Single One to his
community.

The human person belongs, whether he wants to acknowledge it and take it seriously or not, to the community
in which he is born or which he has happened to get into.
But he who has realized what destiny means, even if it

looks like doom, and what being placed there means, even if it looks like being misplaced, knows too that he must acknowledge it and take it seriously. But then, precisely then, he notes that true membership of a community includes the experience, which changes in many ways, and which can never be definitively formulated, of the *boundary* of this membership. If the Single One, true to the historico-biographical hour, perceives the word, if he grasps the situation of his people, his own situation, as a sign and demand upon him, if he does not spare himself and his community before God, then he experiences the boundary. He experiences it in such agony as if the boundary-post had pierced his soul. The Single One, the man living in responsibility, can carry out his political actions as well—and of course omissions are also actions—only from that ground of his being to which the claim of the fearful and kind God, the Lord of history and our Lord, wishes to penetrate.

It is obvious that for the man living in community the ground of personal and essential decision is continually threatened by the fact of so-called collective decisions. I remind you of Kierkegaard's warning : " That men are in a crowd either excuses a man of repentance and responsibility or at all events weakens the Single One's responsibility, because the crowd lets the man have only a fragment of responsibility." But I must put it differently. In practice, in the moment of action, it is only the semblance of a fragment, but afterward, when in your waking dream after midnight you are dragged before the throne and attacked by the spurned calling to be a Single One, it is complete responsibility.

It must, of course, be added that the community to which a man belongs does not usually express in a unified and unambiguous way what it considers to be right and what not right in a given situation. It consists of more or less visible groups, which yield to a man interpretations of destiny and of his task which are utterly different yet all alike claim absolute authenticity. Each knows what benefits the community, each claims your unreserved complicity for the good of the community.

Political decision is generally understood to-day to mean joining such a group. If this is done then everything is finally in order, the time of deciding is over. From then on one has only to share in the group's movements. One no longer stands at the cross-roads, one no longer has to choose the right action out of the possible ones; everything is decided. What you once thought—that you had to answer ever anew, situation by situation, for the choice you made—is now got rid of. The group has relieved you of your political responsibility. You feel yourself answered for in the group; you are permitted to feel it.

The attitude which has just been described means for the man of faith (I wish to speak only of him here), when he encounters it, his fall from faith—without his being inclined to confess it to himself or to admit it. It means his fall in very fact from faith, however loudly and emphatically he continues to confess it not merely with his lips but even with his very soul as it shouts down inmost reality. The relation of faith to the one Present Being is perverted into semblance and self-deceit if it is not an all-embracing relation. " Religion " may agree to be one department of life beside others which like it are independent and autonomous—it has thereby already perverted the relation of faith. To remove any realm basically from this relation, from its defining power, is to try to remove it from God's defining power which rules over the relation of faith. To prescribe to the relation of faith that " so far and no further you may define what I have to do; here your power ends and that of the group to which I belong begins " is to address God in precisely the same way. He who does not let his relation of faith be fulfilled in the uncurtailed measure of the life he lives, however much he is capable of at different times, is trying to curtail the fulfilment of God's rule of the world.

Certainly the relation of faith is no book of rules which can be looked up to discover what is to be done now, in this very hour. I experience what God desires of me for this hour—so far as I do experience it—not earlier than *in* the hour. But even then it is not given me to experience it except by answering before God for this hour as *my*

hour, by carrying out the responsibility for it towards him
as much as I can. What has now approached me, the
unforeseen, the unforeseeable, is word from him, a word
found in no dictionary, a word that has now become word
—and it demands my answer to him. I give the word of
my answer by accomplishing among the actions possible
that which seems to my devoted insight to be the right
one. With my choice and decision and action—commit-
ting or omitting, acting or persevering—I answer the word,
however inadequately, yet properly; I answer for my hour.
My group cannot relieve me of this responsibility, I must
not let it relieve me of it : if I do, I pervert my relation of
faith, I cut out of God's realm of power the sphere of my
group. But it is not as though the latter did not concern
me in my decision—it concerns me tremendously. In my
decision I do not look away from the world, I look at it
and into it, and before all I may see in the world, to
which I have to do justice with my decision, my group to
whose welfare I cling; I may before all have to do justice
to it, yet not as a thing in itself, but before the Face of
God; and no programme, no tactical resolution, no command can tell me how I, as I decide, have to do justice
to my group before the Face of God. It may be that I may
serve it as the programme and resolution and command
have laid down. It may be that I have to serve it otherwise. It could even be—if such an unheard-of thing were
to rise within me in my act of decision—that I might be set
in cruel opposition to its success, because I became aware
that God's love ordains otherwise. Only one thing matters,
that as the situation is presented to me I expose myself to
it as to the word's manifestation to me, to the very ground
where hearing passes into being, and that I perceive what
is to be perceived and answer it. He who prompts me with
an answer in such a way as to hinder my perceiving is
the hinderer, let him be for the rest who he will (12).

I do not in the least mean that a man must fetch the
answer alone and unadvised out of his breast. Nothing of
the sort is meant; how should the direction of those at the
head of my group not enter essentially into the substance
out of which the decision is smelted? But the direction

must not be substituted for the decision; no substitute is
accepted. He who has a master may yield "himself," his
bodily person, to him, but not his responsibility. He must
find his way to that responsibility armed with all the
"ought" that has been forged in the group, but exposed
to destiny so that in the demanding moment all armour
falls away from him. He may even hold firm with all his
force to the "interest" of the group—till in the last
confrontation with reality a finger, hardly to be perceived,
yet never to be neglected, touches it. It is not the "finger
of God," to be sure; we are not permitted to expect that,
and therefore there is not the slightest assurance that our
decision is right in any but a personal way. God tenders
me the situation to which I have to answer; but I have not
to expect that he should tender me anything of my
answer. Certainly in my answering I am given into the
power of his grace, but I cannot measure heaven's share
in it, and even the most blissful sense of grace can deceive.
The finger I speak of is just that of the "conscience," but
not of the routine conscience, which is to be used, is being
used and worn out, the play-on-the-surface conscience,
with whose discrediting they thought to have abolished the
actuality of man's positive answer. I point to the unknown
conscience in the ground of being, which needs to be discovered ever anew, the conscience of the "spark" (13),
for the genuine spark is effective also in the single composure of each genuine decision. The certainty produced
by this conscience is of course only a personal certainty;
it is uncertain certainty; but what is here called person is
the very person who is addressed and who answers.

I say, therefore, that the Single One, that is, the man
living in responsibility, can make even his political decisions properly only from that ground of his being at
which he is aware of the event as divine speech to him;
and if he lets the awareness of this ground be strangled by
his group he is refusing to give God an actual reply.

What I am speaking of has nothing to do with "individualism." I do not consider the individual to be either
the starting-point or the goal of the human world. But I
consider the human person to be the irremovable central

place of the struggle between the world's movement away from God and its movement towards God. This struggle takes place to-day to an uncannily large extent in the realm of public life, of course not between group and group but within each group. Yet the decisive battles of this realm as well are fought in the depth, in the ground or the groundlessness, of the person.

Our age is intent on escaping from the demanding " ever anew " of such an obligation of responsibility by a flight into a protective " once-for-all." The last generation's intoxication with freedom has been followed by the present generation's craze for bondage; the untruth of intoxication has been followed by the untruth of hysteria. He alone is true to the one Present Being who knows he is bound to his place—and just there free for his proper responsibility. Only those who are bound and free in this way can still produce what can truly be called community. Yet even to-day the believing man, if he clings to a thing that is presented in a group, can do right to join it. But belonging to it, he must remain submissive with his whole life, therefore with his group life as well, to the One who is his Lord. His responsible decision will thus at times be opposed to, say, a tactical decision of his group. At times he will be moved to carry the fight for the truth, the human, uncertain and certain truth which is brought forward by his deep conscience, into the group itself, and thereby establish or strengthen an inner front in it. This can be more important for the future of our world than all fronts that are drawn to-day between groups and between associations of groups; for this front, if it is everywhere upright and strong, may run as a secret unity across all groups.

What the right is can be experienced by none of the groups of to-day except through men who belong to them staking their own souls to experience it and then revealing it, however bitter it may be, to their companions—charitably if it may be, cruelly if it must be. Into this fiery furnace the group plunges time and again, or it dies an inward death.

And if one still asks if one may be certain of finding

what is right on this steep path, once again the answer is
No; there is no certainty. There is only a chance; but
there is no other. The risk does not ensure the truth for
us; but it, and it alone, leads us to where the breath of
truth is to be felt.

Attempts at Severance

Against the position outlined here of the Single One in
responsibility there is bound to rise up that powerful
modern point of view, according to which in the last
resort only so-called objectives, more precisely collectives,
are real, while significance is attached to persons only as
the workers or the tools of the collectives. Kierkegaard's
merely religious category, to be sure, may be indifferent to
this point of view: according to his category only the
person is essential and the objective either has only a
secondary existence or, as crowd, is the negative which is
to be avoided. If, however, the Single One as such has
essentially to do with the world, and even with the world
in particular, with the body politic, but not in order, consciously and with the emphasis of faith, henceforth to let
himself be used, but in responsibility for that in which
before God he participates, then he is bound to be opposed
and if possible refuted once for all by that point of view.
It can set about this by means of arguments taken from a
certain contemporary trend of thought which conforms to
the time and is apparently its expedient. It is a trend of
which the representatives, first of all, with all their various
differences, have in common one object of attack—it may
be described as liberalism or individualism or by any other
slogan you please. (In this they usually neglect—as, under-
standably, often happens in cases of this kind—to analyze
the attacked "ism" conceptually, nor do they make a
distinction between what they mean and what they do
not mean, that is, between what is worth contesting and
what should be spared. If such an analysis should be
applied to, say, "liberalism," individual concepts of vary-
ing tendency would arise, towards which it would be

possible to adopt a standpoint in quite different clarity and unambiguousness. Thus, for example, there would be libertinism, the poor mode of thought of the released slave who only knows what is or what ought to be permitted to him, to "man"; on the other hand there would be liberism, the mode of thought of the free-born man for whom freedom is the presupposition of binding, of the true personal entry into a binding relation, no more and no less— a mode of thought worthy of being preserved in the treasure-house of the spirit and defended along with it by everyone who knows about the spirit.) But it is more significant that the representatives of this trend have also a common purpose or at least a common effect: they give the political province an exaggerated autonomy, they contrast public life with the rest of life, they remove it from the responsibility of the Single One who takes part in it.

In order to indicate what might be replied to such arguments from the standpoint of the transformed category of the Single One, two examples of the trend of thought under consideration may be discussed, one concerning the philosophy of the State and the other the theology of the State.

But first I precede these with a third example, less important but also rich in teaching, a historiosophical one.

Oswald Spengler wishes to establish the special sphere of the political, as having a value independent of our therefore inaccessible ethics, by classifying man with beasts of prey. If no longer between tamed individuals yet certainly between the groups, conditions (he says) are always, necessarily and normally, like those between packs of beasts. Here, in his existence within the group, man has remained an unweakened beast of prey, and the Single One has to guard against applying standards which are foreign to the particular sphere.

This is a trivialization of a Nietzschian thesis. Nietzsche believed that the important thing is that the power in history should keep faith with its own nature; if that is repressed then degeneration follows. Nietzsche does not move away from a *presupposition*. The important thing is that the power in history keeps faith with itself as with one of the partners in a dialogical event in which even the most forceful activity can signify a shirking of the answer, a refusal to give an answer.

Nietzsche's thesis speaks the language of history, Spengler's the language of biology. Every attempt to interpret human action in biological terms (however much one must remember biological existence when explaining man) is a trivialization; it is a poor simplification because it means the abandoning of the proper anthropological content, of that which constitutes the category of *man*.

Beasts of prey have no history. A panther can indeed have a biography and a colony of termites perhaps even State annals, but they do not have history in the great distinguishing sense which permits us to speak of human history as "world-history." A life of prey yields no history. Man has acquired history by entering fundamentally on something that would be bound to appear to the beast of prey as senseless and grotesque—namely, on responsibility, and thus on becoming a person with a relation to the truth. Hence it has become impossible to comprehend man from the standpoint of biology alone. "History" is not the sequence of conquests of power and actions of power but the context of the responsibilities of power in time.

Thus the beast of prey thesis means a denial of human essence and a falsification of human history. It is true, as Spengler says in defence of his thesis, that "the great beasts of prey are. *noble* creations of the most perfect kind," but this has no power to prove anything. It is a matter of man's becoming in *his* kind, which is conditioned by *his* evolution *and* his history, just as "noble a creation" as they in theirs : that means that he helps to realize that "freedom of the children of God" towards which, as Paul says, all creatures "crane their necks."

More serious consideration must be given to the conceptual definition of the political offered by a well-known Roman Catholic exponent of Constitutional Law, Carl Schmitt. In his view the political has its own criterion, which cannot be derived from the criterion of another realm. It is the distinction between friend and foe which in his view corresponds to "the relatively autonomous criteria of other oppositions, good and evil in the moral sphere, beautiful and ugly in the æsthetic, and so on." The eventuality of a real struggle, which includes the "possibility of physical killing," belongs to the concept of the foe, and from this possibility the life of man acquires "its specifically *political* tension."

The "possibility of physical killing"—really it should be "the intention of physical killing." For Schmitt's thesis carries a situation of private life, the classic duel situation, over into public life.

This duel situation arises when two men experience a conflict existing between them as absolute, and therefore capable of resolution only in the destruction of the one by the other. There is no reconciliation, no mediation, no adequate expiation, the hand that deals the blow must not be any but the opponent's; but this *is* the resolution. Every classic duel is a masked "judgment of God." In each there is an aftermath of the belief that men can bring about a judgment of God. That is what Schmitt, carrying it over to the relation of peoples to one another, calls the specifically political.

But the thesis rests on an error of method. The essential principle of a realm, the principle that constitutes it as such, cannot be taken from the *labile* state of the formations in this realm, but only from their lasting character. The friend-foe formula derives from the sphere of exposedness of political formations, not from the sphere of their coherence. The radical distinction which Schmitt supposes appears in times in which the common life is threatened, not in times in which it experiences its stability as self-evident and assured. The distinction, therefore, is not adequate to yield the principle of "the political."

But the formula does not even include the whole lability of a political formation. This lability is always twofold—an outer, which is exposed by the neighbour (or attacker become neighbour) pressing on the frontier, and an inner, which is indicated by the rebel. Schmitt calls him the "inner foe," but in this he confuses two fundamentally different kinds of lability. The foe has no interest in the preservation of the formation, but the rebel has—he wants to "change" it: it is precisely *it* he wants to change. Only the former is radical enough to establish the import of the formula. The friend-foe formula comprehends, therefore, only one side of lability and cannot be stretched to include the other.

The oppositions "good and evil in the moral sphere, beautiful and ugly in the æsthetic," which Schmitt sets together with this one, are in distinction from it intended *normatively*, that is, only when the good, the beautiful, are understood in a content of essential significance is there any sense in defining the evil, the ugly. "Friend and foe," however, describes not a normative concept of being but only a concept of an attitude within a situation.

Moreover, it seems to me that behind the common pairs of opposed concepts, good and evil, beautiful and ugly, there stand others in which the negative concept is intimately bound to the positive, being the emptiness to its fulness, the chaos to its cosmos. Behind good and evil as the criteria of the ethical stand direction and absence of direction, behind beautiful and ugly as the criteria of the æsthetic stand form and formlessness. For the realm of the political there is no pair of concepts in the foreground, obviously because it is more difficult, or impossible, to give autonomy to the negative pole in it. I should call the pair in the background order and absence of order, but the concept of order must be freed of the depreciation which sometimes clings to it. Right order is direction and form in the political realm. But these two concepts must not be allowed to petrify. They have their truth only from the conception of a homogeneous *dynamic of order* which is the real principle of the political. The true history of a commonwealth must be understood as its striving to reach the order suited to it. This striving, this wrestling for the realization of true order—wrestling between ideas, plans, outlines of true order that are so different, but also a wrestling that is simultaneously common to them all, not known, not to be expressed—constitutes the political structure's dynamic of order. An order is gained and established again and again as a result. It becomes firm and

inclusive, it consolidates itself as well against the resistance
of whatever dynamic may be left. It stiffens and dies off,
completely renouncing the dynamic which set it going; and
yet it keeps its power for the struggle for true order flaring
up again. The foe threatens the whole dynamic of order
in the commonwealth, the rebel threatens only the order
as it is at the time. Every order considered from the
standpoint of the whole dynamic is called in doubt. That
is the double life of the State : again and again realization
of the political structure, again and again its being called
in doubt. The " high points of concrete politics " are not,
as Schmitt thinks, " at the same time the moments in
which the foe is visualized in concrete clarity as the foe ";
they are the moments in which an order, in face of the
gravest responsibility of the individual confronting himself with it, demonstrates the legitimacy of its static character, its character (however necessarily relative) of fulfilment.

In Schmitt's view all " genuine " political theories pre-
suppose that man is " evil." (Incidentally, why do the
theories that do this do it? Since from Schmitt's point of
view political theory is only a department of practical
politics, the answer along his line would have to be " because it seems to their authors to be politically expedient.")
This " evil," indeed, Schmitt explains as being " in no way
unproblematic " and " dangerous "—and I too take man
to be both—but he finds support for the correctness of his
presupposition in the theological doctrine of the *absolute*
sinfulness of man. He has found a weighty theological
associate in Friedrich Gogarten.

Gogarten explains in his *Political Ethics* that all ethical
problems receive their ethical relevance only from the
political problem. That is, the ethical is valid as the
ethical only by its connexion with man's political being.
In saying this he abandons Kierkegaard's category of the
Single One. Gogarten believes that he is only fighting
against individualism but at the same time he is fighting
against the position of personal life in the rigour of its total
responsibility. If ethical problems receive their relevance
from the political realm, they cannot also receive them

from the religious, not even if the political has a religious basis. But if they do not receive them from the religious realm, then we have reached again, within the life of the "religious" man—even if in a politicized form—the disconnected ethic which Kierkegaard helped us to overcome. Gogarten may speak in theological terms as emphatically as he pleases, he narrows down the Single One's fundamental relation with God when he lets his action receive its validity from some other source, even if it is from destiny, considered in itself, of the community to which the Single One belongs. (And what else are "ethical problems" but man's questions about his actions and their meaning?) True as it is that he, the Single One, cannot win to a legitimate relation with God without a legitimate relation to the body politic, it is nevertheless also true that the defining force has to be ascribed not to the latter but to the former alone. That is, I must always let the boundary between co-operation and non-co-operation within my relation to my community be drawn by God. You say that often you hear nothing? Well, we have to be attentive with the unreserved effort of our being. If even then we hear nothing, then, but only then, may we turn in the direction Gogarten indicates. But if we are not attentive or if we hear but do not obey, then our omission, and not our invoking of some kind of relation of ethical problems to the political, will persist in eternity.

In Gogarten's view man is "radically and therefore irrevocably evil, that is, in the grip of evil." The relevance of the political arises from the fact that "only in the political" does man have, "in face of this recognition, the possibility of existence." The ethical quality of the State consists "in its warding off the evil to which men have fallen prey by its sovereign power and by its right over the life and property of its subjects." (Incidentally, this is a theological version of the old police-state idea.) For "whence shall the State derive sovereign power if not from the recognition of man's fallen state"?

The concept to which Gogarten refers, of the radical evil of man, his absolute sinfulness, is taken from the realm where man confronts God and is significant there alone.

What to my knowledge and understanding is taught by
Christian theology, in whose name Gogarten speaks, is that
man, more precisely, fallen man, considered as being unredeemed, is "before God" (*coram Deo*) sinful and de-
praved. I do not see how his being unredeemed can be
broken off from its dialectic connexion with redemption
(*ab his malis liberemur et servemur*) and used separately.
Nor do I see how the concept of being evil can be translated from the realm of being "before God" into that of
being before earthly authorities, and yet retain its radical
nature. In the sight of God a state of radical evil can be
ascribed to man because God is God and man is man,
and the distance between them is absolute, and because
precisely in this distance and in virtue of it God's redeem-
ing deed is done. In the sight of his fellow-men, of human
groups and orders, man, it seems to me, cannot be properly described as simply sinful, because the distance is
lacking which alone is able to establish the unconditional.
Nothing is changed if a human order is considered as
established or empowered by God. For that absolute distance to man, which establishes the unconditional (but at
the same time discloses the place of redemption)—the distance from which alone man's radical evil could appear
also in face of the body politic—can by no means be
bestowed in this way upon the human order. Hence no
legitimate use can be made in politics or political theory
of the concept of human sinfulness.

In my view, however, man generally is not "radically"
this or that.

It is not radicality that characterizes man as separated
by a primal abyss from all that is merely animal, but it is
his potentiality. If we put him alone before the whole
of nature then there appears embodied in him the character of possibility inherent in natural existence and
which everywhere else hovers round dense reality only like
a haze. Man is the crystallized potentiality of existence.
But he is this potentiality in its factual limitation. The
wealth of possibility in existence from which the animals
are kept away by their exiguous reality is exhibited in man
in a sign that is incomprehensible from the standpoint of

nature. Yet this wealth of possibility does not hold free sway, so that life might be able time and again to follow on wings the anticipation of spirit, but it is confined within narrow limits. This limitation is not essential, but only factual. That means that man's action is unforeseeable in its nature and extent, and that even if he were peripheral to the cosmos in everything else, he remains the centre of all surprise in the world. But he is fettered surprise, only inwardly is it without bands; and his fetters are strong.

Man is not good, man is not evil; he is, in a pre-eminent sense, good and evil together. He who eats of him, as he who ate of that fruit, has the knowledge of good and evil together. That is his limitation, that is the cunning of the serpent: he was to become as God, knowing good and evil; but what he "recognizes," what in being mixed up with it he has recognized as something mixed up, is good and evil together: he has become good and evil together; that is the nakedness in which he recognizes himself. The limitation is only factual, it does not transform his essence or destroy God's work. To ascribe to the serpent the power of destruction is to elevate it to rivalry with God and make it for the time superior to him (as Ahriman was for a time to Ormuzd), since it perverts God's creation. But the serpent in the Bible is not that. It is not an opposing god, it is only the creature which desires to undo man by man's own doing. It is the "cunning" creature, the cunning of the secretly poisonous creature which foments disorder; and out of the disorder comes history which, groping and striving and failing, is concerned with God's order. The primal event pointed out by the images of the Bible does not lie under the principle of contradiction: *A* and *not-A* are here strangely concerned with one another.

Good and evil, then, cannot be a pair of opposites like right and left or above and beneath. "Good" is the movement in the direction of home, "evil" is the aimless whirl of human potentialities without which nothing can be achieved and by which, if they take no direction but remain trapped in themselves, everything goes awry. If

the two were indeed poles the man who did not see them
as such would be blind; but the man would be blinder who
did not perceive the lightning flash from pole to pole,
the " and."

As a condition of the individual soul evil is the con-
clusive shirking of direction, of the total orientation of the
soul by which it stands up to personal responsibility before
God. The shirking can take place from passion or from
indolence. The passionate man refuses by his passion, the
indolent man by his indolence. In both cases the man
goes astray within himself. The real historical dæmonias
are the exploiting by historical powers of this shirking.

But the State *as such* cannot indicate the one direction
of the hour towards God, which changes time and again
by concretion. Only the Single One, who stands in the
depth of responsibility, can do that. And indeed a states-
man can also be this Single One.

Gogarten puts *the* State in place of the historical State,
that is, of the government of the particular time (ἄρχοντες).
This government cannot ward off the " evil" as an
impersonal State but can do it only on the basis of its own
personal responsibility, and is for the rest itself exposed
to the dynamic between good and evil. The State is the
visible form of authority, and for Gogarten authority is
simply what is established, the diaconal; power is full
power. But if the establishment of power is taken seriously,
theologically and biblically seriously, the establishing turns
out to be a precise commission and the power a great duty
of responsibility. The Old Testament records, in the
history of the kings of Israel and the history of foreign
rulers, the degeneration of legitimacy into illegitimacy
and of full power into antagonistic power. As no philosophical concept of the State, so likewise no theological
concept of the State leads beyond the reality of the
human person in the situation of faith. None leads
beyond his responsibility—be he servant or emperor—for
the body politic as man in the sight of God.

The Question

In the human crisis which we are experiencing to-day these two have become questionable—the person and the truth.

We know from the act of responsibility how they are linked together. For the responsible response to exist the reality of the person is necessary, whom the word meets in the happening claiming him; and the reality of the truth is necessary to which the person goes out with united being and which he is therefore able to receive only in the word, as the truth which concerns himself, in his particular situation, and not in any general way.

The question by which the person and the truth have become questionable to-day is the question to the Single One.

The person has become questionable through being collectivized.

This collectivizing of the person is joined in history to a basically different undertaking in which I too participated and to which I must therefore confess now. It is that struggle of recent decades against the idealistic concepts of the sovereign, world-embracing, world-sustaining, world-creating *I*. The struggle was conducted (among other ways) by reference to the neglected creaturely bonds of the concrete human person. It was shown how fundamentally important it is to know in every moment of thought this as well—that the one who thinks is bound, in different degrees of substantiality but never purely functionally, to a spatial realm, to a historical hour, to the genus man, to a people, to a family, to a society, to a vocational group, to a companionship in convictions. This entanglement in a manifold *We*, when known in an actual way, wards off the temptation of the thought of sovereignty: man is placed in a narrow creaturely position. But he is enabled to recognize that this is his genuine width; for being bound means being bound up in relation.

But it came about that a tendency of a quite different origin and nature assumed power over the new insights,

which exaggerated and perverted the perception of bonds
into a doctrine of serfdom. Primacy is ascribed here to a
collectivity. The collectivity receives the right to hold the
person who is bound to it bound in such a way that he
ceases to have complete responsibility. The collectivity
becomes what really exists, the person becomes derivatory.
In every realm which joins him to the whole he is to be
excused a personal response.

Thereby the immeasurable value which constitutes man
is imperilled. The collectivity cannot enter instead of
the person into the dialogue of the ages which the Godhead conducts with mankind. Human perception ceases,
the human response is dumb, if the person is no longer
there to hear and to speak. It is not possible to reduce the
matter to private life; only in the uncurtailed measure of
lived life, that is, only with the inclusion of participation
in the body politic, can the claim be heard and the reply
spoken.

The truth, on the other hand, has become questionable
through being politicized.

The sociological doctrine of the age has exercised a
relativizing effect, heavy with consequences, on the concept of truth, in that it has, in the dependence of the
thought processes on social processes, proved the connection of thought with existence. This relativization was
justified in that it bound the "truth" of a man to his
conditioning reality. But its justification was perverted
into the opposite when its authors omitted to draw the
basic boundary line between what can and what cannot be
understood as conditioned in this way. That is, they did
not comprehend the person in his *total* reality, wooing the
truth and wrestling for it. If we begin with the Single One
as a whole being, who wishes to recognize with his total
being, we find that the force of his desire for the truth can
at decisive points burst the "ideological" bonds of his
social being. The man who thinks "existentially," that is,
who stakes his life in his thinking, brings into his real
relation to the truth not merely his conditioned qualities
but also the unconditioned nature, transcending them, of
his quest, of his grasp, of his indomitable will for the truth,

which also carries along with it the whole personal power
of standing his test. We shall certainly be able to make no
distinction, in what he has, time and again, discovered
as the truth, between what can and what cannot be derived
from the social factor. But it is an ineluctable duty to
accept what cannot be so derived as a border concept and
thus to point out, as the unattainable horizon of the distinction made by the sociology of knowledge, what takes
place between the underivable in the recognizing person
and the underivable in the object of his recognition. This
duty has been neglected. Consequently, the political
theory of modern collectivisms was easily able to assume
power over the principle which lay ready, and t. proclaim what corresponded to the (real or supposed) 'ife
interests of a group as its legitimate and unappealab.
truth. Over against this the Single One could no longer
appeal to a truth which could be recognized and tested by
him.

This marks the beginning of a disintegration of human
faith in the truth, which can never be possessed and yet
may be comprehended in an existentially real relation; it
marks the beginning of the paralysis of the human search
for the truth.

"What I speak of," says Kierkegaard, "is something
simple and straightforward—that the truth for the Single
One only exists in his producing it himself in action."
More precisely, man finds the truth to be true only when
he stands its test. Human truth is here bound up with the
responsibility of the person.

"True is what is Mine," says Stirner. Human truth is
here bound up with the human person's lack of responsibility. Collectivisms translate this into the language of
the group: "True is what is Ours."

But in order that man may not be lost there is need of
persons who are not collectivized, and of truth which is not
politicized.

There is need of persons, not merely "representatives"
in some sense or other, chosen or appointed, who exonerate
the represented of responsibility, but also "represented"
who on no account let themselves be represented with

regard to responsibility. There is need of the person as the ground which cannot be relinquished, from which alone the entry of the finite into conversation with the infinite became possible and is possible.

There is need of man's faith in the truth as that which is independent of him, which he cannot acquire for himself, but with which he can enter into a real relation of his very life; the faith of human persons in the truth as that which sustains them all together, in itself inaccessible but disclosing itself, in the fact of responsibility which awaits test, to him who really woos the truth.

That man may not be lost there is need of the person's responsibility to truth in his historical situation. There is need of the Single One who stands over against all being which is present to him—and thus also over against the body politic—and guarantees all being which is present to him—and thus also the body politic.

True community and true commonwealth will be realized only to the extent to which the Single Ones become real out of whose responsible life the body politic is renewed.

III

EDUCATION

" THE DEVELOPMENT of the creative powers in the child " is the subject of this conference. As I come before you to introduce it I must not conceal from you for a single moment the fact that of the nine words in which it is expressed only the last three raise no question for me.

The child, not just the individual child, individual children, but the child, is certainly a reality. That in this hour, while we make a beginning with the " development of creative powers," across the whole extent of this planet new human beings are born who are characterized already and yet have still to be characterized—this is a myriad realities, but also one reality. In every hour the human race begins. We forget this too easily in face of the massive fact of past life, of so-called world-history, of the fact that each child is born with a given disposition of " world-historical " origin, that is, inherited from the riches of the whole human race, and that he is born into a given situation of " world-historical " origin, that is, produced from the riches of the world's events. This fact must not obscure the other no less important fact that in spite of everything, in this as in every hour, what has not been invades the structure of what is, with ten thousand countenances, of which not one has been seen before, with ten thousand souls still undeveloped but ready to develop—a creative event if ever there was one, newness rising up, primal potential might. This potentiality, streaming unconquered, however much of it is squandered, is the reality *child* : this phenomenon of uniqueness, which is more than just begetting and birth, this grace of beginning again and ever again.

What greater care could we cherish or discuss than that this grace may not henceforth be squandered as before, that the might of newness may be preserved for renewal?

Future history is not inscribed already by the pen of a causal law on a roll which merely awaits unrolling; its characters are stamped by the unforeseeable decisions of future generations. The part to be played in this by everyone alive to-day, by every adolescent and child, is immeasurable, and immeasurable is our part if we are educators. The deeds of the generations now approaching can illumine the grey face of the human world or plunge it in darkness. So, then, with education : if it at last rises up and exists indeed, it will be able to strengthen the light-spreading force in the hearts of the doers—how much it can do this cannot be guessed, but only learned in action.

The child is a reality; education must become a reality. But what does the "development of the creative powers" mean? Is *that* the reality of education? Must education become that in order to become a reality? Obviously those who arranged this session and gave it its theme think this is so. They obviously think that education has failed in its task till now because it has aimed at something different from this development of what is in the child, or has considered and promoted other powers in the child than the creative. And probably they are amazed that I question this objective, since I myself talk of the treasure of eternal possibility and of the task of unearthing it. So I must make clear that this treasure cannot be properly designated by the notion of "creative powers," nor its unearthing by the notion of "development."

Creation originally means only the divine summons to the life hidden in non-being. When Johann Georg Hamann and his contemporaries carried over this term metaphorically to the human capacity to give form, they marked a supreme peak of mankind, the genius for forming, as that in which man's imaging of God is authenticated in action. The metaphor has since been broadened; there was a time (not long ago) when "creative" meant almost the same as "of literary ability"; in face of this lowest condition of the word it is a real promotion for it to be understood, as it is here, quite generally as something dwelling to some extent in all men, in all children of men, and needing

only the right cultivation. Art is then only the province
in which a faculty of production, which is common to all,
reaches completion. Everyone is elementally endowed
with the basic powers of the arts, with that of drawing, for
instance, or of music; these powers have to be developed,
and the education of the whole person is to be built up on
them as on the natural activity of the self.

We must not miss the importance of the reference which
is the starting-point of this conception. It concerns a significant but hitherto not properly heeded phenomenon,
which is certainly not given its right name here. I mean
the existence of an autonomous instinct, which cannot be
derived from others, whose appropriate name seems to me
to be the "originator instinct." Man, the child of man,
wants to make things. He does not merely find pleasure
in seeing a form arise from material that presented itself
as formless. What the child desires is its own share in this
becoming of things : it wants to be the subject of this
event of production. Nor is the instinct I am speaking of
to be confused with the so-called instinct to busyness or
activity which for that matter does not seem to me to exist
at all (the child wants to set up or destroy, handle or hit,
and so on, but never "busy himself"). What is important
is that by one's own intensively experienced action something arises that was not there before. A good expression
of this instinct is the way children of intellectual passion
produce speech, in reality not as something they have
taken over but with the headlong powers of utter newness : sound after sound tumbles out of them, rushing from
the vibrating throat past the trembling lips into the world's
air, and the whole of the little vital body vibrates and
trembles, too, shaken by a bursting shower of selfhood. Or
watch a boy fashioning some crude unrecognizable instrument for himself. Is he not astonished, terrified, at his
own movement like the mighty inventors of prehistoric
times? But it is also to be observed how even in the
child's apparently "blind" lust for destruction his instinct
of origination enters in and becomes dominant. Sometimes
he begins to tear something up, for example, a sheet of
paper, but soon he takes an interest in the form of the

pieces, and it is not long before he tries—still by tearing—to produce definite forms.

It is important to recognize that the instinct of origination is autonomous and not derivatory. Modern psychologists are inclined to derive the multiform human soul from a single primal element—the "libido," the "will to power," and the like. But this is really only the generalization of certain degenerate states in which a single instinct not merely dominates but also spreads parasitically through the others. They begin with the cases (in our time of inner loss of community and oppression the innumerable cases) where such a hypertrophy breeds the appearance of exclusiveness, they abstract rules from them, and apply them with the whole theoretical and practical questionableness of such applications. In opposition to these doctrines and methods, which impoverish the soul, we must continually point out that human inwardness is in origin a polyphony in which no voice can be "reduced" to another, and in which the unity cannot be grasped analytically, but only heard in the present harmony. One of the leading voices is the instinct of origination.

This instinct is therefore bound to be significant for the work of education as well. Here is an instinct which, no matter to what power it is raised, never becomes greed, because it is not directed to "having" but only to doing; which alone among the instincts can grow only to passion, not to lust; which alone among the instincts cannot lead its subject away to invade the realm of other lives. Here is pure gesture which does not snatch the world to itself, but expresses itself to the world. Should not the person's growth into form, so often dreamed of and lost, at last succeed from this starting-point? For here this precious quality may be unfolded and worked out unimpeded. Nor does the new experiment lack demonstration. The finest demonstration I know, that I have just got to know, is this Children's Choir led by the marvellous Bakule of Prague, with which our Conference opened. How under his leadership crippled creatures, seemingly condemned to lifelong idleness, have been released to a life of freely moving persons, rejoicing in their achievement, formidable and forming, who know how to shape sights and sounds in multiform patterns and also how to sing out their risen souls wildly and gloriously; more, how a community of achievement, proclaimed in glance and response, has been welded together out of dull immured solitary creatures : all this seems to prove irrefutably not merely what fruitfulness but also what power, streaming through the whole constitution of man, the life of origination has.

But this very example, seen more deeply, shows us that the decisive influence is to be ascribed not to the release of an instinct but to the forces which meet the released instinct, namely, the educative forces. It depends on them, on their purity and fervour, their power of love and their discretion, into what connexions the freed element enters and what becomes of it.

There are two forms, indispensable for the building of true human life, to which the originative instinct, left to itself, does not lead and cannot lead : to sharing in an undertaking and to entering into mutuality.

An individual achievement and an undertaking are two very different matters. To make a thing is mortal man's pride; but to be conditioned in a common job, with the unconscious humility of being a part, of participation and partaking, is the true food of earthly immortality. As soon as a man enters effectively into an undertaking, where he discovers and practises a community of work with other men, he ceases to follow the originative instinct alone.

Action leading to an individual achievement is a " onesided " event. There is a force within the person, which goes out, impresses itself on the material, and the achievement arises objectively : the movement is over, it has run in one direction from the heart's dream into the world, and its course is finished. No matter how directly, as being approached and claimed, as perceiving and receiving, the artist experiences his dealings with the idea which he faces and which awaits embodiment, so long as he is engaged in this work spirit goes out from him and does not enter him, he replies to the world but he does not meet it any more. Nor can he foster mutuality with his work : even in the legend Pygmalion is an ironical figure.

Yes; as an originator man is solitary. He stands wholly without bonds in the echoing hall of his deeds. Nor can it help him to leave his solitariness that his achievement is received enthusiastically by the many. He does not know if it is accepted, if his sacrifice is accepted by the anonymous receiver. Only if someone grasps his hand not as a " creator " but as a fellow-creature lost in the world, to be his comrade or friend or lover beyond the arts, does he have an awareness and a share of mutuality. An education based only on the training of the instinct of origination would prepare a new human solitariness which would be the most painful of all.

The child, in putting things together, learns much that he can learn in no other way. In making some thing he gets to know its possibility, its origin and structure and connexions, in a way he cannot learn by observation. But there is something else that is not learned in this way, and that is the viaticum of life. The being of the world as an object is learned from within, but not its being as a subject, its saying *I* and *Thou*. What teaches us the saying of *Thou* is not the originative instinct but the instinct for communion.

This instinct is something greater than the believers in the " libido " realize : it is the longing for the world to become present to us as a person, which goes out to us as we to it, which chooses and recognizes us as we do it, which is confirmed in us as we in it. The child lying with half-closed eyes, waiting with tense soul for its mother to speak to it—the mystery of its will is not directed towards enjoying (or dominating) a person, or towards doing something of its own accord; but towards experiencing communion in face of the lonely night, which spreads beyond the window and threatens to invade.

But the release of powers should not be any more than a *presupposition* of education. In the end it is not the originative instinct alone which is meant by the " creative powers " that are to be " developed." These powers stand for human spontaneity. Real education is made possible —but is it also established?—by the realization that youthful spontaneity must not be suppressed but must be allowed to give what it can.

Let us take an example from the narrower sphere of the originative instinct—from the drawing-class. The teacher of the "compulsory" school of thought began with rules and current patterns. Now you knew what beauty was, and you had to copy it; and it was copied either in apathy or in despair. The teacher of the "free" school places on the table a twig of broom, say, in an earthenware jug, and makes the pupils draw it. Or he places it on the table, tells the pupils to look at it, removes it, and then makes them draw it. If the pupils are quite unsophisticated soon not a single drawing will look like another. Now the delicate, almost imperceptible and yet important influence begins—that of criticism and instruction. The children encounter a scale of values that, however unacademic it may be, is quite constant, a knowledge of good and evil that, however individualistic it may be, is quite unambiguous. The more unacademic this scale of values, and the more individualistic this knowledge, the more deeply do the children experience the encounter. In the former instance the preliminary declaration of what alone was right made for resignation or rebellion; but in the latter, where the pupil gains the realization only after he has ventured far out on the way to his achievement, his heart is drawn to reverence for the form, and educated.

This almost imperceptible, most delicate approach, the raising of a finger, perhaps, or a questioning glance, is the other half of what happens in education.

Modern educational theory, which is characterized by tendencies to freedom, misunderstands the meaning of this other half, just as the old theory, which was characterized by the habit of authority, misunderstood the meaning of the first half. The symbol of the funnel is in course of being exchanged for that of the pump. I am reminded of the two camps in the doctrine of evolution, current in the seventeenth and eighteenth centuries, the animalculists, who believed that the whole germ was present in the spermatozoon, and the ovists who believed it was wholly present in the ovum. The theory of the development of powers in the child recalls, in its most extreme expressions, Swammerdam's "unfolding" of the "preformed" organism. But the growth of the spirit is no more an unfolding than that of the body. The dispositions which would be discovered in the soul of a new-born child—if the soul could in fact be analysed—are nothing but capacities to receive and imagine the world. The world engenders the person in the individual. The world, that is the whole environment, nature and society, "educates" the human being: it draws out his powers, and makes him grasp and penetrate its objections. What we term education, conscious and willed, means *a selection by man of the effective world*: it means to give decisive effective power to a selection of the world which is concentrated and manifested in the educator. The relation in education is lifted out of the purposelessly streaming education by all things, and is marked off as purpose. In this way, through the educator, the world for the first time becomes the true subject of its effect.

There was a time, there were times, where there neither was nor needed to be any specific calling of educator or teacher. There was a master, a philosopher or a coppersmith, whose journeymen and apprentices lived with him and learned, by being allowed to share in it, what he had to teach them of his handwork or brainwork. But they also learned, without either their or his being concerned with it, they learned, without noticing that they did, the mystery of personal life: they received the spirit. Such a thing must still happen to some extent, where spirit and person exist, but it is expelled to the sphere of spirituality, of personality, and has become exceptional, it happens only "on the heights." Education as a purpose is bound to be summoned. We can as little return to the state of affairs that existed before there were schools as to that which existed before, say, technical science. But we can and must enter into the completeness of its growth to reality, into the perfect humanization of its reality. Our way is composed of losses that secretly become gains. Education has lost the paradise of pure instinctiveness and now consciously serves at the plough for the bread of life.

It has been transformed; only in this transformation has it become visible.

Yet the master remains the model for the teacher. For if the educator of our day has to act consciously he must nevertheless do it "as though he did not." That raising of the finger, that questioning glance, are his genuine doing. Through him the selection of the effective world reaches the pupil. He fails the recipient when he presents this selection to him with a gesture of interference. It must be concentrated in him; and doing out of concentration has the appearance of rest. Interference divides the soul in his care into an obedient part and a rebellious part. But a hidden influence proceeding from his integrity has an integrating force.

The world, I said, has its influence as nature and as society on the child. He is educated by the elements, by air and light and the life of plants and animals, and he is educated by relationships. The true educator represents both; but he must be to the child as one of the elements.

The release of powers can be only a presupposition of education, nothing more. Put more generally, it is the nature of freedom to provide the place, but not the foundation as well, on which true life is raised. That is true both of inner, "moral" freedom and of outer freedom (which consists in not being hindered or limited). As the higher freedom, the soul's freedom of decision, signifies perhaps our highest moments but not a fraction of our substance, so the lower freedom, the freedom of development, signifies our capacity for growth but by no means our growth itself. This latter freedom is charged with importance as the actuality from which the work of education begins, but as its fundamental task it becomes absurd.

There is a tendency to understand this freedom, which may be termed evolutionary freedom, as at the opposite pole from compulsion, from being under a compulsion. But at the opposite pole from compulsion there stands not freedom but communion. Compulsion is a negative reality; communion is the positive reality; freedom is a possibility, possibility regained. At the opposite pole of being com-

pelled by destiny or nature or men there does not stand
being free of destiny or nature or men but to commune
and to covenant with them. To do this, it is true that one
must first have become independent; but this independence is a foot-bridge, not a dwelling-place. Freedom is the
vibrating needle, the fruitful zero. Compulsion in education means disunion, it means humiliation and rebellious-
ness. Communion in education is just communion, it
means being opened up and drawn in. Freedom in education is the possibility of communion; it cannot be dispensed with and it cannot be made use of in itself; without
it nothing succeeds, b. . neither does anything succeed by
means of it : it is . . run before the jump, the tuning of
the violin, the confirmation of that primal and mighty
potentiality which it cannot even begin to actuali. .

Freedom—I love its flashing face : it flashes forth from
the darkness and dies away, but it has made the heart
invulnerable. I am devoted to it, I am always ready to
join in the fight for it, for the appearance of the flash,
which lasts no longer than the eye is able to endure it, for
the vibrating of the needle that was held down too long
and was stiff. I give my left hand to the rebel and my
right to the heretic : forward ! But I do not trust them.
They know how to die, but that is not enough. I love
freedom, but I do not believe in it. How could one
believe in it after looking in its face ? It is the flash of a
significance comprising all meanings, of a possibility comprising all potentiality. For it we fight, again and again,
from of old, victorious and in vain.

It is easy to understand that in a time when the deterio-
ration of all traditional bonds has made their legitimacy
questionable, the tendency to freedom is exalted, the
springboard is treated as the goal and a functional good
as substantial good. Moreover, it is idle sentimentality to
lament at great length that freedom is made the subject of
experiments. Perhaps it is fitting for this time which has
no compass that people should throw out their lives like a
plummet to discover our bearings and the course we should
set. But truly *their* lives ! Such an experiment, when it is
carried out, is a neck-breaking venture which cannot be

disputed. But when it is talked about and talked around, in intellectual discussions and confessions and in the mutual pros and cons of their life's " problems," it is an abomination of disintegration. Those who stake themselves, as individuals or as a community, may leap and crash out into the swaying void where senses and sense fail, or through it and beyond into some kind of existence. But they must not make freedom into a theorem or a programme. To become free of a bond is destiny; one carries that like a cross, not like a cockade. Let us realize the true meaning of being free of a bond : it means that a quite personal responsibility takes the place of one shared with many generations. Life lived in freedom is personal responsibility or it is a pathetic farce.

I have pointed out the power which alone can give a content to empty freedom and a direction to swaying and spinning freedom. I believe in it, I trust those devoted to it.

This fragile life between birth and death can nevertheless be a fulfilment—if it is a dialogue. In our life and experience we are addressed; by thought and speech and action, by producing and by influencing we are able to answer. For the most part we do not listen to the address, or we break into it with chatter. But if the word comes to us and the answer proceed from us then human life exists, though brokenly, in the world. The kindling of the response in that " spark " of the soul, the blazing up of the response, which occurs time and again, to the unexpectedly approaching speech, we term responsibility. We practise responsibility for that realm of life allotted and entrusted to us for which we are able to respond, that is, for which we have a relation of deeds which may count—in all our inadequacy—as a proper response. The extent to which a man, in the strength of the reality of the spark, can keep a traditional bond, a law, a direction, is the extent to which he is permitted to lean his responsibility on something (more than this is not vouchsafed to us, responsibility is not taken off our shoulders). As we " become free " this leaning on something is more and more denied to us, and our responsibility must become personal and solitary.

From this point of view education and its transformation in the hour of the crumbling of bonds are to be understood.

It is usual to contrast the principle of the "new" education as "Eros" with that of the "old" education as the "will to power."

In fact the one is as little a principle of education as the other. A principle of education, in a sense still to be clarified, can only be a basic relation which is fulfilled in education. But Eros and the will to power are alike passions of the soul for whose real elaboration a place is prepared elsewhere. Education can supply for them only an incidental realm and moreover one which sets a limit to their elaboration; nor can this limit be infringed without the realm itself being destroyed. The one can as little as the other constitute the educational attitude.

The "old" educator, in so far as he was an educator, was not "the man with a will to power," but he was the bearer of assured values which were strong in tradition. If the educator represents the world to the pupil, the "old" educator represented particularly the historical world, the past. He was the ambassador of history to this intruder, the "child"; he carried to him, as the Pope in the legend did to the prince of the Huns, the magic of the spiritual forces of history; he instilled values into the child or he drew the child into the values. The man who reduces this encounter between the cosmos of history and its eternally new chaos, between Zeus and Dionysos, to the formula of the "antagonism between fathers and sons," has never beheld it in his spirit. Zeus the Father does not stand for a generation but for a world, for the olympic, the formed world; the world of history faces a particular generation, which is the world of nature renewed again and again, always without history.

This situation of the old type of education is, however, easily used, or misused, by the individual's will to power, for this will is inflated by the authority of history. The will to power becomes convulsive and passes into fury, when the authority begins to decay, that is, when the

magical validity of tradition disappears. Then the moment
comes near when the teacher no longer faces the pupil as
an ambassador but only as an individual, as a static atom
to the whirling atom. Then no matter how much he
imagines he is acting from the fulness of the objective
spirit, in the reality of his life he is thrown back on himself, cast on his own resources, and hence filled with longing. Eros appears. And Eros finds employment in the new
situation of education as the will to power did in the old
situation. But Eros is not a bearer or the ground or the
principle any more than the will to power was. He only
claims to be that, in order not to be recognized as longing,
as the stranger given refuge. And many believe it.

Nietzsche did not succeed in glorifying the will to power
as much as Plato glorified Eros. But in our concern for
the creature in this great time of concern, for both alike
we have not to consider the myths of the philosophers but
the actuality of present life. In entire opposition to any
glorification we have to see that Eros—that is, not " love,"
but Eros the male and magnificent—whatever else may
belong to him, necessarily includes this one thing, that he
desires to enjoy men; and education, the peculiar essence
bearing this name which is composed of no others, excludes
precisely this desire. However mightily an educator is
possessed and inspired by Eros, if he obeys him in the
course of his educating then he stifles the growth of his
blessings. It must be one or the other : either he takes on
himself the tragedy of the person, and offers an unblem-
ished daily sacrifice, or the fire enters his work and con-
sumes it.

Eros is choice, choice made from an inclination. This is
precisely what education is not. The man who is loving
in Eros chooses the beloved, the modern educator finds his
pupil there before him. From this unerotic situation the
greatness of the modern educator is to be seen—and most
clearly when he is a teacher. He enters the school-room
for the first time, he sees them crouching at the desks,
indiscriminately flung together, the misshapen and the
well-proportioned, animal faces, empty faces, and noble
faces in indiscriminate confusion, like the presence of the

created universe; the glance of the educator accepts and receives them all. He is assuredly no descendant of the Greek gods, who kidnapped those they loved. But he seems to me to be a representative of the true God. For if God " forms the light and creates darkness," man is able to love both—to love light in itself, and darkness towards the light.

If this educator should ever believe that for the sake of education he has to practise selection and arrangement, then he will be guided by another criterion than that of inclination, however legitimate this may be in its own sphere; he will be guided by the recognition of values which is in his glance as an educator. But even then his selection remains suspended, under constant correction by the special humility of the educator for whom the life and particular being of all his pupils is the decisive factor to which his " hierarchic " recognition is subordinated. For in the manifold variety of the children the variety of creation is placed before him.

In education, then, there is a lofty asceticism : an asceticism which rejoices in the world, for the sake of the responsibility for a realm of life which is entrusted to us for our influence but not our interference—either by the will to power or by Eros. The spirit's service of life can be truly carried out only in the system of a reliable counterpoint—regulated by the laws of the different forms of relation—of giving and withholding oneself, intimacy and distance, which of course must not be controlled by reflection but must arise from the living tact of the natural and spiritual man. Every form of relation in which the spirit's service of life is realized has its special objectivity, its structure of proportions and limits which in no way resists the fervour of personal comprehension and penetration, though it does resist any confusion with the person's own spheres. If this structure and its resistance are not respected then a dilettantism will prevail which claims to be aristocratic, though in reality it is unsteady and fever-ish : to provide it with the most sacred names and attitudes will not help it past its inevitable consequence of disintegration. Consider, for example, the relation of doctor and patient. It is essential that this should be a real human relation experienced with the spirit by the one who is addressed; but as soon as the helper is touched by the desire—in however subtle a form—to dominate or to enjoy his patient, or to treat the latter's wish to be dominated or enjoyed by him other than as a wrong condition needing to be cured, the danger of falsification arises, beside which all quackery appears peripheral.

The objectively ascetic character of the sphere of education must not, however, be misunderstood as being so separated from the instinct to power and from Eros that no bridge can be flung from them to it. I have already pointed out how very significant Eros can be to the educator without corroding his work. What matters here is the threshold and the transformation which takes place on it. It is not the church alone which has a testing threshold on which a man is transformed or becomes a lie. But in order to be able to carry out this ever renewed transition from sphere to sphere he must have carried it out once in a decisive fashion and taken up in himself the essence of education. How does this happen? There is an elemental experience which shatters at least the assurance of the erotic as well as the cratetic man, but sometimes does more, forcing its way at white-heat into the heart of the instinct and remoulding it. A reversal of the single instinct takes place, which does not eliminate it but reverses its system of direction. Such a reversal can be effected by the elemental experience with which the real process of education begins and on which it is based. I call it experiencing the other side.

A man belabours another, who remains quite still. Then let us assume that the striker suddenly receives in his soul the blow which he strikes : the same blow; that he receives it as the other who remains still. For the space of a moment he experiences the situation from the other side. Reality imposes itself on him. What will he do? Either he will overwhelm the voice of the soul, or his impulse will be reversed.

A man caresses a woman, who lets herself be caressed. Then let us assume that he feels the contact from two sides —with the palm of his hand still, and also with the woman's skin. The twofold nature of the gesture, as one that takes place between two persons, thrills through the depth of enjoyment in his heart and stirs it. If he does not deafen his heart he will have—not to renounce the enjoyment but—to love.

I do not in the least mean that the man who has had such an experience would from then on have this two-sided sensation in every such meeting—that would perhaps destroy his instinct. But the one extreme experience makes the other person present to him for all time. A transfusion has taken place after which a mere elaboration of subjectivity is never again possible or tolerable to him.

Only an inclusive power is able to take the lead; only an inclusive Eros is love. Inclusiveness is the complete realization of the submissive person, the desired person, the " partner," not by the fancy but by the actuality of the being.

It would be wrong to identify what is meant here with the familiar but not very significant term " empathy." Empathy means, if anything, to glide with one's own feeling into the dynamic structure of an object, a pillar or a crystal or the branch of a tree, or even of an animal or a man, and as it were to trace it from within, understanding the formation and motoriality of the object with the perceptions of one's own muscles; it means to " transpose " oneself over there and in there. Thus it means the exclusion of one's own concreteness, the extinguishing of the actual situation of life, the absorption in pure æstheticism of the reality in which one participates. Inclusion is the opposite of this. It is the extension of one's own concreteness, the fulfilment of the actual situation of life, the complete presence of the reality in which one participates. Its elements are, first, a relation, of no matter what kind, between two persons, second, an event experienced by them in common, in which at least one of them actively participates, and, third, the fact that this one person, without forfeiting anything of the felt reality of his activity, at the same time lives through the common event from the standpoint of the other.

A relation between persons that is characterized in more or less degree by the element of inclusion may be termed a dialogical relation.

A dialogical relation will show itself also in genuine conversation, but it is not composed of this. Not only is the shared silence of two such persons a dialogue, but also their dialogical life continues, even when they are separated in space, as the continual potential presence of the one to the other, as an unexpressed intercourse. On the other hand, all conversation derives its genuineness only from the consciousness of the element of inclusion—even if this appears only abstractedly as an " acknowledgment " of the actual being of the partner in the conversation; but this acknowledgment can be real and effective only when it springs from an experience of inclusion, of the other side.

The reversal of the will to power and of Eros means that relations characterized by these are made dialogical. For that very reason it means that the instinct enters into communion with the fellow-man and into responsibility for him as an allotted and entrusted realm of life.

The element of inclusion, with whose recognition this clarification begins, is the same as that which constitutes the relation in education.

The relation in education is one of pure dialogue.

I have referred to the child, lying with half-closed eyes waiting for his mother to speak to him. But many children do not need to wait, for they know that they are unceasingly addressed in a dialogue which never breaks off. In face of the lonely night which threatens to invade, they lie preserved and guarded, invulnerable, clad in the silver mail of trust.

Trust, trust in the world, because this human being exists—that is the most inward achievement of the relation in education. Because this human being exists, meaninglessness, however hard pressed you are by it, cannot be the real truth. Because this human being exists, in the darkness the light lies hidden, in fear salvation, and in the callousness of one's fellow-men the great Love.

Because this human being exists : therefore he must be really there, really facing the child, not merely there in spirit. He may not let himself be represented by a phantom : the death of the phantom would be a catastrophe for the child's pristine soul. He need possess none of the perfections which the child may dream he possesses; but he must be really there. In order to be and to remain truly present to the child he must have gathered· the child's presence into his own store as one of the bearers of his communion with the world, one of the focuses of his responsibilities for the world. Of course he cannot be continually concerned with the child, either in thought or in deed, nor ought he to be. But if he has really gathered the child into his life then that subterranean dialogic, that steady potential presence of the one to the other is established and endures. Then there is reality *between* them, there is mutuality.

But this mutuality—that is what constitutes the peculiar nature of the relation in education—cannot be one of inclusion, although the true relation of the educator to the pupil is based on inclusion. No other relation draws its inner life like this one from the element of inclusion, but no other is in that regard like this, completely directed to one-sidedness, so that if it loses one-sidedness it loses essence.

We may distinguish three chief forms of the dialogical relation.

The first rests on an abstract but mutual experience of inclusion.

The clearest example of this is a disputation between two men, thoroughly different in nature and outlook and calling, where in an instant—as by the action of a messenger as anonymous as he is invisible—it happens that each is aware of the other's full legitimacy, wearing the insignia of necessity and of meaning. What an illumination! The truth, the strength of conviction, the " standpoint," or rather the circle of movement, of each of them, is in no way reduced by this. There is no " relativizing," but we may say that, in the sign of the limit, the essence of mortal recognition, fraught with primal destiny, is manifested to us. To recognize means for us creatures the fulfilment by each of us, in truth and responsibility, of his own relation to the Present Being, through our receiving all that is manifested of it and incorporating it into our own being, with all our force, faithfully, and open to the world and the spirit. In this way living truth arises and endures. We have become aware that it is with the other as with ourselves, and that what rules over us both is not a truth of recognition but the truth-of-existence and the existence-of-truth of the Present Being. In this way we have become able *to acknowledge*.

I have called this form abstract, not as though its basic experience lacked immediacy, but because it is related to man only as a spiritual person and is bound to leave out the full reality of his being and life. The other two forms proceed from the inclusion of this full reality.

Of these the first, the relation of education, is based on a concrete but one-sided experience of inclusion.

If education means to let a selection of the world affect a person through the medium of another person, then the one through whom this takes place, rather, who makes it take place through himself, is caught in a strange paradox. What is otherwise found only as grace, inlaid in the folds of life—the influencing of the lives of others with one's own life—becomes here a function and a law. But since the educator has to such an extent replaced the master, the danger has arisen that the new phenomenon, the will to educate, may degenerate into arbitrariness, and that the educator may carry out his selection and his influence from himself and his idea of the pupil, not from the pupil's own reality. One only needs to read, say, the accounts of Pestalozzi's teaching method to see how easily, even with the noblest teachers, arbitrary self-will is mixed up with will. This is almost always due to an interruption or a temporary flagging of the act of inclusion, which is not merely regulative for the realm of education, as for other realms, but is actually constitutive; so that the realm of education acquires its true and proper force from the constant return of this act and the constantly renewed connexion with it. The man whose calling it is to influence the being of persons that can be determined, must experience this action of his (however much it may have assumed the form of non-action) ever anew from the other side. Without the action of his spirit being in any way weakened he must at the same time be over there, on the surface of that other spirit which is being acted upon—and not of some conceptual, contrived spirit, but all the time the wholly concrete spirit of this individual and unique being who is living and confronting him, and who stands with him in the common situation of " educating " and " being educated " (which is indeed one situation, only the other is at the other end of it). It is not enough for him to imagine the child's individuality, nor to experience him directly as a spiritual person and then to acknowledge him. Only when he catches himself " from over there," and feels how it affects one, how it affects this other human being, does he recognize the real limit, baptize his self-will in Reality and make it true will, and renew his paradoxical legitimacy. He is of all men the one for whom inclusion may and should change from an alarming and edifying event into an atmosphere.

But however intense the mutuality of giving and taking with which he is bound to his pupil, inclusion cannot be mutual in this case. He experiences the pupil's being educated, but the pupil cannot experience the educating of the educator. The educator stands at both ends of the common situation, the pupil only at one end. In the moment when the pupil is able to throw himself across and experience from over there, the educative relation would be burst asunder, or change into friendship.

We call friendship the third form of the dialogical relation, which is based on a concrete and mutual experience of inclusion. It is the true inclusion of one another by human souls.

The educator who practises the experience of the other side and stands firm in it, experiences two things together, first that he is limited by otherness, and second that he receives grace by being bound to the other. He feels from "over there" the acceptance and the rejection of what is approaching (that is, approaching from himself, the educator)—of course often only in a fugitive mood or an uncertain feeling; but this discloses the real need and absence of need in the soul. In the same way the foods a child likes and dislikes is a fact which does not, indeed, procure for the experienced person but certainly helps him to gain an insight into what substances the child's body needs. In learning from time to time what this human being needs and does not need at the moment, the educator is led to an even deeper recognition of what the human being needs in order to grow. But he is also led to the recognition of what he, the "educator," is able and what he is unable to give of what is needed—and what he can give now, and what not yet. So the responsibility for this realm of life allotted and entrusted to him, the constant responsibility for this living soul, points him to that which seems impossible and yet is somehow granted to us—to self-education. But self-education, here as everywhere, cannot take place through one's being concerned with oneself but only through one's being concerned, knowing what it means, with the world. The forces of the world which the child needs for the building up of his substance must be chosen by the educator from the world and drawn into himself.

The education of men by men means the selection of the effective world by a person and in him. The educator gathers in the constructive forces of the world. He distinguishes, rejects, and confirms in himself, in his self which is filled with the world. The constructive forces are eternally the same : they are the world bound up in community, turned to God. The educator educates himself to be their vehicle.

Then is this the "principle" of education, its normal and fixed maxim?

No; it is only the *principium* of its reality, the beginning of its reality—wherever it begins.

There is not and never has been a norm and fixed

maxim of education. What is called so was always only the norm of a culture, of a society, a church, an epoch, to which education too, like all stirring and action of the spirit, was submissive, and which education translated into its language. In a formed age there is in truth no autonomy of education, but only in an age which is losing form. Only in it, in the disintegration of traditional bonds, in the spinning whirl of freedom, does personal responsibility arise which in the end can no longer lean with its burden of decision on any church or society or culture, but is lonely in face of Present Being.

In an age which is losing form the highly-praised "personalities," who know how to serve its fictitious forms and in their name to dominate the age, count in the truth of what is happening no more than those who lament the genuine forms of the past and are diligent to restore them. The ones who count are those persons who—though they may be of little renown—respond to and are responsible for the continuation of the living spirit, each in the active stillness of his sphere of work.

The question which is always being brought forward—" To where, to what, must we educate?"—misunderstands the situation. Only times which know a figure of general validity—the Christian, the gentleman, the citizen—know an answer to that question, not necessarily in words, but by pointing with the finger to the figure which rises clear in the air, out-topping all. The forming of this figure in all individuals, out of all materials, is the formation of a "culture." But when all figures are shattered, when no figure is able any more to dominate and shape the present human material, what is there left to form?

Nothing but the image of God.

That is the indefinable, only factual, direction of the responsible modern educator. This cannot be a theoretical answer to the question " To what?", but only, if at all, an answer carried out in deeds; an answer carried out by non-doing.

The educator is set now in the midst of the need which he experiences in inclusion, but only a bit deeper in it. He is set in the midst of the service, only a bit higher up,

which he invokes without words; he is set in the *imitatio
Dei absconditi sed non ignoti.*

When all "directions" fail there arises in the darkness
over the abyss the one true direction of man, towards the
creative Spirit, towards the Spirit of God brooding on the
face of the waters, towards Him of whom we know not
whence He comes and whither He goes.

That is man's true autonomy which no longer betrays
but responds.

Man, the creature, who forms and transforms the creation, cannot create. But he, each man, can expose himself
and others to the creative Spirit. And he can call upon the
Creator to save and perfect His image.

IV

THE EDUCATION OF CHARACTER

I

EDUCATION WORTHY of the name is essentially education of character. For the genuine educator does not merely consider individual functions of his pupil, as one intending to teach him only to know or to be capable of certain definite things; but his concern is always the person as a whole, both in the actuality in which he lives before you now and in his possibilities, what he can become. But in this way, as a whole in reality and potentiality, a man can be conceived either as personality, that is, as a unique spiritual-physical form with all the forces dormant in it, or as character, that is, as the link between what this individual is and the sequence of his actions and attitudes. Between these two modes of conceiving the pupil in his wholeness there is a fundamental difference. Personality is something which in its growth remains essentially outside the influence of the educator; but to assist in the moulding of character is his greatest task. Personality is a completion, only character is a task. One may cultivate and enhance personality, but in education one can and one must aim at character.

However—as I would like to point out straightaway—it is advisable not to over-estimate what the educator can even at best do to develop character. In this more than in any other branch of the science of teaching it is important to realize, at the very beginning of the discussion, by fundamental limits to conscious influence, even before asking what character is and how it is to be brought about.

If I have to teach algebra I can expect to succeed in giving my pupils an idea of quadratic equations with two unknown quantities. Even the slowest-witted child will understand it so well that he will amuse himself by solving equations at night when he cannot fall asleep. And even one with the most sluggish memory will not forget, in his old age, how to play with x and y. But if I am concerned with the education of character, everything becomes problematic. I try to explain to my pupils that envy is despicable, and at once I feel the secret resistance of those who are poorer than their comrades. I try to explain that it is wicked to bully the weak, and at once I see a suppressed smile on the lips of the strong. I try to explain that lying destroys life, and something frightful happens : the worst habitual liar of the class produces a brilliant essay on the destructive power of lying. I have made the fatal mistake of *giving instruction* in ethics, and what I said is accepted as current coin of knowledge; nothing of it is transformed into character-building substance.

But the difficulty lies still deeper. In all teaching of a subject I can announce my intention of teaching as openly as I please, and this does not interfere with the results. After all, pupils do want, for the most part, to learn something, even if not overmuch, so that a tacit agreement becomes possible. But as soon as my pupils notice that I want to educate their characters I am resisted precisely by those who show most signs of genuine independent character : they will not let themselves be educated, or rather, they do not like the idea that somebody wants to educate them. And those, too, who are seriously labouring over the question of good and evil, rebel when one dictates to them, as though it were some long-established truth, what is good and what is bad; and they rebel just because they have experienced over and over again how hard it is to find the right way. Does it follow that one should keep silent about one's intention of educating character, and act by ruse and subterfuge? No; I have just said that the difficulty lies deeper. It is not enough to see that education of character is not introduced into a lesson in class; neither may one conceal it in cleverly arranged intervals. Education cannot tolerate such politic action. Even if the pupil does not notice the hidden motive it will have its negative effect on the actions of the teacher himself by depriving him of the directness which is his strength.

Only in his whole being, in all his spontaneity can the educator truly affect the whole being of his pupil. For educating characters you do not need a moral genius, but you do need a man who is wholly alive and able to communicate himself directly to his fellow beings. His aliveness streams out to them and affects them most strongly and purely when he has no thought of affecting them.

The Greek word character means *impression*. The special link between man's being and his appearance, the special connexion between the unity of what he is and the sequence of his actions and attitudes is impressed on his still plastic substance. Who does the impressing? Everything does : nature and the social context, the house and the street, language and custom, the world of history and the world of daily news in the form of rumour, of broadcast and newspaper, music and technical science, play and dream—everything together. Many of these factors exert their influence by stimulating agreement, imitation, desire, effort; others by arousing questions, doubts, dislike, resistance. Character is formed by the interpenetration of all those multifarious, opposing influences. And yet, among this infinity of form-giving forces the educator is only one element among innumerable others, but distinct from them all by his *will* to take part in the stamping of character and by his *consciousness* that he represents in the eyes of the growing person a certain *selection* of what is, the selection of what is " right," of what *should* be. It is in this will and this consciousness that his vocation as an educator finds its fundamental expression. From this the genuine educator gains two things : first, humility, the feeling of being only one element amidst the fullness of life, only one single existence in the midst of all the tremendous inrush of reality on the pupil; but secondly, self-awareness, the feeling of being therein the only existence that *wants* to affect the whole person, and thus the feeling of responsibility for the selection of reality which he represents to the pupil. And a third thing emerges from all this, the recognition that in this realm of the education of character, of wholeness, there is only *one* access to the pupil : his *confidence*. For the adolescent who is frightened and disappointed by an unreliable world, confidence means the liberating insight that there is human truth, the truth of human existence. When the pupil's confidence has been won, his resistance against being educated gives way to a singular happening : he accepts the educator as a person. He feels he may trust this man, that this man is not making a business out of him, but is taking part in his life, accepting him before desiring to influence him. And so he learns to *ask*.

The teacher who is for the first time approached by a boy with somewhat defiant bearing, but with trembling hands, visibly opened-up and fired by a daring hope, who asks him what is the right thing in a certain situation— for instance, whether in learning that a friend has betrayed a secret entrusted to him one should call him to account or be content with entrusting no more secrets to him—the teacher to whom this happens realizes that this is the moment to make the first conscious step towards education of character; he has to answer, to answer under a responsibility, to give an answer which will probably lead beyond the alternatives of the question by showing a third possibility which is the right one. To dictate what is good and evil in general is not his business. His business is to answer a concrete question, to answer what is right and wrong in a given situation. This, as I have said, can only happen in an atmosphere of confidence. Confidence, of course, is not won by the strenuous endeavour to win it, but by direct and ingenuous participation in the life of the people one is dealing with—in this case in the life of one's pupils —and by assuming the responsibility which arises from such participation. It is not the educational intention but it is the meeting which is educationally fruitful. A soul suffering from the contradictions of the world of human society, and of its own physical existence, approaches me with a question. By trying to answer it to the best of my knowledge and conscience I help it to become a character that actively overcomes the contradictions.

If this is the teacher's standpoint towards his pupil, taking part in his life and conscious of responsibility, then everything that passes between them can, without any deliberate or politic intention, open a way to the education of character : lessons and games, a conversation about quarrels in the class, or about the problems of a world-war. Only, the teacher must not forget the limits of education; even when he enjoys confidence he cannot always expect agreement. Confidence implies a break-through from reserve, the bursting of the bonds which imprison an unquiet heart. But it does not imply uncon-ditional agreement. The teacher must never forget that conflicts too, if only they are decided in a healthy atmos-phere, have an educational value. A conflict with a pupil is the supreme test for the educator. He must use his own insight wholeheartedly; he must not blunt the pierc-ing impact of his knowledge, but he must at the same time have in readiness the healing ointment for the heart pierced by it. Not for a moment may he conduct a dia-lectical manœuvre instead of the real battle for truth. But if he is the victor he has to help the vanquished to endure defeat; and if he cannot conquer the self-willed soul that faces him (for victories over souls are not so easily won), then he has to find the word of love which alone can help to overcome so difficult a situation.

§

So far I have referred to those personal difficulties in the education of character which arise from the relation be-tween educator and pupil, while for the moment treating character itself, the object of education, as a simple con-cept of fixed content. But it is by no means that. In order to penetrate to the real difficulties in the education of character we have to examine critically the concept of character itself.

Kerschensteiner in his well-known essay on *The Concept and Education of Character* distinguished between " char-acter in the most general sense," by which he means " a man's attitude to his human surroundings, which is con-stant and is expressed in his actions," and real " ethical character," which he defines as " a special attitude, and one which in action gives the preference before all others to absolute values." If we begin by accepting this distinction unreservedly—and undeniably there is some truth in it —we are faced with such heavy odds in all education of character in our time that the very possibility of it seems doubtful.

The "absolute values" which Kerschensteiner refers to cannot, of course, be meant to have only subjective validity for the person concerned. Don Juan finds absolute and subjective value in seducing the greatest possible number of women, and the dictator sees it in the greatest possible accumulation of power. "Absolute validity" can only relate to universal values and norms, the existence of which the person concerned recognizes and acknowledges. But to deny the presence of universal values and norms of absolute validity—that is the conspicuous tendency of our age. This tendency is not, as is sometimes supposed, directed merely against the sanctioning of the norms by religion, but against their universal character and absolute validity, against their claim to be of a higher order than man and to govern the whole of mankind. In our age values and norms are not permitted to be anything but expressions of the life of a group which translates its own needs into the language of objective claims, until at last the group itself, for example a nation, is raised to an absolute value—and moreover to the only value. Then this splitting up into groups so pervades the whole of life that it is no longer possible to re-establish a sphere of values common to mankind, and a commandment to mankind is no longer observed. As this tendency grows the basis for the development of what Kerschensteiner means by moral character steadily diminishes. How, under these circumstances, can the task of educating character be completed?

At the time of the Arab terror in Palestine, when there were single Jewish acts of reprisal, there must have been many discussions between teacher and pupils on the question : Can there be any suspension of the Ten Commandments, i.e. can murder become a good deed if committed in the interest of one's own group? One such

discussion was once repeated to me. The teacher asked:
"When the commandment tells you 'Thou shalt not bear
false witness against thy neighbour,' are we to interpret it
with the condition, 'provided that it does not profit you'?"
Thereupon one of the pupils said, "But it is not a question of my profit, but of the profit of my people." The
teacher: "And how would you like it, then, if we put our
condition this way: 'Provided that it does not profit your
family'?" The pupil: "But family—that is still something more or less like myself; but the people—that is
something quite different; there all question of *I* disappears." The teacher: "Then if you are thinking, 'we
want victory,' don't you feel at the same time, 'I want
victory'?" The pupil: "But the people, that is something infinitely more than just the people of to-day. It
includes all past and future generations." At this point
the teacher felt the moment had come to leave the narrow
compass of the present and to invoke historical destiny.
He said: "Yes; all past generations. But what was it that
made those past generations of the Exile live? What made
them outlive and overcome all their trials? Wasn't it that
the cry 'Thou shalt not' never faded from their hearts
and ears?" The pupil grew very pale. He was silent for a
while, but it was the silence of one whose words threatened
to stifle him. Then he burst out: "And what have we
achieved that way? This!" And he banged his fist on the
newspaper before him, which contained the report on the
British White Paper. And again he burst out with "Live?
Outlive? Do you call that life? We want to live!"

I have already said that the test of the educator lies in
conflict with his pupil. He has to face this conflict and,
whatever turn it may take, he has to find the way through
it into life, into a life, I must add, where confidence continues unshaken—more, is even mysteriously strengthened.
But the example I have just given shows the extreme difficulty of this task, which seems at times to have reached
an impassable frontier. This is no longer merely a conflict
between two generations, but between a world which for
several millennia has believed in a truth superior to man,

and an age which does not believe in it any longer—will not or cannot believe in it any longer.

But if we now ask, "How in this situation can there be any education of character?", something negative is immediately obvious : it is senseless to want to prove by any kind of argument that nevertheless the denied absoluteness of norms exists. That would be to assume that the denial is the result of reflection, and is open to argument, that is, to material for renewed reflection. But the denial is due to the disposition of a dominant human type of our age. We are justified in regarding this disposition as a sickness of the human race. But we must not deceive ourselves by believing that the disease can be cured by formulæ which assert that nothing is really as the sick person imagines. It is an idle undertaking to call out, to a mankind that has grown blind to eternity : " Look ! the eternal values !" To-day host upon host of men have everywhere sunk into the slavery of collectives, and each collective is the supreme authority for its own slaves; there is no longer, superior to the collectives, any universal sovereignty in idea, faith, or spirit. Against the values, decrees and decisions of the collective no appeal is possible. This is true, not only for the totalitarian countries, but also for the parties and party-like groups in the so-called democracies. Men who have so lost themselves to the collective Moloch cannot be rescued from it by any reference, however eloquent, to the absolute whose kingdom the Moloch has usurped. One has to begin by pointing to that sphere where man himself, in the hours of utter solitude, occasionally becomes aware of the disease through sudden pain : by pointing to the relation of the individual to his own self. In order to enter into a personal relation with the absolute, it is first necessary to be a person again, to rescue one's real personal self from the fiery jaws of collectivism which devours all selfhood. The desire to do this is latent in the pain the individual suffers through his distorted relation to his own self. Again and again he dulls the pain with a subtle poison and thus suppresses the desire as well. To keep the pain awake, to waken the desire—that is the first task of everyone who regrets the obscuring of eternity. It is also the first task of the genuine educator in our time.

The man for whom absolute values in a universal sense do not exist cannot be made to adopt " an attitude which in action gives the preference over all others to absolute values." But what one can inculcate in him is the desire to attain once more to a real attitude, and that is, the desire to become a person following the only way that leads to this goal to-day.

But with this the concept of character formulated by Kerschensteiner and deriving, as we know, from Kant is recognized to be useless for the specifically modern task of the education of character. Another concept has to be found if this task is to be more precisely defined.

We cannot conceal from ourselves that we stand to-day on the ruins of the edifice whose towers were raised by Kant. It is not given to us living to-day to sketch the plan for a new building. But we can perhaps begin by laying the first foundations without a plan, with only a dawning image before our mind's eye.

3

According to Kerschensteiner's final definition character is " fundamentally nothing but voluntary obedience to the maxims which have been moulded in the individual by experience, teaching, and self-reflection, whether they have been adopted and then completely assimilated or have originated in the consciousness through self-legislation." This voluntary obedience " is, however, only a form of self-control." At first, love or fear of other people must have produced in man " the *habit* of self-conquest." Then, gradually, " this outer obedience must be transformed into inner obedience."

The concept of habit was then enlarged, especially by John Dewey in his book, *Human Nature and Conduct.* According to him character is " the interpenetration of habits." Without " the continued operation of all habits in every act" there would be no unified character, but only "a juxtaposition of disconnected reactions to separated situations."

With this concept of character as an organization of self-control by means of the accumulation of maxims, or as a system of interpenetrating habits, it is very easy to understand how powerless modern educational science is when faced by the sickness of man. But even apart from the special problems of the age, this concept can be no adequate basis for the construction of a genuine education of character. Not that the educator could dispense with employing useful maxims or furthering good habits. But in moments that come perhaps only seldom, a feeling of blessed achievement links him to the explorer, the inventor, the artist, a feeling of sharing in the revelation of what is hidden. In such moments he finds himself in a sphere very different from that of maxims and habits. Only on this, the highest plane of his activity, can he fix his real goal, the real concept of character which is his concern, even though he might not often reach it.

For the first time a young teacher enters a class independently, no longer sent by the training college to prove his efficiency. The class before him is like a mirror of mankind, so multiform, so full of contradictions, so inaccessible. He feels "These boys—I have not sought them out; I have been put here and have to accept them as they are—but not as they now are in this moment, no, as they *really* are, as they can become. But how can I find out what is in them and what can I do to make it take shape?" And the boys do not make things easy for him. They are noisy, they cause trouble, they stare at him with impudent curiosity. He is at once tempted to check this or that trouble-maker, to issue orders, to make compulsory the rules of decent behaviour, to say No, to say No to everything rising against him from beneath: he is at once tempted to start from beneath. And if one starts from beneath one perhaps never arrives above, but everything comes down. But then his eyes meet a face which strikes him. It is not a beautiful face nor particularly intelligent; but it is a real face, or rather, the chaos preceding the cosmos of a real face. On it he reads a question which is something different from the general curiosity : " Who are you? Do you know something that concerns me? Do you bring me something? What do you bring?"

In some such way he reads the question. And he, the young teacher, addresses this face. He says nothing very ponderous or important, he puts an ordinary introductory question : " What did you talk about last in geography? The Dead Sea? Well, what about the Dead Sea?" But there was obviously something not quite usual in the question, for the answer he gets is not the ordinary schoolboy answer; the boy begins to *tell a story*. Some months earlier he had stayed for a few hours on the shores of the Dead Sea and it is of this he tells. He adds : " And everything looked to me as if it had been created a day before the rest of creation." Quite unmistakably he had only in this moment made up his mind to talk about it. In the meantime his face has changed. It is no longer quite as chaotic as before. And the class has fallen silent. They all listen. The class, too, is no longer a chaos. Something has happened. The young teacher has started from above.

The educator's task can certainly not consist in educating great characters. He cannot select his pupils, but year by year the world, such as it is, is sent in the form of a school class to meet him on his life's way as his destiny; and in this destiny lies the very meaning of his life's work. He has to introduce discipline and order, he has to establish a law, and he can only strive and hope for the result that discipline and order will become more and more inward and autonomous, and that at last the law will be written in the heart of his pupils. But his real goal which, once he has well recognized it and well remembers it, will influence all his work, is the great character.

The great character can be conceived neither as a system of maxims nor as a system of habits. It is peculiar to him to act from the whole of his substance. That is, it is peculiar to him to react in accordance with the uniqueness of every situation which challenges him as an active person. Of course there are all sorts of similarities in different situations; one can construct types of situations, one can always find to what section the particular situation belongs, and draw what is appropriate from the hoard of established maxims and habits, apply the appropriate maxim, bring into operation the appropriate habit. But what is untypical in the particular situation remains unnoticed and unanswered. To me that seems the same as if, having ascertained the sex of a new-born child, one were immediately to establish its type as well, and put all the children of one type into a common cradle on which not the individual name but the name of the type was inscribed. In spite of all similarities every living situation has, like a new-born child, a new face, that has never been before and will never come again. It demands of you a reaction which cannot be prepared beforehand. It demands nothing of what is past. It demands presence, responsibility; it demands you. I call a great character one who by his actions and attitudes satisfies the claim of situations out of deep readiness to respond with his whole life, and in such a way that the sum of his actions and attitudes expresses at the same time the unity of his being in its willingness to accept responsibility. As his being is unity, the unity of accepted responsibility, his active life, too, coheres into unity. And one might perhaps say that for him there rises a unity out of the situations he has responded to in responsibility, the indefinable unity of a moral destiny.

All this does not mean that the great character is beyond the acceptance of norms. No responsible person remains a stranger to norms. But the command inherent in a genuine norm never becomes a maxim and the fulfilment of it never a habit. Any command that a great character takes to himself in the course of his development does not act in him as part of his consciousness or as material for building up his exercises, but remains latent in a basic layer of his substance until it reveals itself to him in a concrete way. What it has to tell him is revealed whenever a situation arises which demands of him a solution of which till then he had perhaps no idea. Even the most universal norm will at times be recognized only in a very special situation. I know of a man whose heart was struck by the lightning flash of "Thou shalt not steal" in the very moment when he was moved by a very different desire from that of stealing, and whose heart was so struck by it that he not only abandoned doing what he wanted to do, but with the whole force of his passion did the very opposite. Good and evil are not each other's opposites like right and left. The evil approaches us as a whirlwind, the good as a direction. There is a direction, a "yes," a command, hidden even in a prohibition, which is revealed to us in moments like these. In moments like these the command addresses us really in the second person, and the Thou in it is no one else but one's own self. Maxims command only the third person, the each and the none.

One can say that it is the unconditioned nature of the address which distinguishes the command from the maxim. In an age which has become deaf to unconditioned address we cannot overcome the dilemma of the education of character from that angle. But insight into the structure of great character can help us to overcome it.

Of course, it may be asked whether the educator should really start "from above," whether, in fixing his goal, the hope of finding a great character, who is bound to be the exception, should be his starting-point; for in his methods of educating character he will always have to take into consideration the others, the many. To this I reply that the educator would not have the right to do so if a method inapplicable to these others were to result. In fact, however, his very insight into the structure of a great character helps him to find the way by which alone (as I have indicated) he can begin to influence also the victims of the collective Moloch, pointing out to them the sphere in which they themselves suffer—namely, their relation to their own selves. From this sphere he must elicit the values which he can make credible and desirable to his pupils. That is what insight into the structure of a great character helps him to do.

A section of the young is beginning to feel to-day that, because of their absorption by the collective, something important and irreplaceable is lost to them—personal responsibility for life and the world. These young people, it is true, do not yet realize that their blind devotion to the collective, e.g. to a party, was not a genuine act of their personal life; they do not realize that it sprang, rather, from the fear of being left, in this age of confusion, to rely on themselves, on a self which no longer receives its direction from eternal values. Thus they do not yet realize that their devotion was fed on the unconscious desire to have responsibility removed from them by an authority in which they believe or want to believe. They do not yet realize that this devotion was an escape. I repeat, the young people I am speaking of do not yet realize this. But they are beginning to notice that he who no longer, with his whole being, decides what he does or does not, and assumes responsibility for it, becomes sterile in soul. And a sterile soul ceases to be a soul.

This is where the educator can begin and should begin. He can help the feeling that something is lacking to grow into the clarity of consciousness and into the force of desire. He can awaken in young people the courage to shoulder life again. He can bring before his pupils the image of a great character who denies no answer to life and the world, but accepts responsibility for everything essential that he meets. He can show his pupils this image without the fear that those among them who most of all need discipline and order will drift into a craving for aimless freedom : on the contrary, he can teach them in this way to recognize that discipline and order too are starting-points on the way towards self-responsibility. He can show that even the great character is not born perfect, that the unity of his being has first to mature before expressing itself in the sequence of his actions and attitudes. But unity itself, unity of the person, unity of the lived life, has to be emphasized again and again. The confusing contradictions cannot be remedied by the collectives, not one of which knows the taste of genuine unity and which if left to themselves would end up, like the scorpions imprisoned in a box, in the witty fable, by devouring one another. This mass of contradictions can be met and conquered only by the rebirth of personal unity, unity of being, unity of life, unity of action—unity of

being, life and action together. This does not mean a
static unity of the uniform, but the great dynamic unity
of the multiform in which multiformity is formed into
unity of character. To-day the great characters are still
" enemies of the people," they who love their society, yet
wish not only to preserve it but to raise it to a higher level.
To-morrow they will be the architects of a new unity of
mankind. It is the longing for personal unity, from which
must be born a unity of mankind, which the educator
should lay hold of and strengthen in his pupils. Faith in
this unity and the will to achieve it is not a " return " to
individualism, but a step beyond all the dividedness of
individualism and collectivism. A great and full relation
between man and man can only exist between unified and
responsible persons. That is why it is much more rarely
found in the totalitarian collective than in any historically
earlier form of society; much more rarely also in the
authoritarian party than in any earlier form of free association. Genuine education of character is genuine education for community.

In a generation which has had this kind of upbringing
the desire will also be kindled to behold again the eternal
values, to hear again the language of the eternal norm.
He who knows inner unity, the innermost life of which is
mystery, learns to honour the mystery in all its forms. In
an understandable reaction against the former domination
of a false, fictitious mystery, the present generations are
obsessed with the desire to rob life of all its mystery. The
fictitious mystery will disappear, the genuine one will rise
again. A generation which honours the mystery in all its
forms will no longer be deserted by eternity. Its light seems
darkened only because the eye suffers from a cataract; the
receiver has been turned off, but the resounding ether has
not ceased to vibrate. To-day, indeed, in the hour of
upheaval, the eternal is sifted from the pseudo-eternal.
That which flashed into the primal radiance and blurred
the primal sound will be extinguished and silenced, for it
has failed before the horror of the new confusion and the
questioning soul has unmasked its futility. Nothing remains but what rises above the abyss of to-day's monstrous

problems, as above every abyss of every time : the wing-beat of the spirit and the creative word. But he who can see and hear out of unity will also behold and discern again what can be beheld and discerned eternally. The educator who helps to bring man back to his own unity will help to put him again face to face with God.

V

WHAT IS MAN?

Ne connaîtrons-nous jamais l'homme?—ROUSSEAU

SECTION ONE:
THE PROGRESS OF THE QUESTION

1: *Kant's Questions*

I

RABBI BUNAM VON PRZYSUCHA, one of the last great teachers of Hasidism, is said to have once addressed his pupils thus: "I wanted to write a book called *Adam*, which would be about the whole man. But then I decided not to write it."

In these naive-sounding words of a genuine sage the whole story of human thought about man is expressed. From time immemorial man has known that he is the subject most deserving of his own study, but he has also fought shy of treating this subject as a whole, that is, in accordance with its total character. Sometimes he takes a run at it, but the difficulty of this concern with his own being soon overpowers and exhausts him, and in silent resignation he withdraws—either to consider all things in heaven and earth save man, or to divide man into departments which can be treated singly, in a less problematic, less powerful and less binding way.

The philosopher Malebranche, the most significant of the French philosophers who continued the Cartesian investigation, writes in the foreword to his chief work *De la recherche de la vérité* (1674): "Of all human knowledge the knowledge of man is the most deserving of his study. Yet this knowledge is not the most cultivated or the most

developed which we possess. The generality of men neglect
it completely. And even among those who busy themselves
with this knowledge there are very few who dedicate themselves to it—and still fewer who successfully dedicate themselves to it." He himself certainly raises in his book such
genuinely anthropological questions as how far the life of
the nerves which lead to the lungs, the stomach, and the
liver, influences the origin of errors; but he too established
no doctrine of the being of man.

2

The most forcible statement of the task set to philosophical anthropology was made by Kant. In the *Hand-
book* to his lectures on logic, which he expressly acknowledged—though he himself did not publish it and though it
does not reproduce his underlying notes authentically—he
distinguishes between a philosophy in the scholastic sense
and a philosophy in the universal sense *(in sensu cosmico)*.
He describes the latter as " the knowledge of the ultimate
aims of human reason " or as the " knowledge of the
highest maxim of the use of our reason." The field of
philosophy in this cosmopolitan significance may, according to Kant, be marked off into the following questions.
"1. What can I know? 2. What ought I to do? 3. What
may I hope? 4. What is man? Metaphysics answers the
first question, ethics the second, religion the third and
anthropology the fourth." And Kant adds: "Fundamentally all this could be reckoned as anthropology, since
the first three questions are related to the last." This
formulation repeats the three questions of which Kant says,
in the section of his *Critique of Pure Reason* entitled *Of
the ideal of the supreme good,* that every interest of the
reason, the speculative as well as the practical, is united
in them. In distinction from the *Critique of Pure Reason*
he here traces these questions back to a fourth question,
that about the being of man, and assigns it to a discipline
called anthropology, by which—since he is discussing the
fundamental questions of human philosophizing—only

philosophical anthropology can be understood. This, then, would be the fundamental philosophical science.

But it is remarkable that Kant's own anthropology, both what he himself published and his copious lectures on man, which only appeared long after his death, absolutely fails to achieve what he demands of a philosophical anthropology. In its express purpose as well as in its entire content it offers something different—an abundance of valuable observations for the knowledge of man, for example, on egoism, on honesty and lies, on fancy, on fortune-telling, on dreams, on mental diseases, on wit, and so on. But the question, what man is, is simply not raised, and not one of the problems which are implicitly set us at the same time by this question—such as man's special place in the cosmos, his connexion with destiny, his relation to the world of things, his understanding of his fellow-men, his existence as a being that knows it must die, his attitude in all the ordinary and extraordinary encounters with the mystery with which his life is shot through, and so on—not one of these problems is seriously touched upon. The *wholeness* of man does not enter into this anthropology. It is as if Kant in his actual philosophizing had had qualms about setting the question which he formulated as the fundamental one.

A modern philosopher, Martin Heidegger, who has dealt (in his *Kant and the Problem of Metaphysics,* 1929) with this strange contradiction, explains it by the *indefiniteness* of the question, what man is. The way of asking the question about man, he says, has itself become question-able. In Kant's first three questions it is man's *finitude* which is under discussion : " What *can* I know?" involves an inability, and thus a limitation; " What *ought* I to do?" includes the realization that something has not yet been accomplished, and thus a limitation; and " What *may* I hope?" means that the questioner is given one expectation and denied another, and thus it means a limitation. The fourth question is the question about " finitude in man," and is no longer an anthropological question at all, for it is the question about the essence of existence itself. As the basis of metaphysics anthropology is replaced by " fundamental ontology."

Whatever this finding represents, it is no longer Kant. Heidegger has shifted the emphasis of Kant's three questions. Kant does not ask: " What *can* I know?" but " What *can* I *know*?" The essential point here is not that there is something I can do and thus something else that I cannot do; nor is it that there is something I know and thus something else that I do not know; but it is that I *can know* something, and that I can then ask what that is that I can know. It is not my finitude that is under discussion here, but my real participation in knowing what there is to know. And in the same way " What ought I to do?" means that there *is* something I ought to do, and thus that I am not separated from " right " doing, but precisely by being able to *come to know* my " ought " may find the way to the doing. Finally, " W_ at may I hope?" does not assert, as Heidegger thinks, that a " may " is made questionable here, and that in the expectation a want of what may not be expected is revealed; but it asserts, first, that there is something for me to hope (for obviously Kant does not mean that the answer to the third question is " Nothing "), secondly, that I am permitted to hope it, and thirdly, that precisely because I am permitted I can learn what it is that I may hope. That is what *Kant* says. And thus in Kant the meaning of the fourth question, to which the first three can be reduced is, what sort of a being is it which is able to know, and ought to do, and may hope? And the fact that the first three questions can be reduced to this question means that the knowledge of the essence of this being will make plain to me *what*, as such a being, it can know, *what*, as such a being, it ought to do, and *what*, as such a being, it may hope. This also means that indissolubly connected with the finitude which is given by the ability to know *only* this, there is a participation in infinity, which is given by the ability to know at all. The meaning is therefore that when we recognize man's finitude we must *at the same time* recognize his participation in infinity, not as two juxtaposed qualities but as the twofold nature of the processes in which alone man's existence becomes recognizable. The finite has its effect on him and the infinite has its effect on him; he shares in finitude and he shares in infinity.

Certainly Kant in his anthropology has neither answered nor undertaken to answer the question which he put to anthropology—What is man? He lectured on another anthropology than the one he asked for—I should say, in terms of the history of philosophy, an earlier anthropology, one that was still bound up with the uncritical " science of man " of the 17th and 18th centuries. But in formulating the task which he set to the philosophical anthropology he asked for, he has left a legacy.

3

It is certainly doubtful to me as well whether such a discipline will suffice to provide a foundation for philosophy, or, as Heidegger formulates it, a foundation for metaphysics. For it is true, indeed, that I continually learn what I can know, what I ought to do, and what I may hope. It is further true that philosophy contributes to this learning of mine : to the first question by telling me, in logic and epistemology, what being able to know means, and in cosmology and the philosophy of history and so on, what there is to know; to the second question by telling me, in psychology, how the " ought to do " is carried out psychically, and in ethics, the doctrine of the State, æsthetics and so on, what there is to do; and to the third question by telling me, at least in the philosophy of religion, how the " may hope " is displayed in actual faith and the history of faith—whereas it can certainly not tell me what there is to hope, since religion itself and its conceptual elaboration in theology, whose task this is, do not belong to philosophy. All this is agreed. But philosophy succeeds in rendering me such help in its individual disciplines precisely through each of these disciplines *not* reflecting, and not being able to reflect, on the wholeness of man. Either a philosophical discipline shuts out man in his complex wholeness and considers him only as a bit of nature, as cosmology does; or (as all the other disciples do) it tears off its own special sphere from the wholeness of man, delimits it from the other spheres, establishes its own basic principles and develops its own methods. In addition it has to remain open and accessible, first to the ideas of metaphysics itself as the doctrine of being, of what is and of existence, secondly to the findings of the philosophical branch disciplines, and thirdly to the discoveries of philosophical anthropology. But least of all may it make itself dependent on the latter; for in every one of those disciplines the possibility of its achieving anything in thought rests precisely on its objectification, on what may be termed its " de-humanization," and even a discipline like the philosophy of history, which is so concerned with the actual man, must, in order to be able to comprehend man *as a historical being*, renounce consideration of the whole man—of which the kind of man who is living outside history in the unchanging rhythm of nature is an essential part. What the philosophical disciplines are able to contribute to answering Kant's first three questions, even if it is only by clarifying them, or teaching me to recognize the problems they contain, they are able to do only by *not* waiting for the answer to the fourth question.

Nor can philosophical anthropology itself set itself the task of establishing a foundation either for metaphysics or for the individual philosophical sciences. If it attempted to answer the question *What is man?* in such a general way that answers to the other questions could be derived from it, it would miss the very reality of its own subject. For it would reach, instead of the subject's genuine wholeness, which can become visible only by the contemplation of all its manifold nature, a false unity which has no reality. A legitimate philosophical anthropology must know that there is not merely a human species but also peoples, not merely a human soul but also types and characters, not merely a human life but also stages in life; only from the systematic comprehension of these and of all other differences, from the recognition of the dynamic that exerts power within every particular reality and between them, and from the constantly new proof of the one in the many, can it come to see the wholeness of man. For that very reason it cannot grasp man in that absoluteness which, though it does not speak out from Kant's fourth question, yet very easily presents itself when an answer is attempted —the answer which Kant, as I have said, avoided giving. Even as it must again and again distinguish within the human race in order to arrive at a solid comprehension, so it must put man in all seriousness into nature, it must compare him with other things, other living creatures, other bearers of consciousness, in order to define his special place reliably for him. Only by this double way of distinction and comparison does it reach the whole, real man who, whatever his people or type or age, knows, what no being on earth but he can know, that he goes the narrow way from birth towards death, tests out what none but he can, a wrestling with destiny, rebellion and reconciliation, and at times even experiences in his own blood, when he is joined by choice to another human being, what goes on secretly in others.

Philosophical anthropology is not intent on reducing philosophical problems to human existence and establishing the philosophical disciplines so to speak from below instead of from above. It is solely intent on knowing man himself. This sets it a task that is absolutely different from all other tasks of thought. For in philosophical anthropology man himself is given to man in the most precise sense as a subject. Here, where the subject is man in his wholeness, the investigator cannot content himself, as in anthropology as an individual science, with considering man as another part of nature and with ignoring the fact that he, the investigator, is himself a man and experiences his humanity in his inner experience in a way that he simply cannot experience any part of nature—not only in a quite different perspective but also in a quite different dimension of being, in a dimension in which he experiences only this one part of all the parts of nature. Philosophical knowledge of man is essentially man's self-reflection (*Selbstbesinnung*), and man can reflect about himself only when the cognizing person, that is, the philosopher

pursuing anthropology, first of all reflects about himself as
a person. The principle of individuation, the fundamental
fact of the infinite variety of human persons, of whom this
one is only one person, of this constitution and no other,
does not relativize anthropological knowledge; on the
contrary, it gives it its kernel and its skeleton. In order to
become genuine philosophical anthropology, everything
that is discovered about historical and modern man,
about men and women, Indians and Chinese, tramps and
emperors, the weak-minded and the genius, must be built
up and crystallized round what the philosopher discovers
by reflecting about himself. That is a quite different
matter from what, say, the psychologist undertakes when
he completes and clarifies by reference to his own self in
self-observation, self-analysis and experiment, what he
knows from literature and observation. For with him it is
a matter of individual, objectivized processes and phenomena, of something that is separated from connexion with
the whole real person. But the philosophical anthropologist must stake nothing less than his real wholeness, his
concrete self. And more; it is not enough for him to stake
his self as an *object* of knowledge. He can know the
wholeness of the person and through it the wholeness of
man only when he does not leave his *subjectivity* out and
does not remain an untouched observer. He must enter,
completely and in reality, into the act of self-reflection, in
order to become aware of human wholeness. In other
words, he must carry out this act of entry into that unique
dimension as an act of his *life*, without any prepared
philosophical security; that is, he must expose himself to
all that can meet you when you are really living. Here
you do not attain to knowledge by remaining on the
shore and watching the foaming waves, you must make
the venture and cast yourself in, you must swim, alert and
with all your force, even if a moment comes when you
think you are losing consciousness : in this way, and in no
other, do you reach anthropological insight. So long as
you "have" yourself, have yourself as an object, your
experience of man is only as of a thing among things, the
wholeness which is to be grasped is not yet "there"; only

when you *are,* and nothing else but that, is the wholeness there, and able to be grasped. You perceive only as much as the reality of the " being there " incidentally yields to you; but you do perceive that, and the nucleus of the crystallization develops itself.

An example may clarify more precisely the relation between the psychologist and the anthropologist. If both of them investigate, say, the phenomenon of anger, the psychologist will try to grasp what the angry man feels, what his motives and the impulses of his will are, but the anthropologist will also try to grasp what he is doing. In respect of this phenomenon self-observation, being by nature disposed to weaken the spontaneity and unruliness of anger, will be especially difficult for both of them. The psychologist will try to meet this difficulty by a specific division of consciousness, which enables him to remain outside with the observing part of his being and yet let his passion run its course as undisturbed as possible. Of course this passion can then not avoid becoming similar to that of the actor, that is, though it can still be heightened in comparison with an unobserved passion its course will be different : there will be a release which is willed and which takes the place of the elemental outbreak, there will be a vehemence which will be more emphasized, more deliberate, more dramatic. The anthropologist can have nothing to do with a division of consciousness, since he has to do with the unbroken wholeness of events, and especially with the unbroken natural connexion between feelings and actions; and this connexion is most powerfully influenced in self-observation, since the pure spontaneity of the action is bound to suffer essentially. It remains for the anthropologist only to resign any attempt to stay outside his observing self, and thus when he is overcome by anger not to disturb it in its course by becoming a spectator of it, but to let it rage to its conclusion without trying to gain a perspective. He will be able to register in the act of recollection what he felt and did then; for him memory takes the place of psychological self-experience. But as great writers in their dealings with other men do not deliberately register their peculiarities and, so to speak,

make invisible notes, but deal with them in a natural and
uninhibited way, and leave the harvest to the hour of harvest, so it is the memory of the competent anthropologist
which has, with reference to himself as to others, the con-
centrating power which preserves what is essential. In
the moment of life he has nothing else in his mind but just
to live what is to be lived, he is there with his whole being,
undivided, and for that very reason there grows in his
thought and recollection the knowledge of human wholeness.

II : *From Aristotle to Kant*

I

THE man who feels himself solitary is the most readily
disposed and most readily fitted for the self-reflection of
which I am speaking; that is, the man who by nature or
destiny or both is alone with himself and his problematic,
and who succeeds, in this blank solitude, in meeting himself, in discovering man in his own self, and the human
problematic in his own. The times of spiritual history in
which anthropological thought has so far found its depth
of experience have been those very times in which a feeling of strict and inescapable solitude took possession of
man; and it was the most solitary men in whom the
thought became fruitful. In the ice of solitude man becomes most inexorably a question to himself, and just
because the question pitilessly summons and draws into
play his most secret life he becomes an experience to himself.

In the history of the human spirit I distinguish between
epochs of habitation and epochs of homelessness. In the
former, man lives in the world as in a house, as in a home.
In the latter, man lives in the world as in an open field
and at times does not even have four pegs with which to
set up a tent. In the former epochs anthropological
thought exists only as a part of cosmological thought.

In the latter, anthropological thought gains depth and, with it, independence. I will give a few examples of both, which offer a glance at a few chapters of the *pre-history* of philosophical anthropology.

Bernhard Grœthuysen (a pupil of my teacher Wilhelm Dilthey, the founder of the history of philosophical anthropology) rightly said of Aristotle, in a work called *Philosophical Anthropology* (1931), that with him man ceases to be problematic, with him man speaks of himself always as it were in the third person, is only a " case " for himself, he attains to consciousness of self only as " he," not as " I." The special dimension, in which man knows himself as he can know himself alone, remains unentered, and for that reason man's special place in the cosmos remains undiscovered. Man is comprehended only in the world, the world is not comprehended in him. The tendency of the Greeks to understand the world as a self-contained space, in which man too has his fixed place, was perfected in Aristotle's geocentric spherical system. The hegemony of the visual sense over the other senses, which appears among the Greeks for the first time, as a tremendous new factor in the history of the human spirit, the very hegemony which enabled them to live a life derived from *images* and to base a culture on the forming of images, holds good in their philosophy as well. A visual image of the universe (*Weltbild*) arises which is formed from visual sense-impressions and objectified as only the visual sense is able to objectify, and the experiences of the other senses are as it were retrospectively recorded in this picture. Even Plato's world of ideas is a visual world, a world of forms that are seen. But it is not before Aristotle that the visual image of the universe is realized in unsurpassable clarity as a universe of *things*, and now man is a thing among these things of the universe, an objectively comprehensible species beside other species—no longer a sojourner in a foreign land like the Platonic man, but given his own dwelling-place in the house of the world, not, indeed, in one of the highest storeys, but not in one of the lower, either, rather in the respectable middle. The presupposition for a philosophical anthropology in the sense of Kant's fourth question is lacking here.

2

The first to pose the genuine anthropological question anew, and in the first person—more than seven centuries after Aristotle—was Augustine. The solitude out of which he asked the question can only be understood when one realizes that that round and unified world of Aristotle had long since collapsed. It collapsed because the soul of man, divided against itself, could no longer grasp as truth anything but a world which was divided against itself. In place of the sphere which had collapsed there now arose two autonomous and mutually hostile kingdoms, the kingdom of light and the kingdom of darkness. We meet them again in almost every system of that widespread and manifold spiritual movement of gnosis, which at that time seized the embarrassed heirs of the great oriental and antique cultures, split the godhead and emptied value from creation; and in the most consistent of these systems, in Manichæism, there is even, consistently, a double earth. Here man can no longer be a thing among things, and he can have no fixed place in the world. Since he consists of soul and body he is divided between the two kingdoms, he is simultaneously the scene and the prize of the struggle. In each man the original man who fell is manifested; in each man the problematic of being is stated in terms of life. Augustine emerged from the school of Manichæism. Homeless in the world, solitary between the higher and the lower powers, he remains homeless and solitary even after he found salvation in Christianity as a redemption that had *already taken place*. So he asks Kant's question in the first person, and not, indeed, as with Kant, as an objectivized problem, which the hearers of his logic lectures could certainly not understand as a question directed to themselves; but he takes up the question of the psalmist again in real address, with another sense and in another tone : *What is man that thou art mindful of him?* He asks for information from one who can give it : *quid ergo sum, Deus meus? quæ natura mea?* He does not mean only himself; the word *natura* says clearly that in his person he means man, that man whom he calls the *grande profundum*, the great mystery. And he even draws that same anthropological conclusion which we have heard in Malebranche; he does it in his famous accusation of men, that they marvel at mountains, at the waves of the sea and the course of the stars, but "relinquish" themselves without being astonished at themselves. This wonder of man at himself, which Augustine demands as a result of his own self-experience, is something quite different from the wonder with which Aristotle in his metaphysic makes all philosophizing begin. The Aristotelian man wonders at man among the rest, but only as a part of a quite astonishing world. The Augustinian man wonders at that in man which cannot be understood as a part of the world, as a thing among things; and where that former wondering has already passed into methodical philosophizing, the Augustinian wondering manifests itself in its true depth and uncanniness. It is not philosophy, but it affects all future philosophy.

In the post-augustinian west it is not the contemplation of nature, as with the Greeks, but faith which builds a new house in the cosmos for the solitary soul. The Christian cosmos arises; and this was so real for every mediæval Christian that all who read the *Divina Commedia* made in spirit the journey to the nethermost spiral of hell and stepped up over Lucifer's back, through purgatory, to the heaven of the Trinity, not as an expedition into lands as yet unknown, but as a crossing of regions already fully mapped. Once again there is a self-enclosed universe, once again a house in which man is allowed to dwell. This universe is still more finite than that of Aristotle, for here finite time too is taken into the image in all seriousness— the finite time of the Bible, which here appears, however, transformed into a Christian form. The pattern of this image of the universe is a cross, whose vertical beam is finite space from heaven to hell, leading right across the heart of the human being, and whose cross-beam is finite time from the creation of the world to the end of days; which makes time's centre, the death of Christ, fall coveringly and redemptively on the centre of space, the heart of the poor sinner. The mediæval image of the universe is built round this pattern. In it Dante painted life, the life of men and spirits, but the conceptual framework was set up for him by Thomas Aquinas. As of Aristotle, so too it is true of Aquinas, though he was a theologian, and therefore in duty bound to know about the real man who says "I" and is addressed as "Thou," that man speaks here "as it were always in the third person." In Aqui is's world-system man is indeed a separate species of a quite special kind, because in him the human soul, the lowest of the spirits, is substantially united with the human body, the highest of physical things, so that man appears as it were as "the horizon and the dividing line of spiritual and physical nature." But Aquinas knows no special problem and no special problematic of human life, such as Augustine experienced and expressed with trembling heart. The anthropological question has here come to rest again; in man, housed and unproblematic, no impulse stirs to questioning self-confrontation, or it is soon appeased.

3

In the late middle ages there already emerged a new earnestness about man as man. The finite world still hedged man safely in: *hunc mundum haud aliud esse, quam amplissimam quandam hominis domum,* says Carolus Bovillus as late as the sixteenth century. But the same Bovillus cries to man: *homo es, sistere in homine,* and thus takes up the motif that had been expressed by the great Cusa before him: *homo non vult esse nisi homo.* This by itself certainly does not imply that man by his nature steps out of and forth from the world. For Cusa there is not a thing which would not prefer its own being to all being and its own way of being to all other ways of being; all that is wishes in eternity to be nothing but itself, but to be this one thing always more perfectly in the way proper to its nature; it is precisely from this that the harmony of the universe grows, for every being contains everything in a special "contraction."

But with man there is also thought, the reason which measures and values. He has in himself all created things, like God; but God has them in himself as the archetypes, man has them in himself as relations and values. Cusa compares God to the coining master of the mint, and man to the money-changer with his scale of values. God can create all, we can know all; we can know all because we too carry all in ourselves potentially. And soon after Cusa, Pico della Mirandola draws from this proud self-assurance the anthropological conclusion, which again reminds us of the words of Malebranche : *nos autem peculiare aliquid in homine quaerimus, unde et dignitas ei propria et imago divinae substantiae cum nulla sibi creatura communis comperiatur.* Here the theme of anthropology already clearly appears. But it appears without that setting of the problematic which is indispensable for the genuine establishment of anthropology—the deadly earnestness of the question about man. Man steps forth here in such autonomy and such consciousness of power that the real question does not step up to him. These thinkers of the Renaissance affirm that man can know, but the Kantian question, *what* he can know, is still quite foreign to them : he can know all. It is true that the last in the series of these thinkers, Bovillus, excepts God : the human spirit cannot reach God, but Bovillus lets the whole universe be known by man, who has been created outside it as its spectator, in fact, as its eye. So securely are these pioneers of a new era still housed in a secure universe. Cusa, it is true, speaks of the spatial and temporal infinity of the universe, and thus deprives the earth of its central position, and destroys in thought the mediæval pattern. But this infinity is only one that is thought, it is not yet beheld and lived. Man is not yet solitary again, he has still to learn again to ask the solitary man's question.

But at the same time as Bovillus was extolling the universe as man's *amplissima domus,* all the walls of the

house were in fact already crumbling beneath the blows of
Copernicus, the unlimited was pressing in from every side,
and man was standing in a universe which in actual fact
could no longer be experienced as a house. Man was no
longer secure, but though at first he had a heroic enthusiasm for the grandeur of this universe, as with Bruno,
then a mathematical enthusiasm for its harmony, as with
Kepler, yet finally, more than a century after the death
of Copernicus and the publication of his work, the new
reality of man proved itself to be more powerful than the
new reality of the universe. Pascal, a great scientist, a
mathematician and a physicist, young and destined to die
early, experienced beneath the starry heavens not merely,
as Kant did, their majesty, but still more powerfully their
uncanniness : *le silence éternel de ces espaces infinis
m'effraie*. With a clarity that has not since then been surpassed he discerns the twin infinities, that of the infinitely
great and that of the infinitely small, and so comes to
know man's limitation, his inadequacy, the casualness of
his existence : *combien de royaumes nous ignorent!* The
enthusiasm of Bruno and Kepler which as it were skipped
man is here replaced by a terribly clear, melancholy yet
believing sobriety. It is the sobriety of the man who has
become more deeply solitary than ever before, and with a
sober pathos he frames the anthropological question
afresh : *qu'est ce qu'un homme dans l'infini?* Cusa's sovereignty, in which man boasted that he carried all things in
himself and thus that he could know all things, is opposed
here by the insight of the solitary man, who endures being
exposed as a human being to infinity : *Connaissons donc
notre portée: nous sommes quelque chose, et ne sommes
pas tout; ce que nous avons d'être nous dérobe la connais-
sance des premiers principes, qui naissent du néant; et le
peu que nous avons d'être nous cache la vue de l'infini.*
But, in this renewal of anthropological thought, from the
very fact that self-reflection is carried out with such clarity,
there is yeilded man's special place in the cosmos.
*L'homme n'est qu'un roseau, le plus faible de la nature:
mais c'est un roseau pensant. Il ne faut pas que l'univers
entier s'arme pour l'écraser: une vapeur, une goutte d'eau,*

suffit pour le tuer. Mais, quand l'univers l'écraserait, l'homme serait encore plus noble que ce qui le tue, parce qu'il sait qu'il meurt et l'avantage que l'univers a sur lui. L'univers n'en sait rien. This is not the stoic attitude over again; it is the new attitude of the person who has become homeless in infinity, for here everything depends on the knowledge that man's grandeur is born of his misery, that he is different from all things just because even as he passes away he can be a child of the spirit. Man is the being who knows his situation in the universe and is able, so long as he is in his senses, to continue this knowledge. What is decisive is not that this creature of all dares to step up to the universe and know it—however amazing this is in itself; what is decisive is that he knows the relation between the universe and himself. Thereby from out of the midst of the universe something that faces the universe has arisen. And that means that this "from out of the midst" has its own special problematic.

4

We have seen that the strict anthropological question, which refers to man's specific problematic, becomes insistent in times when as it were the original contract between the universe and man is dissolved and man finds himself a stranger and solitary in the world. The end of an image of the universe, that is, the end of a *security* in the universe, is soon followed by a fresh questioning from man who has become insecure, and homeless, and hence problematic to himself. But it can be shown that a *way* leads from one such crisis to the next, and on to the one after that. The crises have something essential in common, but they are not similar. Aristotle's cosmological image of the universe breaks up from within, through the soul's experience of the problem of evil in its depth, and through its feeling of being surrounded by a divided universe; Aquinas's theological image of the universe breaks up from without, through the universe manifesting itself as unlimited. What causes the crisis is on the one occasion a myth, the dualistic myth of gnosis, on the other occasion it is the cosmos of science itself, no longer clothed with any myth. Pascal's solitude is truly historically *later* than Augustine's; it is more complete and harder to overcome. And in fact something new arises that has not existed before; work is carried out on a new *image* of the universe, but a new *house* in the universe is no longer built. Once the concept of infinity has been taken seriously a human dwelling can no longer be made of the universe. And infinity itself must be included in the image of the universe—which is a paradox, for an image, if it is really an image, is limited, yet now the unlimited itself must enter the image. In other words, when the point is reached where the image ends, the point, say—to use the language of modern astronomy—of the nebulæ, which are a hundred million light-years distant from us, then it must be felt with the utmost urgency that the image does not and cannot end. Incidentally it may be noticed, though it is self-evident, that Einstein's concept of finite space would be by no means fit for rebuilding the universe as a house for man, since this "finitude" is essentially different from that which produced the feeling of the universe as a house. And more, it is certainly possible that this concept of the universe, which has been disclosed by the mathematician's genius, freed from sensuality, can one day become accessible to natural human understanding; but it will no longer be in a position to produce a new *image* of the universe, not even a paradoxical image as the Copernican concept could. For the Copernican concept only fulfilled what the human soul had vaguely felt in the hours when the house of universal space, the Aristotelian or the Thomist, seemed too cramped, and it dared to beat on its walls to see if a window could not be thrown out into a world beyond—it fulfilled it, it is true, in a way which deeply perturbed this same human soul, which cannot help being as it is, once and for all. But Einstein's concept of the universe signifies no fulfilment of the spirit's inkling, but the contradiction of all its inklings and imaginings: this universe can still be thought, but it can no longer be imaged, the man who thinks it no longer really lives in it.

The generation which works modern cosmology into its natural thought will be the first, after several millennia of changing images of the universe, which will have to forego the possession of an image of its universe; this very fact, that it lives in a universe which cannot be imaged, will probably be its feeling of the universe, so to speak its image of the universe : *imago mundi nova—imago nulla.*

5

I have far anticipated the course of our investigation. Let us return to our second example and ask how from there we reach our age in its special human homelessness and solitude, and its new setting of the anthropological question.

The greatest attempt to master the situation of post-copernican man, as mediated to us by Pascal, was undertaken shortly after Pascal's death by a man who was destined to die almost as young. Spinoza's attempt, from the point of view of our problem, means that astronomical infinity is both unconditionally accepted and stripped of its uncanniness : extension, of which this infinity is stated and demonstrated, is only one of the infinitely many attributes of infinite substance, and it is one of the two which alone we know—the other is thought. Infinite substance, also called God by Spinoza, in relation to which this infinity of space can be only one of infinitely many attributes, *loves,* it loves itself, and it loves itself also, and especially, in man, for the love of the human spirit for God is only *pars infiniti amoris, quo Deus se ipsum amat.* Here one may say that Pascal's question, what is a man in the infinite, is answered : he is a being in whom God loves himself. Cosmology and anthropology appear here imposingly reconciled, but the cosmos has not again become what it was with Aristotle and Aquinas—a manifold universe, ordered as an image, in which every thing and every being has its place and the being " man " feels himself at home in union with them all. A new security of being in the world is not given; yet for Spinoza this is not necessary: his devotion to the infinite *natura naturans* lifts him above the mere outline character of his *natura naturata,* which is drawn into the system only conceptually, as the aggregate of the divine modes, and in which the kinds and orders of being are not really grasped and united. There is no new house of the universe, no ground-plan of a house and no material for it: a man accepts his homelessness, his lack of a universe, because it enables him to have *adæquata cognitio æternæ et infinitæ essentiæ Dei,* that is, enables him to know how God loves himself in *him.* A man, however, who knows this can no longer be problematic to himself.

In Spinoza's intellectual separatedness reconciliation was effected. But in actual man's concrete life with the actual world, in the unseparated and inseparable life out of which Pascal spoke and expressed at once man's frailty and the world's terror, it became increasingly difficult to effect it. The age of rationalism, which weakened and adapted Spinoza's objectification of being in which world and man are united, breaks off the point of the anthropological question; but it remains embedded in the flesh and secretly festers.

Certainly, one can point to a man who was a true heir of Spinoza in the post-rationalist age and was made happy by Spinoza's " atmosphere of peace," who was "a child of peace" and minded to keep peace "for ever and ever with the whole world," who grasped and penetrated this world in its living fulness, as a whole which gives us in its synthesis with spirit " the most blissful assurance of the harmony of existence." Goethe, who in his place in history appears to us in many respects like a glorious lethal euphoria before the end of an age, was undoubtedly still able to live really in the cosmos; but he, who had plumbed the depths of solitude (" I can speak only with God about many things "), was exposed in his inmost being to the anthropological question. Certainly, man to him was " the first conversation which nature holds with God," yet, like Werther, he heard " the voice of the creature completely driven into itself, lacking itself, and falling irresistibly downwards."

6

Kant was the first to understand the anthropological question critically, in such a way that an answer was given to Pascal's real concern. This answer—though it was not directed metaphysically to the being of man but epistemologically to his attitude to the world—grasped the fundamental problems. What sort of a world is it, which man knows? How can man, as he is, in his altered reality, know at all? How does man stand in the world he knows in this way—what is it to him and what is he to it?

In order to understand the extent to which the *Critique of Pure Reason* may be taken as an answer to Pascal's question we must consider the question once more. To Pascal infinite space is an uncanny thing which makes him conscious of the questionable nature of man, exposed as he is to this world. But what stirs and terrifies him is not the newly discovered infinity of space in contrast to the finitude previously believed of it. Rather it is the fact that, by the impression of infinity, any concept of space, a finite no less than an infinite, becomes uncanny to him, for really to try and imagine finite space is as hazardous a venture as really to try and imagine infinite space, and makes man just as emphatically conscious that he is not a match for the world. When I was about fourteen years of age I myself experienced this in a way which has deeply influenced my whole life. A necessity I could not understand swept over me : I had to try again and again to imagine the edge of space, or its edgelessness, time with a beginning and an end or a time without beginning or end, and both were equally impossible, equally hopeless—yet there seemed to be only the choice between the one or the other absurdity. Under an irresistible compulsion I reeled from one to the other, at times so closely threatened with the danger of madness that I seriously thought of avoiding it by suicide. Salvation came to the fifteen-year-old boy in a book, Kant's *Prolegomena to all Future Metaphysics,* which I dared to read although its first sentence told me that it was not intended for the use of pupils but for future teachers. This book showed me that space and time are only the forms in which my human view of what is, necessarily works itself out; that is, they were not attached to the inner nature of the world, but to the nature of my senses. It further taught that it is just as impossible to all my concepts to say that the world is infinite in space and time as to say that it is finite. "For neither can be inherent in experience," and neither can be situated in the world itself, since the world is given to us only as an appearance "whose existence and connexions take place only in experience." Both can be asserted and both can be proved: between the thesis and the antithesis there exists an irresoluble contradiction, an antinomy of cosmological ideas; being itself is not touched by either. Now I was no longer compelled to torture myself by trying to imagine first the one unimaginable and then the opposite equally unimaginable thing: I could gain an inkling that being itself was beyond the reach alike of the finitude and the infinity of space and time, since it only appeared in space and time but did not itself enter into this appearance. At that time I began to gain an inkling of the existence of eternity as something quite different from the infinite, just as it is something quite different from the finite, and of the possibility of a connexion between me, a man, and the eternal.

Kant's answer to Pascal may be formulated after this fashion : what approaches you out of the world, hostile and terrifying, the mystery of its space and time, is the mystery of your own comprehension of the world and the mystery of your own being. Your question *What is man?* is thus a genuine question to which you must seek the answer.

Here Kant's anthropological question is shown in all clarity as a legacy to our age. No new house in the universe is being planned for man, but he, as the builder of houses, is being required to know himself. Kant sees the age after him in all its uncertainty as an age of self-restraint and self-reflection, as the anthropological age. First—as is clear from that well-known letter of 1793—he saw in the treatment of the fourth question a task which

he set himself, and whose resolution was to follow that of
the first three questions; he did not really set about it, but
he set it in such clarity and urgency that it remained a task
set to following generations, till at last our own generation
is preparing to place itself in its service.

III : *Hegel and Marx*

I

FIRST, however, there follows such a radical alienation
from the anthropological setting of the question as has
probably never happened before in the history of human
thought. I mean the system of Hegel, that is, the system
which has exercised a decisive influence not merely on an
age's way of thought but also on its social and political
action—an influence which can be characterized as the
dispossessing of the concrete human person and the
concrete human community in favour of universal reason,
its dialectical processes and its objective structures. This
influence, as is well-known, has also operated on thinkers
who, though deriving from Hegel, have travelled far from
him, such as Kierkegaard on the one hand, the critic of
modern Christianity, who certainly grasped like no other
thinker of our time the significance of the person, but still
saw the life of the person entirely in the forms of the
Hegelian dialectic as a movement from the æsthetic to
the ethical and from there to the religious, and Marx on
the other hand, who entered with an unexampled earnestness on the actuality of human society, but considered its
development in forms of Hegelian dialectic as a movement
from primitive communal economy to private property
and from there to socialism.

In his youth Hegel accepted Kant's anthropological
setting of the question, which was at that time not published in its final form but whose sense was certainly known
to the young man so deeply engaged with Kant. From
this point his thought proceeded in a genuinely anthro-

pological fashion, in that he sought to reach, by understanding the organic connexion of the spirit's capacities,
what Kant himself knew only as a regulative idea, not as
living being, namely, what the young Hegel himself
called (about 1798) the "unity of the whole man." What
he strove after then has been rightly called an anthropological metaphysic. He took the concrete human person
so seriously that it was by him that he demonstrated his
conception of man's special position. To illustrate this I
quote a beautiful sentence from the notes *The Spirit of
Christianity and its Destiny,* which clearly shows the way
in which Hegel, going beyond Kant, seeks to penetrate
the anthropological problem : " In every man himself
there is light and life, he is the property of light; and he
is not illuminated by a light like a dark body which has
only a reflected brilliance, but his own fuel is being
kindled and there is a flame of its own." It is worth
noticing that Hegel does not speak of a general concept
of man here, but of "every man," that is, of the real
person from whom genuine philosophical anthropology
must seriously begin.

But this setting of the problem will be sought in vain in
the later Hegel, in the one, that is, who has influenced a
century's thought. I should go so far as to say that the
real man will be sought in vain in the later Hegel. If one,
for instance, looks through the section in the *Encyclopædia
of the Philosophical Sciences* which is entitled "Anthropology," one sees that it begins with statements about
what spirit is and signifies, then passes to statements about
the soul as substance. There follow valuable references to
distinctions within mankind and human life, especially
to distinctions of age, of sex, between sleeping and
waking, and so on—but without our being able to relate
all this to a question about the reality and significance of
this human life. Also the chapters about feeling, self-
feeling, and habit, give no help, and even in the chapter
entitled "The real soul" we learn only that the soul is
real as the "identity of the inner with the outer." The
systematic philosopher Hegel no longer begins, like the
young Hegel, with man, but with universal reason; man

is now only the principle in which the universal reason reaches perfect self-consciousness and thus completion. All the contradiction in human life and history does not lead to the anthropological questionableness and question, but presents itself as a "ruse" which the idea makes use of in order to reach its own perfection through the very fact that it overcomes contradiction. The claim is made that Kant's fundamental question *What is man?* is finally answered here; in reality it is obscured, even eliminated. Even the first of Kant's three philosophical questions which precede the anthropological question, the question *What can I know?* is silenced. If man is the place and medium in which the universal reason knows itself, then there is simply no limitation to what man can know. In terms of the idea man knows all things, just as in terms of the idea he realizes all things, that is, all that is in the reason. Both the knowing and the realizing take place in history, in which the perfect State appears as the completion of being and the perfect metaphysic appears as the completion of knowledge. By experiencing both we experience simultaneously and adequately the meaning of history and the meaning of man.

Hegel undertakes to give man a new security, to build a new house of the universe for him. No further house can be built in Copernican space; Hegel builds it in *time* alone, which is "the supreme power of all that is" (1805).

Man's new house is to be time in the form of history whose meaning can be perfectly learned and understood. Hegel's system is the third great attempt at security within western thought; following Aristotle's cosmological attempt and Aquinas's theological attempt it is the logological attempt. All insecurity, all unrest about meaning, all terror at decision, all abysmal problematic is eliminated. The universal reason goes its undeflectable way through history, and knowing man knows this way, rather, his knowledge is the real goal and end of the way in which truth as it realizes itself knows itself in its realization. The stages of the way follow one another in an absolute order: the law of dialectic, in which the thesis is relieved by the antithesis and the antithesis by the synthesis, is sovereign over them. As one goes with sure step from storey to storey and from room to room of a well-built house with its solid foundations and walls and roof, so Hegel's all-knowing man goes through the new world-house, history, whose whole meaning he knows. If only he shares thoroughly in the thought of the new metaphysic his glance is saved from dizziness, for he can survey everything. The young man over whom the dread of the infinite swept since the Copernican revolution, when he opened the window of his room at night and stood solitary in the darkness, is to know peace now; if the cosmos, in its infinite greatness and infinite smallness, denies itself to his heart, the reliable order of history, which " is nothing but the realization of the spirit," takes him and makes him at home. Solitude is overcome, and the question about man is obliterated.

But now there appears a remarkable historical phenomenon. In earlier times it took some centuries for criticism to destroy a cosmic security and to reinvigorate the anthropological question. Now the Hegelian image of the universe had, indeed, tremendous effect for a century, penetrating every realm of the spirit; but the rebellion against it was raised immediately, and with it the demand for an anthropological perspective was renewed. The Hegelian house of the universe is admired, explained, and imitated; but it proves uninhabitable. Thought confirms it and the word glorifies it; but the real man does not set foot in it. In the universe of Aristotle real ancient man felt himself at home; similarly with the real Christian in the universe of Aquinas; the universe of Hegel has never become the real universe for real modern man. In the thought of mankind Hegel succeeded in repressing Kant's anthropological question only for a moment; in the life of man he did not overcome even for a moment the great anthropological unrest which in modern times is first expressed in Pascal's question.

I wish to indicate here only one of the reasons for this phenomenon. An intellectual image of the universe which builds on *time* can never give the same feeling of security as one which builds on space. To grasp this fact we must distinguish sharply between cosmological and anthropological time. We can as it were comprehend cosmological time, that is, make use of the concept of it, as if all time were present in a relative way, even though the future is not given to us at all. Anthropological time, on the other hand, that is, time in respect of actual, consciously willing man, cannot be comprehended, because the future cannot be present, since it depends to a certain extent, in my consciousness and will, on my decision. Anthropological time is real only in the part which has become cosmological time, that is, in the part called the past. This distinction is not identical with Bergson's well-known one, whose *durée* means a flowing present, whereas the anthropological time which I mean functions essentially through the memory—of course, in respect of the present, this is always " open " memory : as soon as we experience something *as time,* as soon as we become conscious of the dimension of time as such, the memory is already in play ; in other words, the pure present knows no specific consciousness of time. It is true that we do not know cosmological time as a whole either, in spite of our knowledge of the regular movements of the stars, and so on ; but our thoughts may be engaged with it as with something real, even in what we do not know of this, and naturally even in what we do not know of future human actions, since in the moment of thought all their causes are present. With the anthropological future, on the other hand, our thoughts cannot be engaged as with something real, since my decision, which will take place in the next moment, has not yet taken place. The same is true of the decisions of other men, since I know, on the basis of the anthropological concept of man as a consciously willing being, that he cannot be understood simply as a part of the world. Within the boundaries of the human world which is given in the problem of human being there is no certainty of the future. The time which Hegel introduced into the groundwork of his image of the universe, cosmological time, is not actual human time but a time in terms of thought. It lies in the power of human thought but not of living human imagination to incorporate perfection in the reality of what is ; it is something which can be thought, but not lived. An intellectual image of the universe, which incorporates " the goal of universal history," has no power in this part of it to give assurance, the unbroken line changes as it were into a dotted line, which even the mightiest philosopher cannot transform for us into a continuous line. The only exception is an image of the universe which is grounded on faith : the power of faith alone can experience perfection as something assured, because it is something guaranteed to us by someone we trust—whom we trust as the guarantor also for what has not yet come to be in our world. In the history of religion we know above all two such great images of the universe, that of Persian Messianism, in which the future final and complete victory of light over darkness is guaranteed to the precise hour, and that of Israelite Messianism, which rejects such precision because it understands man himself, frail, contradictory, questionable man himself as an element that can both contribute to salvation and hinder it; but final and complete salvation is guaranteed to this form of Messianism as well, in faith in the saving power of God which carries out in the midst of history its work on resisting man. In the Christian picture of the universe, as we saw it in its finished form in Aquinas, the effect of Messianism persists, though weakened. In Hegel's system Messianism is secularized, that is, it is transferred from the sphere of faith, in which man feels himself to be bound up with the object of his faith, to the sphere of evident conviction, in which man contemplates and considers the object of his conviction. This has been repeatedly remarked. But it has not been sufficiently observed that in such a transference the element of *trust* cannot be taken over at the same time. Faith in creation may be replaced by a conviction about evolution, faith in revelation by a conviction about increasing knowledge, but faith in salvation will not really be replaced by a conviction about the perfecting of the world by the idea, since only trust in the trustworthy is able to establish a relation of unconditional certainty towards the *future*. I say, not *really* replaced, that is, not in and for real life. For in mere thought a conviction about the self-realization

of an absolute reason in history does not achieve less, even
for man's relation to the future, than a messianic faith in
God; in fact, it achieves even more, since it is, so to speak,
chemically pure and undisturbed by any kind of adultera-
tion by actuality. But thought does not have the power to
build up man's real life, and the strictest philosophical
certainty cannot endow the soul with that intimate certitude that the world which is so imperfect will be brought
to its perfection. In the last resort the problem of the
future does not exist for Hegel, since he saw, in fact, in his
own age and in his own philosophy the beginning of fulfilment, so that the dialectical movement of the idea
through time has really reached its end already. But what
devoted admirer of the philosopher has ever truly shared
in this worldly auto-messianism, that is, not merely with
thought, but—as has continually happened in the history
of religion—with the whole real life?

It is true that there is a significant phenomenon within
the sphere of Hegel's influence which seems to contradict
what I said about the attitude to the future. I mean
Marx's doctrine of history, which is based on the Hegelian
dialectic. Here too a certainty with regard to perfection
is proclaimed, here too Messianism is secularized; yet real
man, in the shape of the modern proletarian masses, has
entered into this certainty and made this secularized Messianism his faith. How is this to be understood? What
Marx has carried out with Hegel's method can be called a
sociological reduction. That is, he does not wish to present any image of the universe; none is necessary any
more. (The representation of an image of the universe
which Engels later—in 1880—attempted, under the title
Dialectic of Nature, a quite derivatory rendering of the
teaching of Hæckel and other evolutionists, completely
contradicts the fundamental restriction made by Marx.)
What Marx wants to give the men of his age is not an
image of the universe but only an image of society, more
precisely, the image of the way by which human society
is to reach its perfection. The Hegelian ideas or universal
reason is replaced by human conditions of production,
from whose transformation proceeds the transformation of

society. Conditions of production are what are essential and basic for Marx; they are the point from which he starts and to which he retraces everything; there is no other origin and no other principle for him. Certainly, they cannot be considered, like Hegel's universal reason, as the first and the last; sociological reduction means an absolute renunciation of a perspective of being in which there exists a first and a last. In Marx the home in which man can dwell—that is, will be able to dwell when it is ready —is built up on conditions of production alone. Man's world is society. In actual fact a security is established by this reduction which the proletarian masses really did accept and take up into their lives, at least for the duration of an age. When the attempt has been made within Marxism, as by Engels, to eliminate this reduction and to present the proletariat with an image of the universe, the proved vital security has been confused with a completely baseless intellectual security and thus robbed of its genuine force.

Certainly, something else, which is particularly important, is added to the reduction. Hegel perceives the beginning of fulfilment in his own age, in which the absolute spirit reaches its goal. Marx simply cannot see the fulfilment beginning in the heyday of capitalism, which has to be relieved by socialism which brings about the fulfilment. He sees, however, in his age something existing in which fulfilment is manifested and guaranteed—namely, the proletariat In the existence of the proletariat the elimination of capitalism, the "negation of the negation," is bodily declared. "When the proletariat," says Marx, "proclaims the dissolution of the hitherto existing world-order, then it is only expressing the mystery of its own existence, for it is the actual dissolution of this world-order." By this fundamental thesis Marx is able to provide the proletariat with a security. Nothing else needs to be believed in but its own continuation, till the hour in which its existence becomes its action. The future appears here as bound to the directly experienced present and assured by it. Thought consequently does not have the power to construct man's real life; but life itself has this power, and the spirit has it, if it acknowledges the power of life and joins to it its own power, which is different in nature and effect.

Marx is both right and wrong in this view of the power of social life proper. He is right, since in fact social life, like all life, itself produces the forces which can renew it. But he is wrong, since human life, to which social life belongs, is distinct from all other kinds of life by the power of decision which is distinct from all other kinds of power : this power is different from them all in that it does not appear as quantity, but reveals the measure of its strength only in action itself. It depends on the direction and force of this power how far the renewing powers of life as such are able to take effect, and even whether they are not transformed into powers of destruction. The development depends essentially on something which cannot be explained in terms of the development. In other words, neither in man's personal nor in his social life must anthropological time be confused with cosmological time, not even when the latter is endowed with the form of the dialectical process, as, for example, in Marx's famous statement that capitalist production breeds its negation "with the necessity of a natural process." With all his sociological reduction he does no more than follow in Hegel's tracks and introduce cosmological time—that is, a time which is alien to man's reality—into his consideration of the future. The problem of human decision, as the origin of events and of destiny, including social events and destiny, does not exist here at all. Such a doctrine can persist in power only so long as it does not clash with a moment in history in which the problematic of human decision makes itself felt to a terrifying degree, I mean a moment in which catastrophic events exercise a frightening and paralysing influence over the power of decision, and repeatedly move it to renunciation in favour of a negative élite of men—men who, knowing no inner restraint, do not act as they do from real decision, but only stick to their power. In such situations the man who is striving for the renewal of social life, socialist man, can only share in the decision of his society's destiny if he believes in his own power of decision and knows that it matters, for only then does he actualize, in the effect which his decision has, the highest strength of his power of decision. In such a moment he can only share in the decision of his society's destiny if the view of life which he holds does not contradict his *experience*.

Hegel as it were compulsorily combined the course of the stars and of history into a speculative security. Marx, who confined himself to the human world, ascribed to it alone a security in regard to the future, which is likewise dialectic, but has the effect of an actual security. To-day this security has perished in the ordered chaos of a terrible historical revulsion. Gone is the calm, a new anthropological dread has arisen, the question about man's being faces us as never before in all its grandeur and terror— no longer in philosophical attire, but in the nakedness of existence. No dialectical guarantee keeps man from falling; it lies with himself to lift his foot and take the step which leads him away from the abyss. The strength to take this step cannot come from any security in regard to the future, but only from those depths of insecurity in which man, overshadowed by despair, answers with his decision the question about man's being.

IV : *Feuerbach and Nietzsche*

I

WITH Marx we are already in the midst of the anthropological rebellion against Hegel. At the same time we can see in perfect clarity in Marx the peculiar character of this rebellion. There is a return to the anthropological limitation of the picture of the universe without a return to the anthropological *problematic* and setting of the question. The philosopher who so rebelled against Hegel, and as whose pupil in this respect Marx has to be regarded, in spite of all differences and even oppositions between them, is Feuerbach. Feuerbach's anthropological reduction precedes Marx's sociological reduction.

In order to understand aright Feuerbach's struggle against Hegel and its significance for anthropology, it is best to begin with the fundamental question, What is the *beginning* of philosophy? Kant, in opposition to rationalism, and based on Hume, had established cognition as the very first thing for philosophizing men, and thus made the decisive philosophical problem what knowing is and how it is possible. This problem then led him, as we saw, to the anthropological question—what kind of a being is man, who knows in this way? Hegel, perfectly conscious of what he was doing, passed over this first thing. In his view, as he expressed it with complete clarity in the first edition of his *Encyclopædia of the Philosophical Sciences* (1817), there must not be *any* immediate object at the beginning of philosophy, since immediacy is by nature opposed to philosophical thought; in other words, philosophy is not permitted, as with Kant and Descartes before him, to start from the situation of the philosophizing man, but it must "anticipate." He carries out this anticipating in the sentence: "Pure being is the beginning," which is straightway explained as follows: "Now, pure being is pure abstraction." On this basis Hegel is able to make the development of the universal reason, instead of that of human cognition, into the object of philosophy. This is the point where Feuerbach puts in his attack The universal reason is only a new concept for God; and as theology, when it said "God," only transferred the human essence itself from earth to heaven, so metaphysics, when it says "universal reason," only transfers the human essence from concrete existence to abstract existence. The new philosophy—so Feuerbach formulates it in his manifesto, *Principles of the Philosophy of the Future* (1843)—has as its principle "not the absolute, that is, the abstract, spirit—in short, not reason *in abstracto*, but man's real, whole being." Unlike Kant, Feuerbach wishes to make the whole being, not human cognition, the beginning of philosophizing. In his view nature too is to be understood only as the "basis

of man." "The new philosophy," he says, "makes man
. . . the exclusive, universal . . . object of philosophy, and
thus makes anthropology . . . the universal science." Thus
the anthropological reduction, the reduction of being to
human existence, is carried out. One could say that Hegel,
in the position he assigns to man, follows the first creation
story, that of the first chapter of *Genesis*, of the creation
of *nature*, where man is created last and given his place in
the cosmos, yet in such a way that creation is not only
ended but also completed in its significance now that the
" image of God " has appeared; while Feuerbach follows
the second creation story, that of the second chapter of
Genesis, of the creation of *history*, where there is no world
but that of man, man in its centre, giving all living things
their true name. Never before has a philosophical anthropology been so emphatically demanded. But Feuerbach's
postulate does not lead beyond the threshold to which
Kant's fourth question led us. More, in one decisive
respect we feel that we are not merely no further advanced
than with Kant, but actually less advanced. For in
Feuerbach's demand the question *What is man?* is not
included at all. Indeed, his demand means a renunciation
of this question. His anthropological reduction of being is
a reduction to *unproblematic* man. But the real man,
man who faces a being that is not human, and is time and
again overpowered by it as by an inhuman fate, yet dares
to know this being and this fact, is not unproblematic;
rather, he is the beginning of all problematic. A philosophical anthropology is not possible unless it begins from
the anthropological *question*. It can be attained only by a
formulation and expression of this question which is more
profound, sharp, strict, and cruel than it has ever been
before. Nietzsche's real significance lies, as we shall see, in
his undertaking of such a deepening and sharpening of
the question.

But we must first continue to deal with Feuerbach, for
the sake of a matter which is extraordinarily important
for the thought of our age about man. By man, whom he
considers as the highest subject of philosophy, Feuerbach
does not mean man as an individual, but man with man

—the connexion of *I* and *Thou*. " The individual man for himself," runs his manifesto, " does not have man's being in himself, either as a moral being or a thinking being. Man's being is contained only in community, in the unity of man with man—a unity which rests, however, only on the reality of the difference between I and Thou." Feuerbach did not elaborate these words in his later writings. Marx did not take up into his concept of society the element of the real relation between the really different *I* and *Thou,* and for that very reason opposed an unreal individualism with a collectivism which was just as unreal. But in those words Feuerbach, passing beyond Marx, introduced that discovery of the *Thou,* which has been called " the Copernican revolution " of modern thought, and " an elemental happening which is just as rich in consequences as the idealist discovery of the I " and " is bound to lead to a new beginning of European thought, pointing beyond the Cartesian contribution to modern philosophy."[1] I myself in my youth was given a decisive impetus by Feuerbach.

2

Nietzsche depends much more solidly on Feuerbach's anthropological reduction than is usually admitted. He falls short of Feuerbach in that he loses sight of the autonomous sphere of the relation between *I* and *Thou* and is content, in respect of inter-human relations, to continue on the line of the French moral philosophers of the seventeenth and eighteenth centuries and complete it by depicting the origin and development of morality. But he far surpasses Feuerbach in that, like no other previous thinker, he brings man into the centre of his thought

[1] Karl Heim, *Ontologie und Theologie,* Zeitschrift für Theologie und Kirche, neue Folge XI (1930), 333; Karl Heim, *Glaube und Denken,* 1.Auflage (1931), 405 ff (in the revised edition of 1934 Heim excised this passage). The English translation, *God Transcendent,* has been made from this third, revised and shortened, and altogether more orthodox edition. For a similar point of view see especially Emil Brunner.

about the universe, and not, as with Feuerbach, man as a clear and unambiguous being, but rather man as a problematic being; and thereby he endows the anthropological question with an unprecedented force and passion.

The questionableness of man is Nietzsche's real great theme, which engages him from his first philosophical efforts till the end. As early as 1874, in his study of Schopenhauer as an educator. he puts a question which is like a marginal note to Kant's fourth question, and in which our age is mirrored as Kant's age is mirrored in his question : " How can man know himself?" And he adds by way of explanation : " He is something dark and veiled." Ten years later comes an explanation of this explanation : man is " the animal that is not yet established." That is. he is not a determined, unambiguous, final species like the others. he is not a finished form, but something that is only becoming. If we regard him as a finished form then he must appear " as the supreme aberration of nature and a self-contradiction," for he is the being which, " in consequence of a violent separation from the animal past," suffers from himself and from the problem of what his life means. But that is only a transition. In truth, man—as Nietzsche finally expresses it in the notes which were brought together posthumously under the title *The Will to Power*—is " as it were an embryo of the man of the future," of the real man, of the real species man. The paradox of the situation consists in the fact that the coming of this real future man is not at all assured; present man, the man of the transition, must first create him out of the material which he himself is. " Man is something fleeting and plastic—one can make of him what one will." Man, *animal* man, " has hitherto had no meaning. His existence on earth has had no goal. ' To what end man?' was a question without an answer." He suffered, ' but it was not the suffering itself which was his problem, but that there was no answer to the cry ' To what end this suffering?' " The ascetic ideal of Christianity wishes to free man from the meaninglessness of suffering; it does this by separating him from the foundations of life and leading him towards nothing. It is from life that man must take the meaning which he has to give to himself. But life is "the will to power"; all great humanity and great culture has developed from the will to power and from a good conscience to it. The ascetic ideals, which gave man a "bad conscience," have suppressed this will. The real man will be he who has a good conscience towards his will to power. That is the man we should "create" and "breed," for whose sake we should "overcome" what is called man. Present man is "no goal, but only a way, an episode, a bridge, a great promise." That is what, in Nietzsche's view, distinguished man from all animals : he is "an animal that may promise"; that is, he treats a bit of the future as something dependent on him for which he answers. No animal can do that. This human quality has arisen out of the contractual relation between creditor and debtor, out of the debtor's obligation. The "leading ethical concept of 'guilt' (*Schuld*) took its origin from the very material concept of 'debts' (*Schulden*)." And human society has elevated by every possible means the quality which has arisen in this way, in order to keep the individual fulfilling his ethical and social duties. As the supreme means it made use of the ascetic ideals. Man must be free of it all, of his bad conscience and of the bad salvation from this conscience, in order to become in truth the way. Now he no longer promises others the fulfilment of his duties, but he promises himself the fulfilment of man.

Whatever of these ideas is meant as an *answer* is wrong. First, the sociological and ethnological presupposition about the history of man's origins is wrong. The concept of guilt is found most powerfully developed even in the most primitive communal forms which we know, where the relation between creditor and debtor is almost non-existent : the man is guilty who violates one of the original laws which dominate the society and which are mostly derived from a divine founder; the boy who is accepted into the tribal community and learns its laws, which bind him henceforth, learns to promise; this promise is often given under the sign of death, which is symbolically carried out on the boy, with a symbolical re-birth. Just because the man has learned to promise in this way it is possible for the contract-relation in private economy to develop between the debtor who promises and the creditor who is promised.

Secondly, the psychological and historical view of the will to power is wrong. Nietzsche's concept of a will to power is not so unambiguous as Schopenhauer's concept of the will to life, on which it was modelled. Sometimes he understands by it the will to acquire ever more and more power; "all purposive happenings," he says, "can be reduced to the purpose of increasing power"; all that lives strives, in his view, "for power, for increase in power," "for a maximal feeling of power." But another time he defines the will to power as the "insatiable desire to display power, or to employ, to practise power." These are two different things. We may, nevertheless, look on them as the two sides, or the two moments, of the same event. At any rate we know that real greatness in history, in the history of the spirit and of culture, as well as in the history of peoples and of states, cannot be characterized by either of these. Greatness by nature includes a power, but not a will to power. Greatness has an inner powerfulness, which sometimes grows suddenly and irresistibly to power over men, sometimes exerts its effect quietly and slowly on a company that is quietly and slowly increasing, sometimes, too, seems to have no effect at all, but rests in itself, and sends out beams which will perhaps catch the glance only of some far time. But greatness strives neither to "increase" nor to "display" power. The great man, whether we comprehend him in the most intense activity of his work or in the restful equipoise of his forces, is powerful, involuntarily and composedly powerful, but he is not avid for power. What he is avid for is the realization of what he has in mind, the incarnation of the spirit. Of course he needs power for this realization; for power—when we strip the concept of the dithyrambic splendour with which Nietzsche equipped it—means simply the capacity to realize what one wants to realize; but the great man is not avid for this capacity—which is, after all, only a self-evident and indispensable means—but for *what* he wishes to be capable of. This is the point from where we can understand the *responsibility* in which the powerful man is placed, namely whether, and how far, he is really serving his goal; and also the point from where we can understand the seduction by power, leading him to be unfaithful to the goal and yield to power alone. When we see a great man desiring power instead of his real goal we soon recognize that he is sick, or more precisely that his attitude to his work is sick. He overreaches himself, the work denies itself to him, the incarnation of the spirit no longer takes place, and to avoid the threat of senselessness he snatches after empty power. This sickness casts the genius on to the same level as those hysterical figures who, being by nature without power, slave for power, for an ever fresh display of power and an ever fresh increase of power, in order that they may enjoy the illusion that they are inwardly powerful, and who in this striving for power cannot let a pause intervene, since a pause would bring with it the possibility of self-reflection and self-reflection would bring collapse. From this point, too, the connexion between power and culture is to be judged. It is an essential element of the history of almost all peoples that the political leadership which is historically important strives to win and to increase the power of the nation; that is, precisely what, as we saw, has a pathological character in personal life is normal in the relation between the historical representatives of the nation and the nation itself. Now again the characters separate in decisive fashion. It is decisively important whether the man who leads longs in his inmost heart, in his deepest desire and dream, to acquire power for his nation for power's sake, or in order that the nation may attain the capacity to realize what in his view appears as their nature and destiny—what he has discovered in his own soul as the sign of a future which is waiting for this nation, to be realized by it. If a man longs in *this* way for power for his nation then what he does in the service of his will or his vocation furthers, enriches and renews the national culture; if he longs for national power in itself then he may achieve the greatest successes—what he does will only

weaken and paralyse the national culture he wishes to
glorify. The heyday of a community's culture is only
rarely identical with the heyday of its power : great,
genuine, spontaneous cultural productivity mostly precedes
the time of intense striving and struggling for power, and
the cultural activity which follows that time is mostly only
a gathering and completing and imitating—unless a conquered people brings a new elemental cultural force to the
powerful conqueror and enters into an association with it
in which the people which has become politically powerless represents culturally the powerful, male, generative
principle. No-one knew more clearly than the historian
Jakob Burckhardt that political predominance and the
capacity to realize the hidden form, the " idea," thus
producing culture, are only seldom compatible. Burckhardt was the man whom Nietzsche admired as he did
scarcely any other of his contemporaries, though Burckhardt more and more set him quietly aside. It is noteworthy that the spark which kindled Nietzsche's enthusiasm for the will to power probably came from a lecture
by Burckhardt which he heard in 1870. We possess these
lectures now in Burckhardt's posthumous book, published
with the title *Reflections on World History*, one of the few
important books about the powers which determine what
we call history. We read there that the real inner incentive
for the great historical individual is not love of glory, not
ambition, but " the sense of power, which as an irresistible
impulse drives the great individual into the light of day."
But Burckhardt understands by that something quite different from the will to power in itself. He sees " the
characteristic of greatness " in " its carrying out a will
which goes beyond the individual." It is possible that the
community and the age are unconscious of this will : " the
individual knows what the nation's will should really be,
and carries it out," because " the force and capacity of
infinitely many are concentrated " in him. There appears
here, as Burckhardt says, " a secret coincidence of the
egoism of the individual " with the greatness of the whole.
But the coincidence can be broken up if the means of
power which are adopted " react on the individual and in

the long run deprive him of the taste for great aims." On the basis of this insight Burckhardt uttered, in another lecture at that time—taking up the words of an earlier historian, Schlosser—the memorable, much-repeated and much-misunderstood words : " Now power in itself is evil, no matter who exercises it. It has no persistence, but is greed and *eo ipso* cannot be fulfilled, hence it is unhappy in itself and is bound to be the cause of unhappiness in others." These words can only be understood in the context of Burckhardt's thoughts, when one notes that he is speaking here of power *in itself.* So long as a man's power, that is, his capacity to realize what he has in mind, is bound to the goal, to the work, to the calling, it is, considered in itself, neither good nor evil, it is only a suitable or an unsuitable instrument. But as soon as this bond with the goal is broken off or loosened, and the man ceases to think of power as the capacity to do something, but thinks of it as a possession, that is, thinks of power in itself, then his power, being cut off and self-satisfied, is evil; it is power withdrawn from responsibility, power which betrays the spirit, power in itself. It corrupts the history of the world. Genuine knowledge of historical reality must rectify in this way Nietzsche's wrong answer to the anthropological question, when he says that man is to be understood, and released from his problematic nature, from the standpoint of the will to power.

As we see, Nietzsche did not give a positive foundation for a philosophical anthropology. But in elevating, as no previous thinker has done, the questionableness of human life to be the real subject of philosophizing he gave the anthropological question a new and unheard-of impulse. Yet it is specially noteworthy that from beginning to end of his thought he endeavoured to overcome the special problem of man in its strict sense. With Augustine, with Pascal, and even with Kant, the pathos of the anthropological question lies in our perceiving something in ourselves that we cannot explain to ourselves from nature and its development alone. For philosophy till Nietzsche, so far as it has an anthropological concern, " man " is not merely a species, but a category. But Nietzsche, who is very strongly determined by the eighteenth century, and whom one would sometimes like to call a mystic of the Enlightenment, does not acknowledge such a category or basic problem. He attempts to follow out a thought indicated by Empedocles, but since then never discussed in a genuinely philosophical fashion : he wants to understand man purely *genetically*, as an animal that has grown out and stepped forth from the animal world. He writes : " We no longer derive man from the 'spirit,' we have put him back among the animals." These could be the words of one of the French encyclopædists. But all the same Nietzsche remains deeply conscious of the specifically human questionableness. It is this very questionableness which he wants to explain by the fact of man's breakaway from the animal world and his aberration from his instincts; man is problematic because he is an " overwrought kind of animal " and thus a " sickness " of the earth. For Kant the problem of man is a *frontier* problem, that is, the problem of a being which belongs, certainly, to nature, but not to nature alone, of a being that is established on the frontier between nature and another realm. For Nietzsche the problem of man is a problem of the *edge,* the problem of a being that has moved from within nature to its utmost edge, to the perilous end of natural being, where there begins, not as for Kant the ether of the spirit but the dizzying abyss of nothing. Nietzsche no longer sees in man a being in himself, a " new thing," which has come out of nature but in such a way that the fact and the way of this coming cannot be grasped by concepts of nature; he sees only a *becoming,* " an attempt, a groping, a missing of the mark," not precisely a being but at best the pre-form of a being, " the animal that is not yet established," thus an extreme piece of nature, where something new has only begun to grow, which till now has certainly seemed very interesting but, considered in respect of its totality, not really a success. Yet two definite things, he thinks, can arise from this indefinite thing. Either man, in virtue of his " growing morality," which suppresses his instincts, will develop in himself " merely the herd animal " and thus " establish " the animal Man as the species

in which the animal world goes into decline, as the deca-
dent animal. Or man will overcome what is "fundamentally amiss" with him, give new life to his instincts, bring
to light his unexhausted possibilities, build up his life on
the affirmation of the will to power, and breed the superman who will be the real man, the successful new being.
For this goal Nietzsche apparently does not think how it
could come to pass that such an "ill-bred" animal could
pull itself out of the bog of its own ambiguity. He demands conscious breeding on a widespread scale, and does
not think of what he himself wrote : "We deny that anything that is being consciously made can be made perfect."
We are, however, not concerned here with these inner
contradictions in Nietzsche's thought, but with something
else. Nietzsche, as we have seen, undertook with passionate earnestness to explain man in terms of the animal
world; the specific problem of man does not thereby fade
out, but has become more visible than ever. Only, from
this point of view, the question ceases to be, *How is it to be
understood that there is such a being as man?* but is *How
is it to be understood that such a being as man has
emerged and stepped forth from the animal world?* But in
spite of all the arguments he brought to bear throughout
his thought Nietzsche had not made this clear. He has
scarcely troubled about what is for us the fundamental
anthropological fact and the most amazing of all earthly
facts—that there is in the world a being who knows the
universe as a universe, its space as space, its time as time,
and knows himself in it as knowing it. But that does not
mean, as has been asserted, that the world exists "over
again" in man's consciousness, but that a *world* in our
sense, a unified, spatio-temporal world of the senses, only
exists in virtue of man, because only the human person is
able to combine into a cosmic unity the data of his own
senses and the traditional data of the whole race. Certainly, if Nietzsche had troubled about this fundamental
fact it would have led him to the sociology he despised,
namely, to the sociology of knowledge and the sociology
of tradition, to that of language, and that of the generations—in brief, to the sociology of human thinking to-

gether, which Feuerbach had in principle already pointed out. The man who knows a world is man *with* man. The problem which Nietzsche neglected, that such a being exists, is only shifted in his view from the realm of the being of a species to the realm of its becoming. If a being has emerged from the animal world who knows about life and about his own life, then the fact and the manner of this emergence cannot be explained by his place in the animal world or comprehended by concepts of nature. For post-nietzschian philosophy man is more than ever not merely a species, but a category. Kant's question *What is man?* is put to us with new urgency by Nietzsche's passionate anthropological concern. We know that to answer it we must invoke not merely the spirit but also nature to tell us what it has to tell; but we know that we have also to approach another power for information, namely, community.

I say "we know." But it is true that modern philosophical anthropology, even in its most significant representatives, has not yet realized this knowledge. Whether it has turned more to the spirit or more to nature, the power of community has not been invoked. If this power is not invoked the others lead not only to fragmentary knowledge but of necessity also to knowledge which is inadequate in itself.

1: *The Crisis and its Expression*

I

ONLY in our time has the anthropological problem reached maturity, that is, come to be recognized and treated as an independent philosophical problem. Besides philosophical development itself, which led to an increasing insight into the problematic nature of human existence, and whose most important points I have presented, two factors which are connected in many ways with this development have contributed to bringing the anthropological problem to maturity. Before discussing the present situation I must indicate the character and significance of these factors.

The first is predominantly sociological in nature. It is the increasing decay of the old organic forms of the direct life of man with man. By this I mean communities which quantitatively must not be too big to allow the men who are connected by them to be brought together ever anew and set in a direct relation with one another, and which qualitatively are of such a nature that men are ever anew born into them or grow into them, who thus understand their membership not as the result of a free agreement with others but as their destiny and as a vital tradition. Such forms are the family, union in work, the community in village and in town. Their increasing decay is the price that had to be paid for man's political liberation in the French Revolution and for the subsequent establishment of bourgeois society. But at the same time human solitude is intensified anew. The organic forms of community offered to modern man—who, as we saw, has lost the feeling of being at home in the world, has lost cosmological security—a life which had the quality of home, a resting in direct connexion with those like him, a sociological security which preserved him from the feeling of being completely exposed. Now this too slipped away from him more and more. In their outer structure many of the old organic forms remained as before, but they decayed inwardly, they steadily lost meaning and spiritual power. The new community forms which undertook to bring the individual anew into connexion with others, such as the club, the trade union, the party, have, it is true, succeeded in kindling collective passions, which, as is said, "fill out" men's lives, but they have not been able to re-establish the security which has been destroyed. All that happens is that the increased sense of solitude is dulled and suppressed by bustling activities; but wherever a man enters the stillness, the actual reality of his life, he experiences the depth of solitude, and confronted with the ground of his existence experiences the depth of the human problematic.

The second factor can be described as one of the history of the spirit, or better, of the soul. For a century man has moved ever deeper into a crisis which has much in common with others that we know from earlier history, but has one essential peculiarity. This concerns man's relation to the new things and connexions which have arisen by his action or with his co-operation. I should like to call this peculiarity of the modern crisis man's lagging behind his works. Man is no longer able to master the world which he himself brought about: it is becoming stronger than he is, it is winning free of him, it confronts him in an almost elemental independence, and he no longer knows the word which could subdue and render harmless the golem (14) he has created. Our age has experienced this paralysis and failure of the human soul successively in three realms. The first was the realm of technique. Machines, which were invented in order to serve men in their work, impressed him into their service. They were no longer, like tools, an extension of man's arm, but man became their extension, an adjunct on their periphery, doing their bidding. The second realm was the economic. Production, immensely increased in order to supply the growing number of men with what they needed, did not reach a reasonable co-ordination; it is as though the business of the production and utilization of goods spread out beyond man's reach and withdrew itself from his command. The third realm was the political. In the first world war, and on both sides, man learned with ever greater horror how he was in the grip of incomprehensible powers, which seemed, indeed, to be connected with man's will but which threw off their bonds and again and again trampled on all human purposes, till finally they brought all, both on this side and on the other, to destruction. Man faced the terrible fact that he was the father of demons whose master he could not become. And the question about the meaning of this simultaneous power and powerlessness flowed into the question about man's being, which now received a new and tremendously practical significance.

It is no chance, but significant necessity, that the most important works in the sphere of philosophical anthropology appeared in the decade after the first world war; nor does it seem to me to be chance that Edmund Husserl, the man in whose school and methods the most powerful attempts of our time to construct an independent philosophical anthropology made their appearance, was a German Jew, that is, the son of a people which experienced more grievously and fatefully than any other the first of those two factors, the increasing decay of the old organic forms of man's common life, and the pupil and adopted son, as he thought, of a people which experienced more grievously and fatefully than any other the second of the two factors, man's lagging behind his works.

Husserl himself, the creator of the phenomenological method in which the two attempts at a philosophical anthrolopogy of which I shall have to speak, those of Martin Heidegger and Max Scheler, were undertaken, never treated the anthropological problem as such. But in his last, unfinished work, a treatise on the crisis of the European sciences, he made, in three separate sentences, a contribution to this problem which seems to me, in view of the man who uttered them and the time when they were uttered, to be important enough to be adduced and have their truth scrutinized at this point, before we pass to the discussion and criticism of phenomenological anthropology.

The first of the three sentences asserts that the greatest historical phenomenon is mankind wrestling for self-understanding. That is, Husserl says that all the effective events which have again and again, as it is usually put, changed the face of the earth, and which fill the books of the historians, are less important than that ever new effort, which is carried out in stillness and is scarcely noticed by the historians, to understand the mystery of man's being. Husserl describes this effort as a wrestling. He means that the human spirit encounters great difficulties, great opposition from the problematic material it is striving to understand—that is, from its own being—and that from the beginning of history it has had to fight them. The history of this struggle is the history of the greatest of all history's phenomena.

Thus Husserl confirms the significance for the growth of man of the historical course of philosophical anthropology —the course from question to question, some of whose stages I have indicated.

The second sentence runs : " If man becomes a ' metaphysical,' a specifically philosophical problem, then he is called in question as a reasoning thing." These words, whose significance was particularly stressed by Husserl, are only true, or only become true, if they mean that the relation of " reason " to non-reason in man must be called in question. In other words, it is not a case of considering reason as the specifically human and considering what is not reason in man as the non-specific, as what man has in common with non-human beings, as what is " natural " in man—as has been done again and again, especially since Descartes. Rather, the depth of the anthropological question is first touched when we also recognize as specifically human that which is not reason. Man is not a centaur, he is man through and through. He can be understood only when one knows, on the one hand, that there is something in all that is human, including thought, which belongs to the general nature of living creatures, and is to be grasped from this nature, while knowing, on the other hand, that there is no human quality which belongs fully to the general nature of living creatures and is to be grasped exclusively from it. Even man's hunger is not an animal's hunger. Human reason is to be understood only in connexion with human non-reason. The problem of philosophical anthropology is the problem of a specific totality and of its specific structure. So it has been seen by Husserl's school, whom Husserl himself, however, was unwilling to acknowledge as his school at the decisive points.

The third sentence runs: "Humanity in general is essentially the existence of man in entities of mankind which are bound together in generations and in society." These words fundamentally contradict the whole anthropological work of the phenomenological school, both that of Scheler who, though a sociologist, scarcely noticed man's social connexions in his anthropological thought, and that of Heidegger, who certainly recognized that these connexions were primary but treated them essentially as the great obstacle to man's attainment of himself. In these words Husserl says that man's essence is not to be found in isolated individuals, for a human being's bonds with his generation and his society are of his essence; we must therefore know what these bonds really mean if we want to know the essence of man. That is to say that an individualistic anthropology either has as its subject man in a condition of isolation, that is, in a condition not adequate to his essence, or in fact does consider man in his bonds of community, but regards their effects as impairing his real essence, and thus is not thinking of that fundamental communion of which Husserl speaks.

2

Before I pass to the discussion of phenomenological anthropology I must refer to the man to whose influence its individualistic character is largely traceable, namely, Kierkegaard. This influence is admittedly of a special nature. The phenomenological thinkers of whom I have

to speak, and pre-eminently Heidegger, have certainly
taken over Kierkegaard's mode of thinking, but they have
broken off its decisive presupposition, without which
Kierkegaard's thoughts, especially those on the connexion
between truth and existence, change their colour and
their meaning. Moreover, as we shall see, they have broken
off not merely the theological aspect of this presupposition but the whole presupposition, including the anthropological aspect, so that the character and thus also the
effect of "existential" thought represented by Kierkegaard have been almost converted into their opposite.

In the first half of the nineteenth century Kierkegaard,
as a single and solitary man, confronted the life of Christ-
endom with its faith. He was no reformer, again and again
he emphasized that he had no "authority" from above;
he was only a Christian thinker, but he was of all thinkers
the one who most forcibly indicated that thought cannot
authorize itself but is authorized only out of the existence
of the thinking man. Yet thought in this latter sense was
not the important thing for him, he really saw in it only
a conceptual translation of faith—either a good or a bad
translation. As for faith, he was intensely convinced that
it is genuine only when it is grounded in and proved by
the existence of the believer. Kierkegaard's criticism of
actual Christianity is an inner one; he does not confront
Christianity, as, for example, Nietzsche does, with an
alleged higher value, and test it by that and reject it.
There is for him no higher, and really no other, value. He
measures the so-called Christianity lived by Christians
against the real Christianity which they profess and proclaim, and rejects this whole so-called Christian life together with its false faith (false because it is not realized),
and its proclamation which has turned into a lie (because
it is self-satisfied). Kierkegaard does not acknowledge
any faith which is not binding. The so-called religious
man, no matter how great the enthusiasm with which he
thinks and speaks of the object of his faith and gives
expression to what he considers to be his faith by taking
part in religious services and ceremonies, is only imagining
that he believes unless the heart of his life is transformed

by it, unless the presence of what he believes in determines his essential attitude from the most secret solitude to public action. Belief is a relation of life to what is believed, a relation of life which includes all life, or it is unreal. Obviously that cannot mean that a man's relation to the object of his faith is established, or can be established, by man. To Kierkegaard's insight as to that of all religious thought this connexion is by nature, first, ontic, that is, concerning not merely a man's subjectivity and life but his objective being, and second, like every objective connexion, two-sided, of which, however, we are able to know only one, the human side. But it can be influenced by man—at least in respect of this human side. That is, it depends on the man to a certain extent, which we cannot measure, if or how far his subjectivity enters his life, in other words, if or how far his faith becomes the substance and form of the life he lives. This question is fraught with destiny, because it does not concern a connexion established by man but one by which man is established, and which, constituting human life and giving it its meaning, should not merely be mirrored in the subjectivity of a religious view and a religious feeling, but bodily fulfilled in the wholeness of human life and "become flesh." Kierkegaard calls the striving for this realization and incarnation of faith an existential striving, for existence is the transition from a possibility in the spirit to a reality in the wholeness of the person. For the sake of this question, fraught with destiny, Kierkegaard makes the stages and condition of life itself, guilt, fear, despair, decision, the prospect of one's own death and the prospect of salvation, into objects of metaphysical thought. He lifts them beyond the sphere of purely psychological consideration, for which they are indifferent events within the course of the soul's life, and looks on them as links in an existential process, in an ontic connexion with the absolute, as elements of an existence "before God." Metaphysics here takes possession of the actuality of the living man with a strength and consistency hitherto unknown in the history of thought. Its ability to do this springs from the fact that man is considered not as an isolated being but in the problematic nature of his bond with the absolute. It is not the I, absolute in itself, of German idealism that is the object of this philosophical thought, the I which makes a world for itself by thinking it, it is the real human person, but considered in the ontic connexion which binds it to the absolute. This connexion is for Kierkegaard a real mutual connexion of person with person, that is, the absolute also enters it as a person. Kierkegaard's anthropology is therefore a theological anthropology. But modern philosophical anthropology has been made possible by it. This philosophical anthropology had to renounce the theological presupposition in order to acquire its philosophical basis. The problem was whether it would succeed in doing that without losing at the same time the metaphysical presupposition of the concrete man's bond with the absolute. As we shall see, it did not succeed.

II : *The Doctrine of Heidegger*

I

WE have seen, in the discussion of Heidegger's interpretation of Kant's four questions, that he wants to establish as the principle of metaphysics not philosophical anthropology but " fundamental ontology," that is, the doctrine of existence as such. By existence he understands a present being which has a relation to its own being and an understanding of it. Man is the only one whom we know as such a present being. But fundamental ontology does not have to do with man in his actual manifold complexity but solely with existence in itself, which manifests itself through man. All concrete human life which is drawn upon by Heidegger concerns him only because (and in so far as) the modes of relation (*Verhalten*) of existence itself are shown in it, both the relation in which it comes to itself and becomes a self and the relation in and through which it fails to do so

Even though Heidegger himself does not regard his

philosophy or wish it to be regarded as philosophical anthropology, we must nevertheless test the genuineness and correctness of its anthropological content, since in philosophical fashion it draws upon concrete human life, which is the subject of philosophical anthropology; that is, against its intention we must subject it to criticism as a contribution to answering the anthropological question.

At the very beginning we must question Heidegger's starting-point. Is the extraction of "existence" from real human life anthropologically justified? Are statements which are made about this separated existence to be regarded in any way as philosophical statements about actual man? Or does the "chemical purity" of this concept of existence not rather make it impossible for the doctrine to stand up to the real facts of its subject—a test which all philosophy and all metaphysics must be able to pass?

Real existence, that is, real man in his relation to his being, is comprehensible only in connexion with the nature of the being to which he stands in relation. To exemplify what I mean I choose one of the most audacious and profound chapters of Heidegger's book, which treats of man's relation to his death. Here everything is perspective, what matters is how man looks to his end, whether he has the courage to anticipate the *whole* of his existence, which is made fully revealed only in death. But only when the subject of discussion is man's relation to his being is death to be limited to the end-point; if one is thinking of objective being itself, then death is also there in the present second as a force which wrestles with the force of life. The state of this struggle at a given time helps to determine man's whole nature at that moment, his existence at that moment, his attitude towards being at that moment; and if man looks now to his end, the manner of this looking cannot be separated from the reality of death's power in this very moment. In other words, man as existence, as comprehension of being that looks towards death, cannot be separated from man as a creature that begins to die when it begins to live, and that cannot possess life without death, or preserving power without destructive and disintegrative power.

Heidegger abstracts from the reality of human life the categories which originate and are valid in the relation of the individual to what is not himself, and applies them to "existence" in the narrower sense, that is, to the relation of the individual to his own being. Moreover he does not do this merely to enlarge the sphere of their validity; in Heidegger's view the true significance and depth and import of these categories is disclosed only in the realm of the individual's relation to himself. But what we find here is that on the one hand they are refined, differentiated, and subtilized, and that on the other hand they are weakened and devitalized. Heidegger's modified categories disclose a curious partial sphere of life, not a piece of the whole real life as it is actually lived, but a partial sphere which receives its independence, its independent character and laws as it were through having the circulation of the blood in the organism arrested at some point and the isolated part examined. We enter a strange room of the spirit, but we feel as if the ground we tread is the board on which a game is being played whose rules we learn as we advance, deep rules which we ponder, and must ponder, but which arose and which persist only through a decision having once been reached to play this intellectual game, and to play it in this very way. And at the same time, it is true, we feel that this game is not arbitrarily chosen by the player, but he is under necessity, it is his fate.

2

I take as an example the concept of guilt (*Schuld*). Heidegger, who always begins from the "everyday" (of which we shall have to say more later), begins here from the situation presented by the German language, which says that someone "owes" something to another (*schuldig ist*), and then from the situation that someone "is

answerable " for something (an etwas Schuld ist), from
where he advances to the situation that someone becomes
guilty in respect of another (schuldig wird), that is, that
he causes a lack in the existence of another, that he
becomes the reason for a lack in the existence of another.
But this too is only indebtedness (eine Verschuldung) and
not the original and real guilt (Schuldigsein) out of which
the indebtedness proceeds and by which it is made possible. Real guilt, according to Heidegger, consists in the
fact that the existence itself is guilty. The existence is
"guilty in the ground of its being." And the existence is
guilty through not fulfilling itself, through remaining in
the so-called "generally human," in "one" (das Man),
and not bringing its own self, the man's self, into being.
The call of conscience sounds into this situation. Who
calls? Existence itself. "In conscience the existence calls
itself." The existence, which by its guilt has not reached
self-being, summons itself to remember the self, to free
itself to a self, to come from the "unreality" to the
"reality" of existence.

Heidegger is right to say that all understanding of
indebtedness must go back to a primal guilt. He is right
to say that we are able to discover a primal guilt. But we
are not able to do this by isolating a part of life, the part
where the existence is related to itself and to its own being,
but by becoming aware of the whole life without reduction, the life in which the individual, in fact, is essentially
related to something other than himself. Life is not lived
by my playing the enigmatic game on a board by myself,
but by my being placed in the presence of a being with
whom I have agreed on no rules for the game and with
whom no rules can be agreed on. This presence before
which I am placed changes its form, its appearance, its
revelation, they are different from myself, often terrifyingly different, and different from what I expected, often
terrifyingly different. If I stand up to them, concern
myself with them, meet them in a real way, that is, with
the truth of my whole life, then and only then am I
"really" there : I am there if I am there, and where this
"there" is, is always determined less by myself than by

the presence of this being which changes its form and its appearance. If I am not really there I am guilty. When I answer the call of present being—" Where art thou?"— with " Here am I," but am not really there, that is, not with the truth of my whole life, then I am guilty. Original guilt consists in remaining with oneself. If a form and appearance of present being move past me, and I was not really there, then out of the distance, out of its disappearance, comes a second cry, as soft and secret as though it came from myself : " Where were you?" *That* is the cry of conscience. It is not my existence which calls to me, but the being which is not I. Now I can answer only the *next* form; the one which spoke can no longer be reached. (This next form can of course sometimes be the same man, but it will be a different, later, changed appearance of him.)

3

We have seen how in the history of the human spirit man again and again becomes solitary, that is, he finds himself alone with a universe which has become alien and uncanny, he can no longer stand up to the universal forms of present being; he can no longer truly meet them. This man, as we recognized him in Augustine, in Pascal, in Kierkegaard, seeks a form of being which is not included in the world, that is, he seeks a divine form of being with which, solitary as he is, he can communicate; he stretches his hands out beyond the world to meet this form. But we have also seen that there is a *way* leading from one age of solitude to the next, that is, that each solitude is colder and stricter than the preceding, and salvation from it more difficult. But finally man reaches a condition when he can no longer stretch his hands out from his solitude to meet a divine form. That is at the basis of Nietzsche's saying, " God is dead." Apparently nothing more remains now to the solitary man but to seek an intimate communication with himself. This is the basic situation from which Heidegger's philosophy arises.

And thereby the anthropological question, which the man who has become solitary discovers ever afresh, the question about the essence of man and about his relation to the being of what is, has been replaced by another question, the one which Heidegger calls the fundamental-ontological question, about human existence in its relation to its *own* being.

There remains, however, one irrefragable fact, that one can stretch out one's hands to one's image or reflection in a mirror, but not to one's real self. Heidegger's doctrine is significant as the presentation of the relations to one another of various "beings" abstracted from human life, but it is not valid for human life itself and its anthropological understanding, however valuable its suggestions for this subject.

4

Human life possesses absolute meaning through transcending in practice its own conditioned nature, that is, through man's seeing that which he confronts, and with which he can enter into a real relation of being to being, as not less real than himself, and through taking it not less seriously than himself. Human life touches on absoluteness in virtue of its dialogical character, for in spite of his uniqueness man can never find, when he plunges to the depth of his life, a being that is whole in itself and as such touches on the absolute. Man can become whole not in virtue of a relation to himself but only in virtue of a relation to another self. This other self may be just as limited and conditioned as he is; in being together the unlimited and the unconditioned is experienced. Heidegger turns away not merely from a relation to a divine unconditioned being, but also from a relation in which man experiences another than himself in the unconditioned, and so experiences the unconditioned. Heidegger's "existence" is monological. And monologue may certainly disguise itself ingeniously for a while as dialogue, one unknown layer after the other of the human self may certainly answer the inner address, so that man makes ever fresh discoveries and can suppose that he is really experiencing a "calling" and a "hearing"; but the hour of stark, final solitude comes when the dumbness of being becomes insuperable and the ontological categories no longer want to be applied to reality. When the man who has become solitary can no longer say "Thou" to the "dead" known God. everything depends on whether he can still say it to the living unknown God by saying "thou" with all his being to another living and known man. If he can no longer do this either, then there certainly remains for him the sublime illusion of detached thought that he is a self-contained self; as man he is lost. The man of "real" existence in Heidegger's sense, the man of "self-being," who in Heidegger's view is the goal of life, is not the man who really lives with man, but the man who can no longer really live with man, the man who now knows a real life only in communication with himself. But that is only a semblance of real life, an exalted and unblessed game of the spirit. This modern man and this modern game have found their expression in Heidegger's philosophy. Heidegger isolates from the wholeness of life the realm in which man is related to himself, since he absolutizes the temporally conditioned situation of the radically solitary man, and wants to derive the essence of human existence from the experience of a nightmare.

5

This seems to be contradicted by Heidegger's statement that man's being is by nature *in the world*, in a world in which man is not merely surrounded by things which are his "gear," that is, which he uses and applies, in order to "take care of" what has to be taken care of, but also by men *together with* whom he is in the world. These men are not, like things, mere being, but, like himself, existence, that is, a being that stands in relation to itself and knows itself. They are for him an object not of "care" but of "carefulness," solicitude; moreover they are this by nature, existentially, even when he passes them by and does not trouble about them, when they " do not concern " him, and even when he treats them with complete inconsiderateness. Further, they are by nature the object of his understanding, for only by the understanding of others do cognition and knowledge become possible at all. This is how it is in the everyday, which is Heidegger's point of departure in a way specially important for him. But of the highest level, which he calls real self-being or resolution, more precisely resolution to be a self, he emphasizes that it does not separate existence from its world or isolate it into a freely moving I. " Resolution," he says, " in fact makes the self into a being with what is to hand, taking care each time, and urges it into a life of solicitude with others." Further, " Real life together is the first thing to arise out of the real self-being of resolution." Thus it looks as though Heidegger fully knew and acknowledged that a relation to others is essential. But this is not actually the case. For the relation of solicitude which is all he considers cannot *as such* be an essential relation, since it does not set a man's life in direct relation with the life of another, but only one man's solicitous help in relation with another man's lack and need of it. Such a relation can share in essential life only when it derives its significance from being the effect of a relation which is essential in itself—such as that between mother and child; of course it can lead to such a relation, as when genuine friendship or love arises between the solicitous person and the object of his solicitude. In its essence solicitude does not come from mere co-existence with others, as Heidegger thinks, but from essential, direct, whole relations between man and man, whether those which are objectively based on ties of blood, or those which arise by choice and can either assume objective, institutional forms or, like friendship, shrink from all institutional forming and yet touch the depth of existence. It is from these direct relations, I say, which have an essential part in building up the substance of life, that the element of solicitude incidentally arises, extending after that, beyond the essential relations, into the merely social and institutional. In man's existence with man it is not solicitude, but the essential relation, which is primal. Nor is it any different if we set aside the problem of origin, and undertake the pure analysis of existence. In *mere* solicitude man remains essentially with himself, even if he is moved with extreme pity; in action and help he inclines towards the other, but the barriers of his own being are not thereby breached; he makes his assistance, not his self, accessible to the other; nor does he expect any real mutuality, in fact he probably shuns it; he " is concerned with the other," but he is not anxious for the other to be concerned with him. In an essential relation, on the other hand, the barriers of individual being are in fact breached and a new phenomenon appears which can appear only in this way : one life open to another—not steadily, but so to speak attaining its extreme reality only from point to point, yet also able to acquire a form in the continuity of life; the other becomes present not merely in the imagination or feeling, but in the depths of one's substance, so that one experiences the mystery of the other being in the mystery of one's own. The two participate in one another's lives in very fact, not physically, but ontically. This is certainly something which comes to a man in the course of his life only by a kind of grace, and many will say that they do not know it; but even he to whom it has not come has it in his existence as a constitutive principle, because the conscious or unconscious *lack* of it plays an essential part in determining the nature and character of his existence. And certainly, in the course of their life many will be given the opportunity of it which they do not fulfil in their existence; they acquire relations which they do not make real, that is, which they do not use to open themselves to another; they squander the most precious, irreplaceable and irrecoverable material; they pass their life by. But then this very void penetrates the existence and permeates its deepest layer. The " everyday," in its inconspicuous, scarcely perceptible part, which is nevertheless accessible to an analysis of existence, is interwoven with what is " not the everyday."

But we have seen that, according to Heidegger, even on

the highest level of self-being man does not pass beyond
" a life of solicitude with others." The level which Heidegger's man can reach is that of the free self which, as
Heidegger emphasizes, is not separated from the world,
but is only now mature and resolute for right existence
with the world. But this mature resolute existence with the
world knows nothing of an *essential* relation. Heidegger
would perhaps reply that it is only the self which has become free that is really capable of love and friendship.
But since self-being is here an ultimate, *the* ultimate,
which the existence is able to reach, there is absolutely no
starting-point for understanding love and friendship still
as essential relations. The self which has become free
certainly does not turn its back on the world, its resolution
includes the resolve really to be with the world, to act in it
and on it, but it does not include the belief that in this
life with the world the barriers of the self can be
breached, nor even the desire that it should happen.
Existence is completed in self-being; there is no ontic
way beyond this for Heidegger. What Feuerbach pointed
out, that the individual does not have the essence of man
in himself, that man's essence is contained in the unity of
man with man, has entirely failed to enter Heidegger's
philosophy. For him the individual has the essence of man
in himself and brings it to existence by becoming a " resolved " self. Heidegger's self is *a closed system*.

6

" Everyone," said Kierkegaard, " should be chary about
having dealings with ' others ' and should essentially speak
only with God and with himself." And he uttered this
" should " as he looked to the goal and the task which he
set to man, namely, to become a Single One. Heidegger
seems to set man the same goal. But with Kierkegaard " to
become a Single One " means only the presupposition to
entry into a relation with God : only by having become
a Single One can man enter into this relation. Kierkegaard's Single One is an open system, even if open solely

to God. Heidegger knows no such relation; and since he does not know any other essential relation his " to become a self " means something quite different from Kierkegaard's " to become a Single One." Kierkegaard's man becomes a Single One *for* something, namely for the entry into a relation with the absolute; Heidegger's man does not become a self for something, since he cannot breach his barriers, and his participation in the absolute—so far as there is such a thing for him—consists in his barriers and nothing else. Heidegger speaks of man becoming "opened" to his self; but this self itself to which he becomes opened is by nature closedness and reserve. What Kierkegaard says appears here in a modified form : "Everyone should essentially speak only with himself." But in fact Heidegger leaves out the "should" as well. What he means is that everyone can essentially speak only with himself; what he speaks with others cannot be essential—that is, the word cannot transcend the individual's essence and transfer him into another essential life, which does not arise but is between the beings and grows by their essential relation with one another. Heidegger's man is certainly pointed towards being with the world and towards an understanding and solicitous life with others; but in the essentiality of his existence, wherever his existence is essential, he is alone. With Kierkegaard's man anxiety and dread become essential as anxiety about the relation with God and dread lest he miss it. With Heidegger they become essential as anxiety about the growth of self-being and dread lest it be missed. In his anxiety and dread Kierkegaard's man stands " alone before God," Heidegger's man stands before himself and nothing else, and—since in the last resort one cannot stand before oneself—he stands in his anxiety and dread before nothing. In order to become a Single One and to enter into the Single One's relation with the absolute, Kierkegaard's man has to renounce the essential relation to another, as Kierkegaard himself renounced the essential relation to another, to his fiancée—a renunciation which shapes the great theme of his works and journals. Heidegger's man has no essential relation to renounce. In

Kierkegaard's world there is a *Thou* spoken with the very being to the other person, even if only to tell this person direct (as in a letter from Kierkegaard to his fiancée long after the engagement was broken off) or indirectly (as often in his books) why the essential relation had to be renounced. In Heidegger's world there is no such *Thou*, no true *Thou* spoken from being to being, spoken with one's own being. One does not say this *Thou* to the man for whom one is merely solicitous.

7

Heidegger's " openness " of the existence to itself thus in truth involves its being finally closed—even though it appears in humane forms—to all genuine bonds with the other and with otherness. This becomes still clearer if we pass from the person's relation to individuals to his relation to an anonymous generality, to what Heidegger calls " one " (*das Man*). Here, too, Kierkegaard, with his concept of the " crowd," has anticipated him. The crowd, in which a man finds himself when he tries to advance to self-reflection, that is, the general, the impersonal, the faceless and formless, the average and the levelled down, this " crowd " is " untruth " for Kierkegaard. On the other hand the man who breaks out of it, escapes from its influence and becomes a Single One, is as a Single One the truth. For to Kierkegaard there is no other possibility of man's becoming truth, human (that is, conditioned) truth except by confronting unconditioned or divine truth and entering into the decisive relation with it. One can do this only as a Single One, through having become a person with the complete and independent responsibility of singleness. But one may only become a Single One through disengaging oneself from the crowd, which deprives one of, or at least weakens, personal responsibility. Heidegger takes over Kierkegaard's concept and develops it in the subtlest fashion. But the growth of the Single One—or, as he says, of self-being—has with him lost its goal of entering into relation with divine truth and thereby becoming human truth. The action which engages man's life—freeing himself from the crowd—retains its central place in Heidegger, but it loses its meaning, which is to lead man out beyond himself.

Heidegger's "one" is not something definite, but is the general condition into which we are born. All are this "one," not as an aggregate of individuals but as the faceless and nameless mass in which nothing individual can be recognized. Its real character is to be the "average," and it is with this that the "one" in its being is essentially concerned. "Every title of precedence," says Heidegger, "is noiselessly suppressed. Everything original is smoothed out in a trice as common knowledge. All that was once fought for is now plausible. Every mystery loses its power." The "one" has the tendency to "level" every possibility of being and to reduce human existence to a uniform flatness. Every interpretation of the world and of existence is arranged in advance by the "public." Almost in the same words as Kierkegaard uses Heidegger says that the "one" deprives the actual human life of its responsibility. If it is asked who then is this "one," the answer can only be that it is "no-one." Actual human life is handed over to this mighty no-one, and thus deprived of independence and reality. Instead of being concentrated in the self, it is dispersed in the "one," and has first to find itself. The power of the "one" causes existence to be fully absorbed by it. The life to which this happens flees from itself, from its power to be a self, it misses its own existence. Only the life which "fetches itself back" from this dispersal (which is, incidentally, a gnostic concept by which the gnostics meant the concentration and salvation of the soul which is lost in the world) attains to self-being.

We have seen that Heidegger does not look on the highest level as an isolation, but as resolution to co-existence with others. We have also seen, however, that this resolution only confirms the relation of solicitude on a higher plain, but knows nothing of any essential relation with others or any real *I-Thou* with them which could breach the barriers of the self. Whereas in the relation between persons, a relation is affirmed even for the self which has become free—namely, the relation of solicitude —in Heidegger there is lacking any corresponding reference for the relation to the impersonal "multitude" of men. The "one," and all that belongs to it, the "idle talk," "curiosity" and "ambiguity" which are dominant there and which are shared in by the man who has fallen a prey to the "one"—all this is purely negative, and destructive of the self : nothing positive takes its place; anonymous generality as such is repudiated, but there is nothing to replace it.

What Heidegger says about the "one" and a man's relation to it is right in essential traits. It is also right that a man has to disengage himself from it in order to reach self-being. But something is lacking here, without which what is right in itself becomes wrong.

As we have seen, Heidegger secularizes the Single One of Kierkegaard, that is, he severs the relation to the absolute for which Kierkegaard's man becomes a Single One. And as we have seen, he does not replace this "for" with any other worldly and human "for." He ignores the decisive fact that only the man who has become a Single One, a self, a real person, is able to have a complete relation to his life to the other self, a relation which is not beneath but above the problematic of the relations between man and man, and which comprises, withstands and overcomes all this problematic situation. A *great* relation exists only between real persons. It can be strong as death, because it is stronger than solitude, because it breaches the barriers of a lofty solitude, subdues its strict law, and throws a bridge from self-being to self-being across the abyss of dread of the universe. It is true that the child says *Thou* before it learns to say *I*; but on the height of personal existence one must be truly able to say *I* in order to know the mystery of the *Thou* in its whole truth. The man who has become a Single One—even if we limit ourselves to immanence—is there *for* something : he has become "this Single One" for something, for the perfect realization of the *Thou*.

8

But is there on this level something corresponding to the essential *Thou* in the relation to the multitude of men, or is Heidegger here finally right?

What corresponds to the essential *Thou* on the level of self-being, in relation to a host of men, I call the essential *We*.[1]

The person who is the object of my mere solicitude is not a *Thou* but a *He* or a *She*. The nameless, faceless crowd in which I am entangled is not a *We* but the " one." But as there is a *Thou* so there is a *We*.

Here we have to do with a category essential for our consideration, which it is important to clarify. It cannot be straightway grasped from out of current sociological categories. It is true that a *We* can arise in every kind of group, but it cannot be understood from the life of any single one of the groups. By *We* I mean a community of several independent persons, who have reached a self and self-responsibility, the community resting on the basis of this self and self-responsibility, and being made possible by them. The special character of the *We* is shown in the essential relation existing, or arising temporarily, between its members; that is, in the holding sway within the *We* of an ontic directness which is the decisive presupposition of the *I-Thou* relation. The *We* includes the *Thou* potentially. Only men who are capable of truly saying *Thou* to one another can truly say *We* with one another.

As we have said, no particular kind of group-formation *as such* can be adduced as an example of the essential *We*, but in many of them the variety which is favourable to the arising of the *We* can be seen clearly enough. For example, in revolutionary groups we find a *We* most readily among those whose members make it their labour among the people to waken and teach quietly and slowly; in religious groups we find it among those who strive for an

[1] I shall not discuss in this connection the *primitive We*, to which the essential *We* is related in the same way as the essential *Thou* to the primitive *Thou*.

unemphatic and sacrificial realization of faith in life. In both cases it is enough to prevent the *We* arising, or being preserved, if a single man is accepted, who is greedy of power and uses others as means to his own end, or who craves for importance and makes a show of himself.

The essential *We* has hitherto been all too little recognized, both in history and in the present, because it is rare, and because group-formations have hitherto been considered mostly in respect of their energies and effects and not their inner structure—though the direction of the energy and the nature of the effects (even if not often their visible and measurable compass) depend most closely on the inner structure.

For more precise understanding I must point out that beside the constant forms of the essential *We* there are also transient forms, which nevertheless merit attention. Among these is to be reckoned, for example, the closer union which is formed for a few days among the genuine disciples and fellow-workers of a movement when an important leader dies. All impediments and difficulties between them are set aside, and a strange fruitfulness, or at all events incandescence, of their life with one another is established. Another transient form is seen when in face of a catastrophe which appears inevitable the really heroic element of a community gathers together within itself, withdraws from all idle talk and fuss, but in it each is open to the others and they anticipate, in a brief common life, the binding power of a common death.

But there are still other, remarkable structures which include men hitherto unknown to one another, and which are at least very close to the essential *We*. Such a structure can arise in, say, a terrorist régime, when adherents of an opinion which is opposed by the régime, hitherto strangers to one another, perceive that they are brothers and meet not as members of a party but in genuine community.

We can see that even in the sphere of the relation to a host of men there is an essential relation which takes up the man who has reached self-being—in fact, can truly take up no-one but him. Here only is the realm where a man is truly saved from the " one." A man is truly saved from the "one" not by separation but only by being bound up in genuine communion.

9

Let us now summarize our comparison of Kierkegaard's man and Heidegger's man.

In virtue of his nature and his situation man has a three-fold living relation. He can bring his nature and situation to full reality in his life if all his living relations become essential. And he can let elements of his nature and situation remain in unreality by letting only single living relations become essential, while considering and treating the others as unessential.

Man's threefold living relation is, first, his relation to the world and to things, second, his relation to men—both to individuals and to the many—third, his relation to the mystery of being—which is dimly apparent through all this but infinitely transcends it—which the philosopher calls the Absolute and the believer calls God, and which cannot in fact be eliminated from the situation even by a man who rejects both designations.

The relation to things is lacking in Kierkegaard, he knows things only as similes. In Heidegger it can be found only as a technical, purposive relation. But a purely technical relation cannot be an essential one, since it is not the whole being and whole reality of the thing one is related to which enter into the relation, but just its applicability to a definite aim, its technical suitability. An essential relation to things can only be a relation which regards them in their essential life and is turned towards them. The fact of art can only be understood in the connexion of an essential with a technical relation. Nor is it to the purpose even in an analysis of everyday existence that things should be present only as "gear." The technical is only what can be easily surveyed, easily explained, it is the co-ordinated. But besides, and in the midst of this, there is a manifold relation to things in their wholeness, their independence, and their purposelessness. The man

who gazes without purpose on a tree is no less " everyday "
than the one who looks at a tree to learn which branch
would make the best stick. The first way of looking belongs to the constitution of the " everyday " no less than
the second. (Besides, it can be shown that even genetically,
in human development, the technical does not come first
in time, and that what in its late form is called the
æsthetic does not come second.)

The relation to individual men is a doubtful thing to
Kierkegaard, because in his view an essential relation to
God is obstructed by an essential relation to human companions. In Heidegger the relation to individual men
appears only as a relation of solicitude. A relation of mere
solicitude cannot be essential; in an essential relation
which includes solicitude the essentiality is derived from
another realm which is lacking in Heidegger. An essential
relation to individual men can only be a direct relation
from life to life in which a man's reserve is resolved and
the barriers of his self-being are breached.

The connexion with the faceless, formless, nameless
many, with the " crowd," with the " one," appears in
Kierkegaard, and following him in Heidegger, as the preliminary situation which must be overcome for self-being
to be attained. In itself this is true; that nameless human
all and nothing in which we are immersed is in fact like a
negative womb from which we have to emerge in order to
come into the world as a self. But it is only one side of
the truth, and without the other side it becomes untrue.
The genuineness and adequacy of the self cannot stand
the test in self-commerce, but only in communication with
the whole of otherness, with the medley of the nameless
crowd. A genuine and adequate self also draws out the
spark of self-being wherever it touches the crowd, it makes
self be bound to self, it founds the opposition to the
" one." it founds the communion of individuals, it shapes
the form of community in the stuff of social life.

Man's third living relation is that which is called respec-
tively the relation to God or to the Absolute or to the
mystery. We have seen that this is the sole essential rela-

tion for Kierkegaard, while it is completely lacking in Heidegger.

The essential relation to God, which Kierkegaard means, presupposes, as we saw, a renunciation of every essential relation to anything else, to the world, to community, to the individual man. It can be understood as a subtraction which, reduced to a crude formula, appears this: Being − (World + Man) = Object (the object or partner of the essential relation); it comes into existence by leaving out everything except God and myself. But a God reached only by renunciation of the relation to the whole being cannot be the God of the whole being whom Kierkegaard means, cannot be the God who has made and preserves and holds together all that is. Though the history of creation which is left to its own resources may be called separation, the goal of the way can only be communion, and no essential relation to this God can stand outside this goal. The God of Kierkegaard can only be either a demiurge outgrown by and suffering from his creation, or a saviour who is a stranger to creation, approaching it from without and taking pity on it. Both are gnostic figures. Of the three great Christian philosophers of solitude, Augustine, Pascal and Kierkegaard, the first is thoroughly conditioned by gnosticism, the presuppositions of the last touch on it—obviously without his knowing it —and only Pascal has nothing to do with it, perhaps because he comes by way of science and never abandons it, and because science can come to terms with faith but not with gnosis, which itself claims to be the true science.

Heidegger's philosophical secularization of Kierkegaard had to abandon the religious conception of a bond of the self with the Absolute, a bond in real mutual relation of person with person. But neither does it know any other form of a bond between the self and the Absolute or between the self and the dimly apparent mystery of being. The Absolute has its place in Heidegger's philosophy only in the sphere to which the self penetrates in its relation to itself, that is, where the question about the entry into a *connexion* with it ceases to be asked. Heidegger, influenced by Hölderlin, the great poet of this mystery, has undoubtedly had a profound experience of the mystery of being which is dimly apparent through all that is; but he has not experienced it as one which steps before us and challenges us to yield the last thing, so hard fought for, the being at rest in one's own self, to breach the barriers of the self and to come out from ourselves to meet with essential otherness.

Besides man's threefold living relation there is one other, that to one's own self. This relation, however, unlike the others, cannot be regarded as one that is real as such, since the necessary presupposition of a real duality is lacking. Hence it cannot in reality be raised to the level of an essential living relation. This is expressed in the fact that every essential living relation has reached its completion and transfiguration, that to things in art, that to men in love, that to the mystery of religious manifestation, while man's relation to his own life and his own self has not reached, and obviously cannot reach, such a completion and transfiguration. (It could perhaps be maintained that lyric poetry is such a completion and transfiguration of man's relation to his own self. But it is rather the tremendous refusal of the soul to be satisfied with self-commerce. Poetry is the soul's announcement that even when it is alone with itself on the narrowest ridge it is thinking not of itself but of the Being which is not itself, and that this Being which is not itself is visiting it there, perplexing and blessing it.)

For Kierkegaard this relation is given meaning and is consecrated by the relation to God. For Heidegger it is essential in itself and it is the only essential relation. That means, that man can attain to his real life only as a system which in respect of his essential relation is a closed system. In contrast to this, the anthropological view which considers man in his connexion with being must regard this connexion as supremely realizable only in an open system. Connexion can mean only connexion with the integrality of his human situation. Neither the world of things, nor his fellow-man and community, nor the mystery which points beyond these, and also beyond himself, can be dismissed from a man's situation. Man can attain to existence only if his whole relation to his situation becomes existence, that is, if every kind of living relation becomes essential.

The question what man is cannot be answered by a consideration of existence or of self-being as such, but only by a consideration of the essential connexion of the human person and his relations with all being. Consideration of existence or self-being as such yields only the concept and outline of an almost ghostly spiritual being, that possesses, indeed, bodily contents of its basic sensations, its dread of the universe, its anxiety about existence, its feeling of primal guilt, yet possesses even these in a way that has nothing to do with the body. This spiritual being lurks in man, lives its life and settles the accounts of this life with itself; but it is not man, and our question is about man. If we try to grasp man on the far side of his essential connexion with the rest of being then we understand him, as Nietzsche does, to be a degenerate animal, or, as Heidegger does, to be a separated spiritual being. Only when we try to understand the human person in his whole situation, in the possibilities of his relation to all that is not himself, do we understand man. Man is to be understood as the being who is capable of the threefold living relation and can raise every form of it to essentiality.

10

"No age," writes Heidegger in his *Kant and the Problem of Metaphysics*, "has known so much, and so many different things, about man as ours. . . . And no age has known less than ours of what man is." In his book *Being and Time* he has tried to give us a knowledge of man by the analysis of his relation to his own being. This analysis he did in fact give, on the basis of a separation of this relation from all other essential human relations. But in this way one does not learn what man is, but only what the edge of man is. One can also say, one learns what man is on the edge—the man who has reached the edge of being. When I read Kierkegaard in my youth, I regarded Kierkegaard's man as the man on the edge. But Heidegger's man is a great and decisive step out from Kierkegaard in the direction of the edge where *nothing* begins.

III : *The Doctrine of Scheler*

I

THE second significant attempt of our time to treat the problem of man as an independent philosophical problem has likewise come from the school of Husserl : it is the "anthropology" of Scheler.

Scheler, indeed, did not complete his work on this subject, but what has been published of articles and addresses on anthropology, by himself and posthumously, is sufficient to show us his point of view and to make it possible for us to form a judgment.

Scheler expresses clearly the situation in our time from which anthropology starts. "We are the first epoch in which man has become fully and thoroughly 'problematic' to himself; in which he no longer knows what he essentially is, but at the same time also *knows* that he does not know." It is now a case of beginning, in this situation of his extreme problematic condition, with the systematic comprehension of what he is (*Wesen*). Scheler, unlike Heidegger, refuses to abstract from the concreteness of the whole man present to him and to consider his " existence " (*Dasein*), namely his relation to his being (*Sein*), as what is metaphysically the only essential. He has to do with the sheer concreteness of man, i.e. he wants to treat what on his understanding divides man from other living creatures only in connexion with what he has in common with them; and he wants to treat it in such a way that it may be recognizable precisely in relation to what is common, by its standing out in its specific character from what is common.

For such a treatment, as Scheler rightly recognizes, the history of anthropological thought in the widest sense, both the philosophical and the pre-philosophical and extra-philosophical, that is, the "history of man's consciousness of himself," can have only an introductory significance. By means of discussion of all "mystical, religious, theological and philosophical theories of man" freedom must be won from all theories. "Only," says Scheler, "by being willing to make a complete *tabula rasa* of all traditions about this question, and by learning to look in extreme methodical aloofness and astonishment on the being called man, can we reach tenable insights again."

That is indeed the real, genuine philosophical method, and is especially to be recommended in face of a subject that has become so problematic as this. All philosophical discovery is the uncovering of what is covered by the veil woven from the threads of a thousand theories. Without such an uncovering we shall not be able to master the problem of man at this late hour. But we have to investigate whether Scheler employs with all strictness in his anthropological thought the method which he sets forth. We shall see that he does not. If Heidegger considers instead of the real man only a metaphysical essence and composition, a metaphysical homunculus, Scheler lets his consideration of the real man be permeated by a metaphysic, and moreover one which, though independently achieved and of independent value, is deeply influenced by Hegel and Nietzsche, however much it seeks to rid itself of these influences. But a metaphysic which permeates the consideration in this way can no less than all anthropological theories prevent the glance being directed "in extreme aloofness and astonishment on the being called man."

Of the two named influences it must be said that Scheler's earlier anthropological writings are more determined by Nietzsche, the later more by Hegel. Scheler has followed both, as we shall see, in his over-estimation of the significance of time for the absolute. Nietzsche admittedly wishes to know nothing of the absolute itself, all idea of absoluteness is for him—not essentially different than for

Feuerbach—merely a game and a projection of man. But in wanting to find the *meaning* of human life in its transition to a "superman" he establishes so to speak a relative absolute, and this no longer has its content in a supra-temporal being but only in becoming, in time. But for Hegel, at whom Scheler arrives by way of Nietzsche, the absolute itself attains complete and final realization of its own being and consciousness only in man and his perfection. Hegel sees the substance of the universal spirit in its "producing itself," in its "knowing and realizing itself and its truth" in an "absolute process," "step by step," culminating in history. Scheler's metaphysic—which has essentially determined his anthropology in its later form —is to be understood from this starting-point, in the doctrine, namely, of the "ground of things," which "is realized in the temporal course of the world-process," and about the human self as "the only place of the becoming of God which is accessible to us and at the same time a true part of the process of this becoming of God"; so that the becoming is dependent on it and it on the becoming. The absolute, or God, is thereby far more radically than with Hegel introduced into time and made dependent on it. God is not, but he is becoming; thus he is inserted into time, in fact he is its product. And even if there is, in passing, talk about a supra-temporal being which only manifests itself in time, for such a being there is no genuine place in a doctrine of a God who is becoming. There is in truth no other being but that of time, in which the becoming takes place.

This basic assumption of Scheler's metaphysic must, however, by no means be confused with Heidegger's teaching about time as the essence of human existence and thereby of existence in general. Heidegger relates only existence to time and does not overstep the boundary of existence. But Scheler lets being itself be resolved in time. Heidegger is silent about eternity, in which perfection *is*; Scheler denies this eternity.

2

Scheler reached this later metaphysic of his after a Catholic period in which he confessed a theism. All theism is a variety of that conception of eternity for which time can signify only the manifestation and effect but not the origin and development of a perfect being. Heidegger comes from the neighbouring Protestant realm of the same Christian theism. But he only draws a line between himself and theism, Scheler breaks with it.

I wish to insert a personal recollection here, for it seems to me to have a significance that goes beyond the personal. Since my own thoughts over the last things reached, in the first world war, a decisive turning-point, I have occasionally described my standpoint to my friends as the "narrow ridge." I wanted by this to express that I did not rest on the broad upland of a system that includes a series of sure statements about the absolute, but on a narrow rocky ridge between the gulfs where there is no sureness of expressible knowledge but the certainty of meeting what remains, undisclosed. When I met Scheler a few years after the war, after we had not seen one another for some time—he had at that time completed that break with the church's thought, without my knowing—he surprised me by saying, "I have come very near your narrow ridge." In the first moment I was nonplussed, for if there was anything I did not expect from Scheler it was the giving up of the supposed knowledge about the ground of being. But in the next moment I answered, "But it is not where you think it is." For in the meantime I had understood that Scheler did not really mean that standpoint which I had then, and have had since then; he confused it with a point of view which I had cherished and upheld for a long time, and which indeed was not far from his new philosophy of the becoming God. Since 1900 I had first been under the influence of German mysticism from Meister Eckhart to Angelus Silesius, according to which the primal ground (*Urgrund*) of being, the nameless, impersonal godhead, comes to "birth" in the human soul; then

I had been under the influence of the later Kabbala and of Hasidism, according to which man has the power to unite the God who is over the world with his *shekinah* dwelling in the world. In this way there arose in me the thought of a realization of God through man; man appeared to me as the being through whose existence the Absolute, resting in its truth, can gain the character of reality. It was this point of view of mine which Scheler meant in his remark; he saw me as still holding it; but it had long since been destroyed in me. He on the other hand surpassed it by his idea of a "becoming of God." But he too had had a decisive experience during the war, which for him was translated into a conviction of the original and essential powerlessness of the spirit.

3

Primal and present being, the world's ground, has according to Scheler two attributes, spirit and impulse. In this connexion one thinks of Spinoza; but with him the two attributes are two of infinitely many, the two which we know. For Scheler the life of absolute being consists in this duality. Further, with Spinoza the two attributes of thought and extension stand to one another in a relation of perfect unity; they correspond to and complete one another. With Scheler the attributes of spirit and impulse stand in a primal tension with one another which is fought out and resolved in the world process. In other words, Spinoza grounds his attributes in an eternal unity which infinitely transcends the world and time; Scheler—in fact though not explicitly—limits being to time and the world process which takes place in time. With Spinoza, when we turn from the world to what is not the world, we have the feeling of an incomprehensible and over-mastering fulness; with Scheler, when we do this, we have the feeling of a meagre abstraction, even a feeling of emptiness. Scheler, who speaks in his lecture on Spinoza of the " air of eternity of the very godhead," which the reader of Spinoza breathes in " in deepest draughts," no longer gives his own reader this air to breathe. In truth the man of our time scarcely knows with living knowledge anything of an eternity which bears and swallows all time as the sea a fleeting wave; though even to him a way to eternal being still stands open, in the content of eternity of each moment into which the whole existence is put and lived.

But in still another important point Scheler differs from Spinoza. He does not, like Spinoza, give the second of his attributes a static denomination, like extension, corporeal or material nature, but the dynamic denomination *impulse*. That is, he substitutes for Spinoza's attributes Schopenhauer's two fundamental principles, the will, which he terms impulse, and the idea, which he terms spirit.

4

With regard to the attribute of spirit in the ground of being, Scheler asserts, in an incidental remark which acquires essential significance for the understanding of his thought, that it is also possible to term this attribute the godhead, *deitas*, in the ground of being. The godhead is thus for him not the world's ground itself, but only one of two opposed principles within it. Moreover it is that of the two which possesses " as spiritual being no kind of original power or force " and hence is not able to exert any kind of positive creative effect. Over against it stands the " almighty " impulse, the world fantasy which is charged with infinitely many images and lets them grow to reality, but in its origin is blind to spiritual ideas and values. In order to realize the godhead with the wealth of ideas and values that are latent in it the world's ground must " lift the brakes " of the impulse, must release it and set the world-process on its course. But since the spirit has no energy of its own it can influence the world-process only by holding ideas and meaning before the primal powers, the life-impulses, and guiding and sublimating them till in ever higher ascent spirit and impulse penetrate one another, impulse being given spirit and spirit being given life. The decisive place of this event is the living being " in which the primal being begins to know and comprehend itself, to understand and to redeem itself," and in which " the relative becoming of God "—namely, man—begins. " Being in itself becomes a being worthy to be called divine existence only to the extent that it realizes, in and through man, the eternal *dietas* in the impulse of world-history."

This dualism, fed on Schopenhauer's philosophy, goes back to the gnostic idea of two primal gods, a lower, related to matter, who creates the world, and a higher, purely spiritual god who redeems the world. Only, in Scheler's thought the two have become attributes of the one world's ground. This cannot be termed a god, since it contains a godhead only alongside a non-divine principle and is only destined to become a god. But it appears to us as much like a man as any kind of divine image, as the transfigured likeness of a modern man. In this man the sphere of the spirit and the sphere of impulse have fallen apart more markedly than ever before. He perceives with apprehension that an unfruitful and powerless remoteness from life is threatening the separated spirit, and he perceives with horror that the repressed and banished impulses are threatening to destroy his soul. His great anxiety is to reach unity, a feeling of unity and an expression of unity, and in deep self-concern he ponders on the way. He believes he finds it by giving his impulses their head, and he expects his spirit to guide their working. It is a misleading way, for the spirit as it is here can indeed hold ideas and values before, but can no longer make them credible to, the impulses. Nevertheless, this man and his way have found their transfiguration in Scheler's " world's ground."

5

Scheler's idea of the world's ground shows, behind the philosophical influences it has received, an origin in the constitution of the modern soul. This origin has introduced into it a deep and insoluble contradiction. Scheler's basic thesis, which is very understandable from the spirit's experiences in our time, affirms that the spirit in its pure form is simply without any power at all. He comes across this powerless spirit present in primal being itself as its attribute. Thereby he makes an empirically *developed* powerlessness which he comes across into one primally existing. But it is an inner contradiction of his conception of the world's ground that in this the spirit is in origin powerless. The world's ground "releases" the impulse in order that it may produce the world, in order, that is, that the spirit may be realized in the history of this world. But by what force did the world's ground bind its impulse and by what force does it now release it? By what other than that of the one of its two attributes which seeks for realization, that of the *deitas,* of the spirit? The impulse cannot itself yield the power to keep itself bound, and if it is to be released this can only happen by the same power which is so superior to its power that it could keep it bound. Scheler's conception of the world's ground demands in fact an original preponderant power of the spirit—a power so great that it is able to bind and to release all the motive-force from which the world proceeds.

It may be objected that this is not a positive creative power of its own. But this objection rests on a confusion of power and force—a compulsion which, indeed, Scheler himself makes many times. Concepts are formed from our highest experiences of a certain kind, which we recognize as being repeated. But our highest experiences of power are not those of a force which produces a direct change, but those of a capacity to set these forces directly or indirectly in motion. Whether we use the positive expression "to set in motion" or the negative expression "to release" is irrelevant. Scheler's choice of words veils the fact that even in his world's ground the spirit has the power to set the forces in motion.

6

Scheler asserts that in the face of his thesis of an original powerlessness of the spirit the thought of a " creation of the world from nothing " falls to the ground. He means, of course, the biblical story of the creation, for which a later theology has coined the misleading description of a creation from nothing. The biblical story does not know the idea of " nothing," an idea which would harm the mystery of the " beginning." The Babylonian epic of the creation of the world makes the god Marduk strike amazement into the assembly of the gods by causing a garment to rise up out of nothing; such magic tricks are alien to the biblical story of the creation. What it at the very beginning calls " to create " heaven and earth—in a word that originally means " to hew out "—is left wholly in mystery, in a process taking place within the godhead. This process is described falsely by later theology in the language of bad philosophy, but gnosis draws it out of mystery into the world and thereby subdues the alogical to the logic which reigns in the world as such. After this beginning there is a " spirit "—which is, indeed, something quite different from a " spiritual being," namely, the source of all motion, of all spiritual and natural motion—upon the face of the " waters " which are obviously charged with germinal forces, since they can make living beings " swarm forth " from them. The creation by the Word which is reported is not to be separated from the effect of the spirit which sets the forces in motion. Forces are set going, and the spirit has the power over them.

Scheler's " world's ground," too, is only one of the countless gnostic attempts to strip the mystery from the biblical God.

7

But let us return from the world's origin to its existence, from the divine spirit to our own which is known to us in our experience. What about this?

In man, says Scheler, the spiritual attribute of present being itself is becoming manifest " in the unity of concentration of the person gathering himself to himself." On the ladder of becoming, primal present being, in the building-up of the world, is always more and more bent back on itself, "in order to become aware of itself on ever higher levels and in ever new dimensions, in order finally to possess and to comprehend itself wholly in man." But the human spirit, in which this Hegelian ladder culminates, is, precisely as spirit, in its origin without any power. It acquires power only by letting itself "be supplied with energy" by the life-instincts, i.e. by man's sublimating his instinctive energy to spiritual capacity. Scheler depicts this process in this way: first the spirit guides the will by instilling into it the ideas and values which are to be realized; then the will as it were starves out the impulses of the instinctive life by mediating to them the conceptions they would use in order to attain to an instinctive *action*; finally the will places "the conceptions, appropriate to the ideas and values," "before the waiting instincts" "like bait before their eyes," until they execute the project of will set by the spirit.

Is the man of whose inner life this presentation—based on the concept of modern psycho-analysis—is given, really *man*? Or is it not rather a certain kind of man, namely that in which the sphere of the spirit and the sphere of the instincts have been made so separate and independent from one another that the spirit from its height can bring before the instincts the fascinating magnificence of ideas, as in gnostic lore the daughters of light appear to the mighty princes of the planets in order to make them burn in love and lose the force of their light?

8

Scheler's description may fit many who are ascetics by a decision of the will and who have reached contemplation by way of asceticism. But the existential asceticism of so many great philosophers is not to be understood as the spirit in them depriving the instincts of life-energy, or having it conveyed into itself. This asceticism is rather to be understood in terms of a high measure of concentrated power having been allotted, and an unqualified mastery lent, to thought in the primal constitution of their life. What happens in them between the spirit and the instincts is not, as with Scheler's man, a struggle conducted from the side of the spirit by great strategical and peda-gogic means, against which the instincts offer a resistance which is first violent and is then gradually overcome. But what happens is, as it were, the two-sided carrying-out of an original contract which assures to the spirit unassail-able mastery and which the instincts now fulfil—in indi-vidual instances grudgingly but in most actually with pleasure.

But the ascetic type of man is not, as seems to Scheler, *the* basic type of spiritual man. This is shown most clearly of all in the realm of art. If you try to understand a man like Rembrandt or Shakespere or Mozart with this type as your starting-point, you will notice that it is pre-cisely the mark of artistic genius that it does not need to be ascetic in its being. It too will have constantly to carry out ascetic acts of denial, of renunciation, of inner trans-formation; but the real conduct of its spiritual life is not based on asceticism. There is here no endless negotiation between spirit and instincts; the instincts listen to the spirit, so as not to lose connexion with the ideas, and the spirit listens to the instincts so as not to lose connexion with the primal powers. Certainly the inner life of these men does not run in a smooth harmony; in fact it is pre-cisely they who know, as scarcely any other, the dæmonic realm of conflict. But it is a mistaken and misleading implication to identify the dæmons with the instincts; they often have a purely spiritual face. The true negotiations and decisions take place, in the life of these and in general of great men, not between spirit and instincts but between spirit and spirit, between instincts and instincts, between one product of spirit and instinct and another product of spirit and instinct. The drama of a great life cannot be reduced to the duality of spirit and instinct.

It is altogether precarious to want to show, as Scheler does, the being of man and of his spirit on the basis of the philosopher-type, his qualities and experiences. The philosopher is an immensely important human type, but he represents a remarkable exceptional case of the spiritual life rather than its basic form. But even he is not to be understood on the basis of that duality.

9

Scheler wishes to represent to us, in the act of forming ideas, the particular nature of the spirit as a specific good of man, in distinction from technical intelligence which he shares with the animals. He gives this example.

A man has a pain in his arm. The intelligence asks how it has arisen and how it can be removed, and answers the question with the help of science. But the spirit takes the same pain as an example of that character of existence, namely, that the world is shot through with pain, it asks about the nature of pain itself and from there it goes on to ask what the ground of things must be like, that something like pain should be possible at all. That is, man's spirit abolishes the character of reality of the empirical pain which the man has felt. Moreover, the spirit does not merely exclude, as Husserl supposed, the judgment about the actuality of the pain and treat it according to its nature, but it removes " experimentally " the whole impression of reality, it carries out the " basically ascetic act by which reality is stripped off " and thus rises above the pain-tormented impulse of life.

I contest, even in respect of the philosopher, so far as he takes the discovery of a mode of being as the starting-point of his thought, whether the decisive act of forming ideas is of this character. The nature of pain is not recognized by the spirit as it were standing at a distance from it, sitting in a box and watching the drama of pain as an unreal example. The man whose spirit does this may have all sorts of brilliant thoughts about pain, but he will not recognize the nature of pain. This is recognized by pain being discovered in very fact. That is, the spirit does not remain outside and strip off reality, it casts itself into the depths of this real pain, takes up its abode in the pain, gives itself over to the pain, permeates it with spirit, and the pain itself in such nearness as it were discloses itself to him. The recognition does not happen by the stripping off of reality but by the penetration into this definite reality, a penetration of such a kind that the nature of pain is exposed in the heart of this reality. Such a penetration we call spiritual.

The first question is therefore not, as Scheler supposes, " What then really is *pain itself* apart from the fact that *I* feel it *here now*?" There is no " apart from " this fact. The nature of pain is disclosed to me by this very pain that I have here now, its being mine, its being now, its being here, its defined and particular being, the perfected presence of this pain. Under the penetrating touch of the spirit the pain itself as it were communicates with the spirit in dæmonic speech. Pain—and every real happening of the soul—is to be compared not with a drama but with those early mysteries whose meaning no-one learns who does not himself join in the dance. The spirit translates out of the dæmonic speech, which it learned in intimate touch with the pain, into the speech of ideas. It is this translation which takes place in a differentiation and removal from the object. "Contemplating" thought is with the philosopher too, so far as he is really empowered by the being of the world to proclaim it, not first but second.

The first thing is the discovery of a mode of being in communion with it, and this discovery is pre-eminently a spiritual act. Every philosophical idea springs from such a discovery. Only a man who has communicated in his spirit with the pain of the world in the ultimate depth of his own pain, without any kind of " apart from," is able to recognize the nature of pain. But for him to be able to do this there is a presupposition, that he has already really learned the depth of the pain of other lives—and that means, not with " sympathy," which does not press forward to being, but with great love. Only then does his own pain in its ultimate depth light a way into the suffering of the world. Only participation in the existence of living beings discloses the meaning in the ground of one's own being.

10

But to learn more precisely what spirit is we must not be content with investigating it where it has reached expression in achievement and a calling. It must also be sought out where it is still a *happening*. For the spirit in its original reality is not something that is but something that happens; more precisely, it is something that is not expected but suddenly happens.

Consider a child, especially at the age when it has absorbed speech but not yet the accumulated wealth of tradition in the language. It lives with things in the world of things, with what we adults also know and also with what we no longer know, what has been scared away from us by the wealth of tradition, by concepts, by all that is sure and stable. And suddenly the child begins to speak, it tells its story, falls silent, again something bursts out. How does the child tell what it tells? The only correct designation is *mythically*. It tells precisely as early man tells his myths which have become an inseparable unity composed from dream and waking sight, from experience and "fantasy" (but is fantasy not originally also a kind of experience?). Then suddenly the spirit is there. But without any preceding "asceticism" and "sublimation." Of course the spirit was in the child before it tells its story; but not as such, not for itself, but bound up with "instinct"—and with things. Now the spirit steps forth itself, independently—in the *word*. The child "has spirit" for the first time when it speaks; it has spirit because it wants to speak. Before it now speaks the mythical images were not there separately but inserted and mingled into the substance of life. But now they are there—in the word. Only because the child has the *spiritual instinct* to the word do these images come forward now, and at the same time become independent: they exist and can be spoken. The spirit begins here as an instinct, as an instinct to the word, that is, as the impulse to be present with others in a world of streaming communication, of an image given and received.

Or consider a typical peasant, as he still exists, although the social and cultural conditions for his existence seem to have disappeared. I mean a peasant who all his life seemed able to think only purposively and technically, who bore in mind only what he needed for his work and the immediate condition of his life. But now he begins to age, to have to make an effort to carry out his job. And then it happens that on his day off he can be seen standing there staring into the clouds, and if he is asked he replies, after a while, that he has been studying the weather and you see that it is not true. At the same time he can occasionally be seen with his mouth quite unexpectedly opening—to utter a saying. Before this he had of course uttered sayings, but traditional and known ones, which were mostly humorously pessimistic utterances about " the way of things." He still utters the same kind now, and preferably if something has gone amiss, if he has experienced the " contraryness " of things (which Scheler takes as the fundamental nature of all experience of the world), that is, if he has once more experienced the contradiction which reigns in the world. But now he makes, time and again, remarks of a quite different kind, such as were not heard from him earlier, and unknown to tradition. And he utters them staring ahead, often only whispering as though to himself, they can barely be caught : he is uttering his own insights. He does not do this when he has experienced the contrariness of things, but for example when the ploughshare has sunk softly and deeply into the soil as though the furrows were deliberately opening to receive it, or when the cow has been quickly and easily delivered of her calf as though an invisible power were helping. That is, he utters his own insights if he has experienced the *grace* of things, if he has once again experienced despite all contrariness that man participates in the being of the world. Certainly the experience of grace is only made possible by the experience

of contrariness and in contrast to it. But here too it holds
true that the spirit arises from concord with things and in
concord with instincts.

II

In his first anthropological treatise, written during his
theistic period, Scheler makes true man begin with the
"God-seeker." Between the beast and *homo faber*, the
maker of tools and machines, there exists only a difference
of degree. But between *homo faber* and the man who
begins to go out beyond himself and to seek God there
exists a difference of kind. In his last anthropological
works, whose underlying position is no longer theism but
that idea of a becoming God, the philosopher takes the
place of the religious man. Between *homo faber* and the
beast, so Scheler expounds here, there exists no difference
of kind, for intelligence and the power of choice belong
also to the beast. Man's special position is established by
means of the principle of spirit as absolutely superior to all
intelligence and standing altogether outside all that we call
life. Man as a being in the order of living things is
"without any doubt a cul-de-sac of nature," while "as a
potential spiritual being" he is "the bright and glorious
way *out* of this cul-de-sac." Man is therefore "not a static
being, not a fact, but only a potential direction of a
process."

That is almost exactly the same as Nietzsche says about
man, except that here the "spirit" takes the place of
Nietzsche's "will to power" which makes man into real
man. But the basic definition of a "spiritual" being is for
Scheler his existential separability from the organic, from
"life" and all that belongs to life. To a certain extent—
with the essential limitations I have formulated above—
this is true of the philosopher; it is not true of the spiritual
existence of man in general, and especially it is not true of
spirit as a happening. In his early and in his later work
Scheler draws two different lines of division through mankind, but both are inadmissible and full of self-contradic-

tion. If the religious man is something different from the existential actuation of all that lives in the "non-religious" man as dumb need, as stammering dereliction, as despair crying out, then he is a monster. Man does not begin where God is sought, but where God's farness means suffering without the knowledge of what is causing it. And a "spiritual" man, in whom a spirit dwells which is not found anywhere else, and which understands the art of cutting itself free from all life, is only a curiosity. If the spirit as a calling wants to be in its essence something different from the spirit as a happening then it is no longer the true spirit but an artificial product usurping the spirit's place. The spirit is inserted in sparks into the life of all, it bursts out in flames from the life of the most living man, and from time to time there burns somewhere a great fire of the spirit. All this is of *one* being and *one* substance. There is no other spirit but that which is nourished by the unity of life and by unity with the world. Certainly it experiences being separated from the unity of life and being thrown into abysmal contradiction to the world. But even in the martyrdom of spiritual existence true spirit does not deny its primal community with the whole of being; rather it asserts it against the false representatives of being who deny it.

12

The spirit *as a happening*, the spirit I have indicated in the child and the peasant, proves to us that it is not inherent in spirit, as Scheler contends, to arise by repression and sublimation of the instincts. Scheler, as is well-known, takes these psychological categories from Sigmund Freud's ideas, among whose greatest services is that he has formed them. But though these categories have general validity, the central position which Freud gives them, their dominating significance for the whole structure of personal and communal life, and especially for the origin and development of the spirit, is not based on the general life of man but only on the situation and qualities of the typical man of to-day. But this man is sick, both in his relation to others and in his very soul The central significance of repression and sublimation in Freud's system derives from analysis of a pathological condition and is valid for this condition. The categories are psychological, their dominating power is pathopsychological. It can, indeed, be shown that nevertheless their significance is valid not only for our time but also for others akin to it, that is, for times of a pathological condition similar to our own, times like our own when a crisis is arising. But I know no such deep-reaching and comprehensive crisis in history as ours, and that indicates the extent of the significance of those categories. If I were to express our crisis in a formula I should like to call it the crisis of confidence. We have seen how epochs of security of human existence in the cosmos alternate with epochs of insecurity; but in the latter there still reigns for the most part a *social* certainty, one is borne along by a small organic community living in real togetherness. Being able to have confidence within this community compensates for cosmic insecurity; there is connexion and certainty. Where confidence reigns man must often, indeed, adapt his wishes to the commands of his community; but he must not repress them to such an extent that the repression acquires a dominating significance for his life. They often coalesce with the needs of the community, which are expressed by its commands. This coalescence, indeed, can really take place only where everything really lives with everything within the community, where, that is to say, there reigns not an enjoined and imagined but a genuine and elementary confidence. Only if the organic community disintegrates from within and mistrust becomes life's basic note does the repression acquire its dominating importance. The unaffectedness of wishing is stifled by mistrust, everything around is hostile or can become hostile, agreement between one's own and the other's desire ceases, for there is no true coalescence or reconciliation with what is necessary to a sustaining community, and the dulled wishes creep hopelessly into the recesses of the soul. But now the ways of the spirit are also changed. Hitherto it was the characteristic

of its origin to flash forth from the clouds as the concentrated manifestation of the wholeness of man. Now there
is no longer a human wholeness with the force and the
courage to manifest itself. For spirit to arise the energy
of the repressed instincts must mostly first be "sub-
limated," the traces of its origin cling to the spirit and it
can mostly assert itself against the instincts only by convulsive alienation. The divorce between spirit and instincts
is here, as often, the consequence of the divorce between
man and man.

13

In opposition to Scheler's conception it must be said of
the spirit that in its beginning it is pure power, namely
man's power to grasp the world, from inner participation
in it and from strict and close struggle with it, in picture
and sound and idea. First comes man's intimate participation in the world, intimate with it in strife as in peace.
Here the spirit as a separate being is not yet present, but
it is contained in the force of the primitively concentrated
participation. Only with the tremendous impulse not
merely to perceive the world in wrestling or in playing
with it, but also to grasp it; only with the passion to
bind the experienced chaos to the cosmos, does the spirit
arise as a separate being. The picture emerges distinctly
from the wild flickering light, the sound from the wild
tumult of the earth, the idea from the wild confusion of all
things : in this way the spirit arises as spirit. But there
cannot be imagined any primal stage of the spirit in which
it does not wish to express itself : the picture itself strives
to be painted on the roof of a cave, and the reddle is at
hand, the sound strives to be sung, and the lips are opening
in a magic song. Chaos is subdued by form. But form
wishes to be perceived by others besides him who produced it : the picture is shown with passion, the singer
sings to the listeners with passion. The impulse to form
is not to be divorced from the impulse to the word. From
participation in the world man reaches participation in

souls. The world is bound up, and given order; it can be spoken between man and man, now for the first time it becomes a world between man and man. And again the spirit is pure power; with gesture and words the man of the spirit subdues the resistance of the friends of chaos and gives order to community. The powerlessness of the spirit which Scheler considers to be original is always an accompanying circumstance of the disintegration of community. The world is no longer received, it no longer binds and orders what is human, participation in souls is forbidden to the spirit and it turns aside and cuts free from the unity of life, it flees to its citadel, the citadel of the brain. Hitherto man thought with his whole body to the very finger-tips; from now on he thinks only with his brain. Only now does Freud receive the object of his psychology and Scheler the object of his anthropology— the sick man, cut off from the world and divided into spirit and instincts. So long as we suppose that this sick man is *man*, the normal man, man in general, we shall not heal him.

Here I must break off the presentation and criticism of Scheler's anthropology. In a genetic study it would remain to be shown that the essential difference between man and beast, the difference which establishes the essential life of man, is not his separation from instinctive connexion with things and living beings but on the contrary his different and new way of turning to things and living beings. It would remain to be shown that the primary relation is not the technical relation common to man and beast, above which man then rises, but that man's specific primitive technique, the invention of independent tools suited to their purpose and able to be used again and again, has become possible only through man's new relation to things as to something that is inspected, is independent, and lasting. It would further remain to be shown that in the same way in relation with other men the original and defining characteristic is not the instinctive in general, above which man only later rises in the struggle of the spirit with a turning to men as persons who are there, apart from my need, independent and lasting, and that the origin of speech is to be understood only on the basis of such a turning to others. Here as there a unity of spirit and instinct and a formation of new spiritual instincts obviously stand at the beginning. And here as there man's essential life is not to be grasped from what unrolls in the individual's inner life nor from the consciousness of one's own self, which Scheler takes to be the decisive difference between man and beast, but from the distinctiveness of his relation to things and to living beings.

IV : *Prospect*

IN two significant modern attempts we have seen that an individualistic anthropology, an anthropology which is substantially concerned only with the relation of the human person to himself, with the relation within this person between the spirit and its instincts, and so on, cannot lead to a knowledge of man's being. Kant's question *What is man?* whose history and effects I have discussed in the first part of this work, can never be answered on the basis of a consideration of the human person as such, but (so far as an answer is possible at all) only on the basis of a consideration of it in the wholeness of its essential relations to what is. Only the man who realizes in his whole life with his whole being the relations possible to him helps us to know man truly. And since, as we have seen, the depths of the question about man's being are revealed only to the man who has become solitary, the way to the answer lies through the man who overcomes his solitude without forfeiting its questioning power. This means that a *new* task in life is set to human thought here, a task that is new in its context of *life*. For it means that the man who wants to grasp what he himself is, salvages the tension of solitude and its burning problematic for a life with his world, a life that is renewed in spite of all, and out of this new situation proceeds with his thinking. Of course this presupposes the beginning of a new process of overcoming the solitude—despite all the vast difficulties—by reference to which that special task of thought can be perceived and expressed. It is obvious that at the present stage reached by mankind such a process cannot be effected by the spirit alone; but to a certain extent knowledge will also be able to further it. It is incumbent on us to clarify this in outline.

Criticism of the individualistic method starts usually from the standpoint of the collectivist tendency. But if individualism understands only a part of man, collectivism understands man only as a part : neither advances to the wholeness of man, to man as a whole. Individualism sees man only in relation to himself, but collectivism does not see *man* at all, it sees only " society." With the former man's face is distorted, with the latter it is masked.

Both views of life—modern individualism and modern collectivism—however different their causes may be, are essentially the conclusion or expression of the same human condition, only at different stages. This condition is characterized by the union of cosmic and social homelessness, dread of the universe and dread of life, resulting in an existential constitution of solitude such as has probably never existed before to the same extent. The human person feels himself to be a man exposed by nature—as an unwanted child is exposed—and at the same time a person isolated in the midst of the tumultuous human world. The first reaction of the spirit to the awareness of this new and uncanny position is modern individualism, the second is modern collectivism.

In individualism the human being ventures to affirm this position, to plunge it into an affirmative reflexion, a universal *amor fati*; he wants to build the citadel of a life-system in which the idea asserts that it wills reality as it is. Just because man is exposed by nature, he is an individual in this specially radical way in which no other being in the world is an individual; and he accepts his exposure because it means that he is an individual. In the same way he accepts his isolation as a person, for only a monad which is not bound to others can know and glorify itself as an individual to the utmost. To save himself from the despair with which his solitary state threatens him, man resorts to the expedient of glorifying it. Modern individualism has essentially an imaginary basis. It founders on this character, for imagination is not capable of actually conquering the given situation.

The second reaction, collectivism, essentially follows upon the foundering of the first. Here the human being tries to escape his destiny of solitude by becoming completely embedded in one of the massive modern group formations. The more massive, unbroken and powerful in its achievements this is, the more the man is able to feel that he is saved from both forms of homelessness, the social and the cosmic. There is obviously no further reason for dread of life, since one needs only to fit oneself into the "general will" and let one's own responsibility for an existence which has become all too complicated be absorbed in collective responsibility, which proves itself able to meet all complications. Likewise, there is obviously no further reason for dread of the universe, since technicized nature—with which society as such manages well, or seems to—takes the place of the universe which has become uncanny and with which, so to speak, no further agreement can be reached. The collective pledges itself to provide total security. There is nothing imaginary here, a dense reality rules, and the "general" itself appears to have become real; but modern collectivism is essentially illusory. The person is joined to the reliably functioning "whole," which embraces the masses of men; but it is not a joining of man to man. Man in a collective is not man with man. Here the person is not freed from his isolation, by communing with living beings, which thenceforth live with him; the "whole," with its claim on the wholeness of every man, aims logically and successfully at reducing, neutralizing, devaluating, and desecrating every bond with living beings. That tender surface of personal life which longs for contact with other life is progressively deadened or desensitized. Man's isolation is not overcome here, but overpowered and numbed. Knowledge of it is suppressed, but the actual condition of solitude has its insuperable effect in the depths, and rises secretly to a cruelty

which will become manifest with the scattering of the
illusion. Modern collectivism is the last barrier raised by
man against a meeting with himself.

When imaginings and illusions are over, the possible and
inevitable meeting of man with himself is able to take place
only as the meeting of the individual with his fellow-man
—and this is how it must take place. Only when the
individual knows the other in all his otherness as himself,
as man, and from there breaks through to the other, has he
broken through his solitude in a strict and transforming
meeting.

It is obvious that such an event can only take place if
the person is stirred up as a person. In individualism the
person, in consequence of his merely imaginary mastery of
his basic situation, is attacked by the ravages of the fictitious, however much he thinks, or strives to think, that he
is asserting himself as a person in being. In collectivism
the person surrenders himself when he renounces the directness of personal decision and responsibility. In both
cases the person is incapable of breaking through to the
other : there is genuine relation only between genuine persons.

In spite of all attempts at revival the time of individualism is over. Collectivism, on the other hand, is at the
height of its development, although here and there appear
single signs of slackening. Here the only way that is left is
the rebellion of the person for the sake of setting free the
relations with others. On the horizon I see moving up,
with the slowness of all events of true human history, a
great dissatisfaction which is unlike all previous dissatisfactions. Men will no longer rise in rebellion—as they
have done till now—merely against some dominating tendency in the name of other tendencies, but against the
false realization of a great effort, the effort towards community, in the name of the genuine realization. Men will
fight against the distortion for the pure form, the vision of
the believing and hoping generations of mankind.

I am speaking of living actions; but it is vital knowledge
alone which incites them. Its first step must be to smash
the false alternative with which the thought of our epoch

is shot through—that of "individualism or collectivism." Its first question must be about a genuine third alternative —by "genuine" being understood a point of view which cannot be reduced to one of the first two, and does not represent a mere compromise between them.

Life and thought are here placed in the same problematic situation. As life erroneously supposes that it has to choose between individualism and collectivism, so thought erroneously supposes that it has to choose between an individualistic anthropology and a collectivist sociology. The genuine third alternative, when it is found, will point the way here too.

The fundamental fact of human existence is neither the individual as such nor the aggregate as such. Each, considered by itself, is a mighty abstraction. The individual is a fact of existence in so far as he steps into a living relation with other individuals. The aggregate is a fact of existence in so far as it is built up of living units of relation. The fundamental fact of human existence is man with man. What is peculiarly characteristic of the human world is above all that something takes place between one being and another the like of which can be found nowhere in nature. Language is only a sign and a means for it, all achievement of the spirit has been incited by it. Man is made man by it; but on its way it does not merely unfold, it also decays and withers away. It is rooted in one being turning to another as another, as this particular other being, in order to communicate with it in a sphere which is common to them but which reaches out beyond the special sphere of each. I call this sphere, which is established with the existence of man as man but which is conceptually still uncomprehended, the sphere of "between." Though being realized in very different degrees, it is a primal category of human reality. This is where the genuine third alternative must begin.

The view which establishes the concept of "between" is to be acquired by no longer localizing the relation between human beings, as is customary, either within individual souls or in a general world which embraces and determines them, but in actual fact *between* them.

"Between" is not an auxiliary construction, but the real place and bearer of what happens between men; it has received no specific attention because, in distinction from the individual soul and its context, it does not exhibit a smooth continuity, but is ever and again re-constituted in accordance with men's meetings with one another; hence what is experience has been annexed naturally to the continuous elements, the soul and its world.

In a real conversation (that is, not one whose individual parts have been preconcerted, but one which is completely spontaneous, in which each speaks directly to his partner and calls forth his unpredictable reply), a real lesson (that is, neither a routine repetition nor a lesson whose findings the teacher knows before he starts, but one which develops in mutual surprises), a real embrace and not one of mere habit, a real duel and not a mere game—in all these what is essential does not take place in each of the participants or in a neutral world which includes the two and all other things; but it takes place between them in the most precise sense, as it were in a dimension which is accessible only to them both. Something happens to me—that is a fact which can be exactly distributed between the world and the soul, between an "outer" event and an "inner" impression. But if I and another come up against one another, "happen" to one another (to use a forcible expression which can, however, scarcely be paraphrased), the sum does not exactly divide, there is a remainder, somewhere, where the souls end and the world has not yet begun, and this remainder is what is essential. This fact can be found even in the tiniest and most transient events which scarcely enter the consciousness. In the deadly crush of an air-raid shelter the glances of two strangers suddenly meet for a second in astonishing and unrelated mutuality; when the All Clear sounds it is forgotten; and yet it did happen, in a realm which existed only for that moment. In the darkened opera-house there can be established between two of the audience, who do not know one another, and who are listening in the same purity and with the same intensity to the music of Mozart, a relation which is scarcely perceptible and yet is one of elemental dialogue, and which has long vanished when the lights blaze up again. In the understanding of such fleeting and yet consistent happenings one must guard against introducing motives of feeling : what happens here cannot be reached by psychological concepts, it is something ontic. From the least of events, such as these, which disappear in the moment of their appearance, to the pathos of pure indissoluble tragedy, where two men, opposed to one another in their very nature, entangled in the same living situation, reveal to one another in mute clarity an irreconcilable opposition of being, the dialogical situation can be adequately grasped only in an ontological way. But it is not to be grasped on the basis of the ontic of personal existence, or of that of two personal existences, but of that which has its being between them, and transcends both. In the most powerful moments of dialogic, where in truth " deep calls unto deep," it becomes unmistakably clear that it is not the wand of the individual or of the social, but of a third which draws the circle round the happening. On the far side of the subjective, on this side of the objective, on the narrow ridge, where *I* and *Thou* meet, there is the realm of " between."

This reality, whose disclosure has begun in our time, shows the way, leading beyond individualism and collectivism, for the life decision of future generations. Here the genuine third alternative is indicated, the knowledge of which will help to bring about the genuine person again and to establish genuine community.

This reality provides the starting-point for the philosophical science of man; and from this point an advance may be made on the one hand to a transformed understanding of the person and on the other to a transformed understanding of community. The central subject of this science is neither the individual nor the collective but man with man. That essence of man which is special to him can be directly known only in a living relation. The gorilla, too, is an individual, a termitary, too, is a collective, but *I* and *Thou* exist only in our world, because man exists, and the *I*, moreover, exists only through the relation to the *Thou*. The philosophical science of man, which includes anthropology and sociology, must take as its starting-point the consideration of this subject, "man with man." If you consider the individual by himself, then you see of man just as much as you see of the moon; only man with man provides a full image. If you consider the aggregate by itself, then you see of man just as much as we see of the Milky Way; only man with man is a completely outlined form. Consider man with man, and you see human life, dynamic, twofold, the giver and the receiver, he who does and he who endures, the attacking force and the defending force, the nature which investigates and the nature which supplies information, the request begged and granted—and always both together, completing one another in mutual contribution, together showing forth man. Now you can turn to the individual and you recognize him as man according to the possibility of relation which he shows; you can turn to the aggregate and you recognize it as man according to the fulness of relation which he shows. We may come nearer the answer to the question what man is when we come to see him as the eternal meeting of the One with the Other.

(1) p. 29. There is a typical example here, which could be multiplied many times, of a play of words in the German which cannot be reproduced in the English. "This is not superstition (*Aberglaube*), but perverse knowledge (*Aberwissen*)." And of course this is more than a *play* of words, since this perverse knowledge leads direct to gnosis, which is very different from the theme, faith.

(2) p. 35. The significance of *responsibility* (and the point of the whole section, indeed of the whole of *Dialogue*) is brought out more acutely in the German than in the English. *Wort, Antwort, antworten, verantworten*, etc., are part of a closely interrelated situation in which speech and response, answering for and being responsible for, and so on, are more intimately connected than the English version can hope to show. If the reader will remember that "responsibility" carries in itself the root sense of being "answerable," then the significance of the "word" in actual life will not be lost. Buber's teaching about the "word" always carries a strict reference to "lived life," and is very far from being an abstraction, theological or other.

(3) p. 39. The German *Genosse*, Hebrew רע, English *companion*, is not the same, Buber means, as the "nearest" (*der Nœchste*, the usual word for neighbour). In the Septuagint the change of sense had already begun, since the word used there, πλήσιος (Lev. xix. 18), means near, near-dweller; Luther completes the change, and in his as in the English vernacular version of the Bible the real sense of the injunction, to meet the other in real objective love, is dissipated in the notion of "universal unreserve."

(4) p. 41. "Reflexion" for *Rückbiegung* is by no means a perfect rendering. Buber, however, makes clear that he is here describing the essence of the "monological" life, in which the other is not really met as the other, but merely as a part of the monological self, in an *Erlebnis* or inner

experience which has no objective import : what happens is that the self "curves back on itself" (cf. *I and Thou*, esp. pp. 115-6, where the same attitude is considered in relation to God).

(5) p. 43. *Ungrund:* for this difficult notion cf. Berdyaev, *Spirit and Reality*, pp. 144-5, where Berdyaev, discussing Boehme's conception of *Ungrund*, says :

> *Ungrund* is not being, but a more primeval and deeper stratum of being. *Ungrund* is *nothingness* as distinct from *something* in the category of being; it is not εὐχ ὄν but μὴ ὄν. But it is not μὴ ὄν in the Greek sense. Boehme goes beyond the limits of Greek thought, of Greek intellectualism and ontology. Like *Eckhart's Gottheit* Boehme's *Ungrund* goes deeper than God.

But for Buber *Ungrund* is less vague and more modest than this, being recognized as the undifferentiated basic unity of the life of the soul.

6) p. 48. "Knowing" ("*erkennen*") is used in the Biblical sense of lovers "knowing" each other—which of course is not limited to the physical, but means a connexion comprehending the whole being of the beloved.

(7) p. 49. I vow it faithfully to myself and myself to it. I vow, I have faith" : here again the German (*ich gelobe es mir an und mich ihm, ich gelobe, ich glaube*) shows in a way the English cannot the intimate connexion between language and thought.

(8) p. 50. "The indwelling of the Present Being between them" : *die Einwohnung des Seienden zwischen ihnen*, refers to the Shekinah or Divine Presence. This usage derives from the Old Testament reference to "the place where the Lord God causes his name to dwell" (cf. e.g. Deut. xii. 11). God comes to be described as "the One who causes his name to dwell there" (scil. the Temple), and then simply as "dwelling" (שכינה). For a full discussion of this usage (which recurs in Buber, as of central significance to his teaching), see Strack-Billerbeck, *Kommentar zum Neuen Testament*, II, 314.

(9) p. 60. *The Question to the Single One.* The German

which I have rendered by the cumbrous and none too clear phrase "the Single One" is *der Einzelne,* which is a fairly precise rendering of Kierkegaard's *hiin Enkelte.* It is a pity that in the English translations of Kierkegaard no effort seems to have been made by the translators to avoid the use of the word "individual," which is highly misleading. For every man is *individuum,* but not everyone is an *Einzelner* or *Enkelte.* In fact, the whole course of Kierkegaard's life, and the whole force of his teaching, is directed towards "becoming a Single One," and this is not a natural or biological category but, as Kierkegaard reiterates, it is "the spirit's category," and a rare thing. The reader's complaisance is invited, therefore, as it was decided better to make the English a little odd rather than customary and misleading.

(10) p. 61. All Kierkegaard's works, and a selection of the Journals, are now available in English. An English translation of Stirner's book, by S. C. Byington, was published under the title *The Ego and his Own,* London (A. C. Fifield) and New York (E. C. Walker), 1913.

(11). p. 73. "Love your neighbour as one like yourself" : this departure from the customary rendering of the Authorized Version is again an effort to render the original more precisely (in this case the Hebrew of Lev. xix. 18) in order to keep before the reader the stark objectivity of the command—the other whom you are required to "love" being one with a real life of his own, and not one whom you are invited to "acquire."

(12) p. 92. "The Hindered" (*der Hinderer*) : this is the best rendering of the Hebrew שׂטן ("Satan"). See, for example, the story of Balaam in Numbers xxii, where the *Authorized Version* gives (v. 22) "adversary," and paraphrases (v. 32) by "to withstand." But the true meaning is given in the most concrete rendering that English can supply—short of being imprisoned in a proper name.

(13) p. 93. "Spark" : the allusion is to the "Fünklein" of Eckhart. Cf. e.g., "the soul has something in it, a spark of speech *redelicheit*) that never dies," and "the soul's spark, which is untouched by time and space" (*Meister Eckhart,* ed. Pfeiffer, 1857, pp. 39 and 193.) There is an

English translation by Evans, *Master Eckhart*, 1924. It is to be noted, however, that in Buber *Fünklein* has throughout a more ethical connotation than in Eckhart.

(14). p. 193. *Golem* is originally a Hebrew word. cf. *I and Thou*, p. 44, i. 17, where I paraphrazed it as " animated clod without soul." The allusion is to the clay figure, possessed of no divine soul, made by a Rabbi in order to prevent attacks on Jews. Its end is either its destruction by the Rabbi, or his by it; for it could only destroy or be destroyed. (cf. H. L. Held, *Das Gespenst des Golem* (1927), pp. 85, 94.)

INDEX OF NAMES

253